MEDIA AND POLITICS IN AMERICA

A Reference Handbook

Other Titles in ABC-CLIO's
CONTEMPORARY
WORLD ISSUES
Series

Books in the Contemporary World Issues series address vital issues in today's society such as terrorism, sexual harassment, homelessness, AIDS, gambling, animal rights, and air pollution. Written by professional writers, scholars, and nonacademic experts, these books are authoritative, clearly written, up-to-date, and objective. They provide a good starting point for research by high school and college students, scholars, and general readers, as well as by legislators, businesspeople, activists, and others.

Each book, carefully organized and easy to use, contains an overview of the subject; a detailed chronology; biographical sketches; facts and data and/or documents and other primary-source material; a directory of organizations and agencies; annotated lists of print and nonprint resources; and an index.

Readers of books in the Contemporary World Issues series will find the information they need in order to better understand the social, political, environmental, and economic issues facing the world today.

MEDIA AND POLITICS IN AMERICA

A Reference Handbook

Guido H. Stempel III

A B C CLIO

Santa Barbara, California   Denver, Colorado   Oxford, England

Library of Congress Cataloging-in-Publication Data

Stempel, Guido Hermann, 1928–
    Media and politics in America : a reference handbook /
Guido H. Stempel, III.
        p. cm. — (Contemporary world issues)
Includes bibliographical references and index.
    ISBN 1-57607-845-0 (hardcover) — ISBN 1-57607-846-9 (e-book)
    1. Mass media—Political aspects—United States—History.
2. United States—Politics and government. I. Title. II. Series.
P95.82.U6 S74 2002
302.23'0973—dc21
                                        2002154378

07 06 05 04 03   10 9 8 7 6 5 4 3 2 1

This book is also available on the World Wide Web as an e-book. Visit www.abc-clio.com for details.

ABC-CLIO, Inc.
130 Cremona Drive, P.O. Box 1911
Santa Barbara, California 93116-1911

This book is printed on acid-free paper ∞.
Manufactured in the United States of America

Contents

Preface

This book is a gateway to knowledge about political communication. It is not about media on one hand and about politics on the other, but rather about how the two entities connect and interact in ways that are basic to our political system. I am trying to do two things in this book. First, I provide background to help you understand political communication. I begin with a chapter on the history and evolution of political communication. That chapter is followed by a discussion of problems in political communication today, many of which are long standing. The third chapter describes the process of news communication, looking at what the media do, what politicians do, and what the public does. Chapter four is an annotated chronology of political communication. Chapter five includes brief biographical sketches of major figures in political communication. Chapter six deals with legal documents and court cases that are vital in understanding political communication.

I believe that background information prepares one to move ahead in the ever changing field of political communication, so I provide you with two chapters dealing with resources you can use. Chapter seven offers names of associations, organizations, and government agencies. The final chapter provides information on various resources, both print and electronic, including books, articles, websites, and videos.

It is my hope that this combination of background and resources will enable you to keep up with a rapidly changing field. At this writing, the part that the Internet will play in political communication is just beginning to evolve. It could be that websites will replace television advertisements in political campaigns. They cost less, and there is some evidence that they are as effective. It also could be that websites will replace media news coverage of campaigns; but perhaps it is more likely that they simply will cause media coverage to change.

I wrote this book both for those who are involved in political communication or intend to follow it as a career and for those whose role will simply be that of citizens. This book may mean different things to these two groups, but political communication affects us all, and we need to understand it. I wrote with the intent that this is a changing field and that our knowledge about it is expanding. I hope this book will be of help to those who participate in the expansion of our knowledge of political communication.

1

History and Evolution of Political Communication

M edia and politics are separate entities in the United States, each with its own objectives and goals. Yet, they cannot advance without each other. The media need politics and politicians because what politicians do is, by any definition, news, and therefore must be reported by the media. Politicians need visibility. They need to be known by the public, and media coverage is a major factor in achieving this objective. This means that media and politics must interact with each other, and that even though they are separate, they do influence each other.

In the inception of this country, there were neither media nor politics of the kind to which one is accustomed today. In the seventeenth century the only newspapers available to the colonists were British newspapers brought here by ship. The content of those papers had little to do with the colonies, and by the time newspapers arrived the news was stale.

The first newspaper ever published in the colonies, *Publick Occurrences Both Foreign and Domestic,* in 1690, lasted just one issue. The first continuous newspaper was the *Boston News-Letter,* founded in 1704 and published by authority—that is, with the permission of the government. Later, the *New England Courant* was founded in 1721 and published not with authority, but in spite of it, an example of the spirit of journalism that would prevail in the colonies. The *Courant* was established by James Franklin, older brother of Benjamin Franklin. James Franklin fell into enough trouble with the government that he ended up in jail, and his younger brother, then only sixteen years old, took over the paper (Emery and Emery, 23–33).

The *Courant's* difficulties with government officials were minor compared to the court case involving New York Governor William Cosby and John Peter Zenger, editor of the *New York Weekly Journal.*

1

For his criticism of Cosby, Zenger was jailed and charged with criminal libel. The case initially appeared to be fairly simple and to soon be forgotten. Instead, it was a genuine landmark case that caused changes in the law both in the colonies and in Great Britain. British law stated that in a criminal libel case, the prosecutor had to show only that the defendant had published the libel. Therefore, the one thing the jury had to determine was whether or not the evidence supported that accusation. However, Andrew Hamilton, the uncle of Alexander Hamilton, came from Philadelphia to defend Zenger and to offer a new perspective. He argued that the jury should determine whether or not the libelous material was true. There was no basis in British law for that argument, but the jury accepted the argument and acquitted Zenger (Eberhard, 156).

The significance of the verdict was not merely legal—it was political as well. Because the jury's verdict was contrary to established British law, it could have been thrown out and a new trial ordered. However, the colonial government of New York did not do that because the verdict was a sign of growing dissatisfaction with British rule in the colonies. The jury had defied the government, just as Zenger had, and the government was not ready to risk another confrontation. There were similar happenings elsewhere in the colonies.

However, the dissent eventually subsided because of the need for common defense. The French and the British had been at war since 1689, and the colonies were oftentimes involved. King George's War, from 1739 to 1748, was fought mainly in New England. The French and Indian War, from 1756 to 1763, was fought on the frontier, then primarily in Pennsylvania and New York (Emery and Emery, 47–48).

When the war was over, the British renewed dissent with the passage of the Stamp Act in 1765, which taxed all forms of paper as well as other goods, so naturally the newspapers and many others opposed it. It brought into the fray two of the great political communicators of Revolutionary America—Patrick Henry and Samuel Adams. Henry, a great orator of the Revolution, said to the Virginia House of Burgesses in response to the Stamp Act:

> Tarquin and Caesar each had his Brutus, Charles the First his Cromwell, and George the Third may profit by their example. (Morley and Everett, 270)

This reference to rebels who had overthrown rulers led to cries of treason, but Henry responded, "If this be treason, make the most of it." It was Henry, however, who made the most of it, becoming one of the major voices of the Revolution. There was no radio or television to broadcast what Henry had to say, but the word certainly got around.

Adams established the Committees of Correspondence, which circulated materials in opposition to the British throne. Adams decided that a continental congress—that is, a body representing all the colonies—was necessary, and led the Assembly of Massachusetts to commence this formation by selecting its representatives. The colonies were on the way to separation from Great Britain (Emery and Emery, 47).

Jefferson and Political Communication

Thus, the stage was set for Thomas Jefferson and the Declaration of Independence, dated 4 July 1776. In an exemplary piece of political communication, Jefferson began by stating the need to tell the British why the colonists were declaring independence. The second paragraph is a statement of the political philosophy of the country. In the third paragraph, he listed twenty-seven specific grievances of the colonies against the mother country. In some ways, it is more important than the Constitution because it was the Declaration of Independence that provided the basis for our becoming a separate country, and it stated the principles for which the new country stood. The Constitution, which was written eleven years later, followed those principles. In the Declaration of Independence Jefferson wrote:

> We hold these Truths to be self-evident, that all Men are created equal, that they are endowed by their Creator with certain unalienable Rights, that among these are Life, Liberty and the Pursuit of Happiness.

Few people, however, remember the next phrase, a part that may be more important:

> That to secure these Rights, Governments are instituted among Men, deriving their just powers from the Consent of the Governed.

At the time this was written, it was intended to mean that governments exist to secure rights, not to gratuitously grant them as some politicians would have the public believe. The power comes from the people and not from divine right of kings, presidents, or speakers of the House. Furthermore, this provision demands that the people be informed of what their government is doing. That requirement, in turn, ultimately leads to the necessity of the First Amendment—that is, the press must be separated from the government. Otherwise, if the government controlled the media, the people would get only a biased account of the government's actions.

Our government evolved slowly after the end of the Revolutionary War. A constitution was not drawn up until 1787, and the Bill of Rights, amending the Constitution, was not written until 1789. Moreover, the Bill of Rights was not ratified until 1791. The First Amendment states:

> Congress shall make no law respecting an establishment of religion, or prohibiting the free exercise thereof, or abridging the freedom of speech, or of the press; or the right of the people peaceably to assemble, and to petition the Government for a redress of grievances.

This statement means that the people of the United States would be free to express themselves and the press would free to publish. However, the First Amendment became a political dialogue because though it is what the founding fathers intended and what communication at that time was largely about, times have changed. There are those today who argue that the First Amendment protects only political communication—forget about *The Simpsons,* MTV, professional football, or Martha Stewart. Yet the Supreme Court has broadened its perspective so that nearly all mass communication is protected by the First Amendment. It must be added that the Supreme Court, over the years, has spent an enormous amount of time determining exactly what the amendment means.

Jefferson was a supporter of the First Amendment. Eleven years after the Declaration of Independence, he wrote:

> The way to prevent these irregular interpositions of the people is to give them full information thro' the channels of the public papers & to contrive that those papers should penetrate the whole mass of the people. The basis of our Governments being the opinions of the people, the very first object should be to keep that right; and were it

left to me to decide whether we should have a Government without newspapers or newspapers without government, I should not hesitate to prefer the latter—but I should mean that every man should receive those papers and be capable of reading them. (Tebbel and Watts, 53)

However, Jefferson had one more role to play in establishing press freedom. Just seven years after the ratification of the amendment, there was a major threat in the form of the Alien and Seditions Acts. They were inspired by conflicts the colonies were having with the French, but they included a broad definition of sedition. It was interpreted by the administration of John Adams to cover virtually any criticism of the president, and it was used to prosecute and convict fourteen persons who had criticized the president, however mildly. The acts became a central issue of the presidential campaign of 1800, and with Jefferson's victory, they were allowed to lapse. Had Adams been reelected in 1800, the Alien and Sedition Acts might have been renewed, and the history of political communication would have been far different.

Jefferson, however, became somewhat disillusioned with the press during his presidency. Midway through his term of office, in 1805, he wrote:

During the course of administration and in order to disturb it, the artillery of the press has been leveled against us, charged with whatever its licentiousness could dare. These abuses of an institution so important to freedom and science, are deeply to be regretted, inasmuch as they tend to lessen its usefulness and sap its safety. (Levy, 367)

In 1814, five years after he was out of office, he wrote:

I deplore, with you, the putrid state to which our newspapers have passed, and the malignity, the vulgarity, and mendacious spirit of those who write for them. . . . As vehicles of information, they have rendered themselves useless. (ibid., 373)

Many have concluded from these statements that Jefferson had turned against the press and perhaps was having second thoughts about the First Amendment. However, by 1823, his presidency now fourteen years behind him, he reasserted his belief in the press and the First Amendment:

This formidable censor of public functionaries, by arranging them at the tribunal of public opinion, produces reform peaceably, which otherwise must be done by revolution. It is also the best instrument for enlightening the mind of man and improving him as a rational, moral, and social being. (ibid., 376)

Jefferson had returned to the vision he had offered in the Declaration of Independence, a vision that remains valid more than two centuries after he first wrote it.

There is no better answer than "consent of the governed," providing that it is an informed consent, to use a term that did not exist in Jefferson's time. Ultimately, both the media and politicians, as well as the people, are better off when consent is achieved.

The Road to a Two-Party System

George Washington was unopposed for president in 1888 and again in 1892. Yet, political divisions were beginning to appear. Washington had John Adams, who would be elected president in 1796, as his vice president and Alexander Hamilton as his secretary of the treasury. Both were Federalists. Washington's first secretary of state was Thomas Jefferson, who as a Republican would defeat Adams in 1800. There were fundamental differences between the two parties. They differed on the role of federal government: the Federalists believed in a strong government and appealed particularly to business interests, the Republicans emphasized the rights of the people.

In 1896, under the Constitutional provision then in place, Jefferson, who had the second higest number of electoral votes, became vice president under Adams, resulting in a president of one party and a vice president of the other party. The Twelfth Amendment, ratified in 1803, changed the procedures to separate the votes for president and vice president.

The Federalists were never again able to elect a president. Jefferson won reelection easily in 1804, and James Madison and James Monroe also won two terms running as Democratic Republicans, as the party became known. In 1820, Monroe got all but one of the electoral votes. That one was denied him by an elector who did not want to see Monroe match Washington's record of a unanimous vote. Historians have called the time of Monroe's presidency "the era of good feeling." It did not last.

1824 saw the most bizarre presidential election in U.S. history. Four candidates received electoral votes, but nobody had a majority. The four candidates—Andrew Jackson, John Quincy Adams, Henry Clay, and William H. Crawford—were all Democratic Republicans. Because nobody had a majority of the electoral votes, the selection of the president fell to the House, and Adams was the winner.

Jackson returned four years later and won the presidency. That marked a new era in that he was from Tennessee, whereas Washington, Jefferson, Madison, and Monroe were from Virginia, and the two Adamses were from Massachusetts. Virginia and Massachusetts were the leaders of the American Revolution and were among the thirteen original states. With Jackson's election, leadership would come from the frontier, and the role of Virginia and Massachusetts was greatly reduced. The party was now the Democratic Party.

The Whig Party became the opposition in the 1840s and elected William Henry Harrison in 1840 and Zachary Taylor in 1848. The Democrats, however, won in 1844, 1852, and 1856. The party of Thomas Jefferson had won thirteen of fifteen presidential elections.

The Republican Party was founded in 1854, and elected Abraham Lincoln as president in 1860. The Republicans then won the next five presidential elections and thirteen of the next seventeen presidential elections. Nonetheless, with the establishment of the Republican Party, there was a two-party system for the first time since 1800, and the political alignment of 1860 remains today. There is, however, no unanimity within the parties. There are factions, and the power of various factions varies over time. In some democratic countries, the factions become parties and the result is a multiparty system in which no one party has a majority. In the United States, there are struggles between the factions inside the parties.

There was another important change in the early nineteenth century. The popular vote for president was not counted until 1824. The electoral college selected the president, with electors being chosen by each of the states. It is still the electoral college that makes the choice. In the presidential election of 2000, as in 1888, the popular vote winner was not the electoral college winner. There have been proposals to change the electoral college before every session of Congress for two centuries, but it has not been changed. The election of 2000 raised the question of the need to change the electoral college. The obvious problem is that a state gets one vote for each member of the House of Representatives, and one for each senator. The House is apportioned according to population, but the Senate is not. Any attempt to adjust that distribution would reduce the political influence of smaller states, and the senators from those states would block such an attempt if it ever reached the Senate.

In the 1824 election, slightly less than 400,000 people voted (Stempel, *The Practice of Political Communication,* 4). That number was 4 percent of the nearly 10 million people in the country. The number of votes tripled in 1828 and continued to rise in the following years. However, the fact of a popular vote did change political strategy. And the change in politics fit with a major change in the media.

A Press for the Masses

The press of the era of Adams and Jefferson was a partisan press, financed by the political parties and individual politicians. In content, it much resembled what one receives in mailings from political parties today. Truth was incidental and personal attack was a staple of this press. Opinion exceeded facts. As the Jeffersonian Republicans became dominant, the press increasingly presented a one-sided picture. However, this was a press for the elite. As indicated in the previous section, relatively few people were really participating in the electoral process.

This changed in the 1830s with the advent of the penny press. Ben Day started it with the *New York Sun* in 1833. With a price of one cent and sensational content, it was aimed at the masses, not the elite. It became more noted for the moon hoax, a series of made-up articles about life on the moon, than for anything it did in the way of political coverage (Emery and Emery, 117–121).

Day's *Sun* was soon eclipsed by James Gordon Bennett's *New York Herald,* founded in 1835. Bennett revolutionized news coverage. He was the first to cover Wall Street, and he fought a successful battle to be allowed to cover the U.S. Senate. Bennett and the Herald also covered New York society and the courts. He said he was "willing to cover anything the Good Lord was willing to let happen." But Bennett had no desire to become involved in politics. The prospectus that appeared in the first issue of the *Herald* said, "We shall support no party, be the organ of no faction or coterie, and care nothing for the election of any candidate from President on down to constable." Within fifteen months, the *Herald* had a circulation of 40,000, far and away the largest in the country (Stewart and Tebbel, 59–71).

Horace Greeley, who founded the *New York Tribune* six years later, had a different outlook on politics. He supported the Whig Party and advocated socialism and social reform. The Whig Party faded in the 1850s, and thereafter Greeley became one of the founders of the Republican Party. He helped engineer the nomination of Lincoln in 1860. However, Greeley's paper did not belong to the party, and to his credit he created the editorial page, thus separating news from opinion. Greeley also established a national weekly edition of the *Tribune,* and by the time of the Civil War, it had a circulation of more than 200,000. Henry Raymond founded the *New York Times* in 1851 when he, like Bennett before him, had a clear commitment to nonpartisan coverage of the news.

What worked in New York was copied in other parts of the country, and a mass press independent of political influence prevailed. No longer could a politician fund a newspaper to parrot his views. Now the newspaper decided whether or not what the politician was saying or doing was of importance and interest to the general public. Political participation was increasing, in part because politicians encouraged public participation in political processes (Emery and Emery, 123, 130–131).

The Press and Politics in the Civil War

The Civil War led to new dynamics between the press and government. Slavery had been an issue for years, but now it became *the* issue. Greeley had long opposed slavery and began pressing Lincoln during his first year in office. By the end of 1861, he was calling for freeing of slaves in conquered areas. On 20 August 1862, he ran his famous "Prayer of Twenty Million" editorial calling for abolition. Lincoln responded by letter to Greeley:

> My paramount object in this struggle is to save the Union, and it is not either to save or destroy Slavery. If I could save the Union without freeing any slave, I would do it; and if I could save it by freeing all the slaves, I would do it; and if I could save it by freeing some and leaving others alone, I would also do that. (ibid., 158)

Yet by 23 September 1862, Lincoln announced his preliminary Emancipation Proclamation to be effective 1 January 1863. Greeley's pressure on the issue had had an effect, and a journalist had influenced national policy perhaps to a greater extent than had ever been the case before (ibid.).

Bennett did not favor abolition and was sympathetic to the South. That was of some concern to the Lincoln administration because the *Herald* was read more widely in Great Britain than any other U.S. paper, and the British wanted Southern cotton for their mills. Bennett, however, was basically supportive of the war effort (ibid., 159).

Henry Raymond, an early critic of Lincoln, became a staunch supporter when the war started. He became chairman of the Republican National Committee in 1863 and managed Lincoln's campaign for reelection in 1864 (Stewart and Tebbel, 126). The *Times* supported Lincoln editorially, as did the *Tribune*, but the *Herald* did not.

Two things produced conflict between the press and the government. One was that there was an element of the press that strongly supported the South. Those newspapers became known as copperheads, and some were suspended because of their support for the South. The other was the reporting of the war, with reporters enjoying unusual access to battles and more freedom than in other wars. Some journalism historians feel that reporting was more irresponsible than it would be later in World War I and World War II. However, more of the reporting was based on first-hand observation and less on official headquarters reports than has been the case since.

Military censorship was inevitable. First came censorship of the telegraph, because the government felt telegraph reporting was providing useful current information to the South. Then in 1862 reporters were required to submit copy to provost marshals for approval before transmission. The understanding was that only military matters could be deleted. Further restrictions were put in place in 1864, and that made it possible for General William Sherman to march to the sea through Southern territory without ever having his plan disclosed by the press (Emery and Emery, 160–162).

Exposés and Muckraking

Although Bennett, Greeley, and Raymond had been aggressive in their reporting, they did not deal in exposés—that would happen after the Civil War; and perhaps the growth of cities and the growth in the size of businesses had something to do with it. In New York City, the Tweed Ring stole $200 million from the city in the late 1860s and early 1870s. They frightened some publications into silence, but they met their match in the *New York Times* and *Harper's Weekly*. The *Times* got documentation and broke the story in 1871, and *Harper's* supported the *Times* editorially as well as providing the cartoons of Thomas Nast (Emery and Emery, 176–178; Stewart and Tebbel, 128–129).

A year later, the *New York Sun* broke what became known as the Credit Mobilier affair. The *Sun* proved that promoters of the Union Pacific and Central Pacific Railroads were influencing legislators and others whose help was needed to get federal land grants to build railroads (ibid., 177–178). This disclosure was followed by a series of scandals in the Grant administration. Though President Grant himself was not implicated in any of them, his party lost control of the House of Representatives in the next election. For sixteen of the next twenty-two years, control of Congress and the presidency was split between the two parties, and little political progress was made.

This period of exposés did not last long. Perhaps because there was eventually less corruption or perhaps it was the changing of the guard. Greeley died just after the presidential election in 1872, in which he was the Democratic and losing candidate. That same year Bennett turned over the *Herald* to his son, James Gordon Bennett Jr. Raymond died in 1869, and George Jones became publisher of the *New York Times*, but despite the Tweed Ring exposé, the *Times* faltered in the next few years.

Ultimately, magazines, not newspapers, took up exposés, partly because of considerable growth in the magazine field in the last twenty years of the nineteenth century, which was largely the result of an act of Congress in 1879 that gave magazines cheap postage rates. The act gave magazines the opportunity to go after mass circulation, and exposés became an integral part of that effort. The exposés became known as muckraking, and the early part of the twentieth century was termed the Muckraking Era.

The target, however, was not the corruption of politicians, but business, which was undergoing consolidation into monopoly. Concentration of economic power, which had begun in the 1880s, intensified in the first decade of the twentieth century to such an extent that it became a political issue. More than 5,000 organizations had merged into about 300 trusts, and further consolidation left much of the country's financial power in the hands of either the Morgan interests or the Rockefeller interests. With this concentration of power came abuse, and the muckrakers went after it.

The best known of the muckrakers probably was Ida Tarbell, who took on Standard Oil and John D. Rockefeller in *McClure's Magazine*. She documented Standard Oil's practices in eliminating competitors and made Standard Oil the symbol of monopoly against the public interest (Burriss, 142).

Samuel Hopkins Adams in *Collier's* and Edward W. Bok in the *Ladies Home Journal* turned attention to the false claims for patent medicines, and Upton Sinclair's exposés of the meatpacking industry in his novel, *The Jungle*, led to the establishment of the Pure Food and Drug Act in 1906 (Emery and Emery, 263).

Both Theodore Roosevelt and Woodrow Wilson understood these concerns and made some reforms. A Supreme Court case prevented a railroad monopoly west of the Mississippi and blunted the tide of concentration. Roosevelt's conservation policies saved natural resources from further exploitation. Forests, minerals, and sources of water power, acquired cheaply and often by means of fraud, were being used carelessly and wastefully by expoliters. In the Wilson years, the creation of the Federal Reserve System gave the country a modern currency and credit system, and the Clayton Act prevented abusive use of court injunctions against labor unions.

The muckrakers influenced the political processes and changed the course of U.S. history. The tradition of the muckrakers lives on in the investigative journalism of the current era. Politicians have to face the reality that every facet of their lives may be made public if their actions are called into question.

Two Waves of Sensationalism

By the last quarter of the nineteenth century, the three men who had greatly influenced journalism and politics, James Gordon Bennett, Horace Greeley, and Henry Raymond, were gone.

Their place on the stage was taken by two men who raised sensationalism to a level few could have imagined. The men were Joseph Pulitzer, publisher of the *New York World*, and William Randolph Hearst, publisher of the *New York Journal*. Their brand of sensationalism became know as yellow journalism. The name came from a comic strip character "The Yellow Kid," created by Richard Outcault for Pulitzer's *World*. Hearst soon hired Outcault for the *Journal,* but the *World* responded by having someone else draw a similar character.

The two combatants, Pulitzer and Hearst, could hardly have been any less alike. Pulitzer, born in Hungary in 1847, came to this country penniless as a military conscript in 1864. After spending a year in the army, Pulitzer went to New York City. He wanted to learn English, and legend has it that a practical joker told him that St. Louis would be the best place to learn English. Pulitzer took the advice, not realizing that St. Louis had one of the largest concentrations of German immigrants. After several years, he got a job on the German-language paper, the *Westliche Post* and soon acquired a partial interest in it. In 1878, he bought the *St. Louis Dispatch,* which was $30,000 in debt. Pulitzer soon bought the *Post,* and the *St. Louis Post-Dispatch* was soon a thriving newspaper. That success led him to buy the *New York World* in 1883 (Stewart and Tebbel, 86–102).

Pulitzer told the readers of the *World* that he would advocate taxing luxuries, inheritances, large incomes, and monopolies; fight for abolishing special privileges for corporations; and seek civil service reform and severe punishment for corrupt officials.

His *World* was more sensational than anything New Yorkers had seen, with large, titillating headlines, explicit coverage of crime and sex, and many pictures. Likewise, there were stunts, the best known of which was Nellie Bly's trip around the world in 1889. Her goal was the beat eighty days, the time suggested by Jules Verne in *Around the World in Eighty Days.* The *World* ran a guessing contest as to how long the trip would take and got a million entries. Nellie Bly pleasantly surprised everybody by finishing in seventy-two days, eight days less than Verne's book suggested.

Although Pulitzer wanted his paper to appeal to the working class, he included an editorial page that offered a sophisticated intellectual liberal appeal. He was thus appealing to two very different kinds of readers. Pulitzer's approach was a success. The newspaper's circulation went from 15,000 to 60,000 in the first year and reached 250,000, the largest of any U.S. newspaper, in 1887.

Hearst, on the other hand, was born into wealth (Stewart and Tebbel, 103–120). His father had made a fortune mining silver and became a U.S. senator. Hearst went to Harvard, where he was expelled after a year for various pranks. While he was there he became aware of Pulitzer's *World* and wanted to emulate him. Hearst asked his father if he could take over the *San Francisco Examiner,* a faltering newspaper that the elder Hearst had acquired for political reasons. He made the *Examiner* a successful newspaper, doubling its circulation in a year, and that feat whetted his appetite for a direct confrontation with Pulitzer. He bought the *New York Journal* in 1895, a move made possible when his mother gave him $7.5 million from the sale of stock in Anaconda Copper. It's worth keeping that in mind when assessing whether or not Hearst's sensationalism was financially successful. Did Hearst make more money with his journalism than he would have had if he had simply kept the Anaconda stock?

Hearst's way of operating was to hire the best talent he possibly could, and the *Journal* did not make money at the outset. He did much of what Pulitzer did—he attacked corporations, exposed abuses in the meatpacking industry, and urged an eight-hour workday and women's suffrage. The *Journal* quickly became competitive with the *World*, passing the 400,000 mark in circulation in 1896. On the day following the 1896 election in which William McKinley defeated William Jennings Bryan, both the *Journal* and the *World* sold 1.5 million copies.

Yellow journalism is most remembered for exciting interest in the Spanish-American War. Historians now doubt that the *Journal* and the *World* started the war, or that the war would not have happened without the papers. They did, however, certainly agitate for action against Spain because of the oppression of Cuba for at least two years before the onset of war. Hearst sent Frederic Remington, the famous Western artist, to Cuba to draw pictures of the war. Legend has it that Remington wired Hearst that he could not find a war and Hearst wired back, "You furnish the pictures, and I'll furnish the war" (Emery and Emery, 236). Hearst later denied this, but in light of other things Hearst was doing to stir things up in Cuba, the story is believable.

The climax came when the battleship USS *Maine* blew up in Havana Harbor. Both the *Journal* and the *World* had artists' drawings of the explosion covering more than half of the front page. The *Journal's* drawing left nothing to the imagination, showing a bomb planted beneath the ship. Both papers left no doubt that the Spanish had blown up the USS *Maine*. But certain as Hearst and Pulitzer were, nobody else to this day knows exactly what happened to the battleship. Yet, "Remember the Maine" became the battle cry of the war, thanks largely to Pulitzer and Hearst.

Both papers continued sensational coverage of what was a popular, short, and highly successful war, and they had plenty of company as other papers joined in. About 500 reporters, artists, and photographers went to Florida, Cuba, and Puerto Rico.

Small fleets of press boats went with the Navy into action, and correspondents were with the armed forces everywhere. Hearst outdid them all, however, with a small fleet of boats carrying *Journal* staffers. They even published a special edition of the *Journal* from one of the boats. Hearst himself led an assault on a beach where he captured twenty-six stranded Spanish sailors and made them prisoners of war.

Though the war coverage sold lots of papers for Hearst and Pulitzer—1.5 million each a day frequently—it was a drain on the financial resources. Hearst could stand that better than Pulitzer, and Pulitzer backed away from the sensational competition with Hearst. With the war over, Hearst had trouble because of his sensationalism. There was public objection to some of the extremes. Furthermore, Hearst had been a harsh critic of McKinley almost from the moment he ascended the political stage. The criticism reached its height when in February 1901, the *Journal* published Ambrose Bierce's quatrain following the assassination of Governor Goebel of Kentucky:

> The bullet that pierced Goebel's breast
> Can not be found in all the West;
> Good reason, it is speeding here
> To stretch McKinley on his bier. (Littlefield, 77).

Seven months later McKinley was assassinated by an anarchist who was said to have a copy of the *Journal* in his pocket. That the public reacted by hanging Hearst in effigy and boycotting his paper was hardly a surprise. The wave of sensationalism was soon to ebb.

Both Pulitzer and Hearst were active in politics. In 1872 Pulitzer had supported the liberal Republican movement and helped nominate Horace Greeley as the candidate for president. When Greeley lost and the liberal Republican movement failed, he turned to the Democratic Party and supported it strongly on his editorial pages. In 1880, Pulitzer was a delegate to the Democratic convention and an unsuccessful candidate for Congress. Five years later he was actually elected to Congress, but resigned in disgust a few months later. That was his last political activity, in part because failing health was restricting his activity.

Hearst's political career was more extensive. He was elected to Congress in 1902 as a Democrat and unsuccessfully sought the Democratic nomination for president in 1904. He ran against Charles Evans Hughes for governor of New York in 1906 and lost in part because he turned his back on the corrupt Tammany machine that controlled New York City politics. Had he won in 1906, he could have been in position to win the Democratic nomination and the presidency in 1912. As governor of New York and media titan, he might have been a more attractive candidate than the New Jersey governor, Woodrow Wilson.

Hearst nonetheless stayed involved in politics, and in 1932 was a significant factor in the nomination of Franklin D. Roosevelt for president. Before Roosevelt's first term was over, however, Hearst had broken with him over New Deal policies. He became conservative, and by the time of his death in 1951, he was a right-wing extremist, which seemed something of a paradox, given his earlier populist attitudes.

The story of Adolph Ochs and the *New York Times* is part of the story of the era of yellow journalism (Stewart and Tebbel, 129–137). The *Times* was in serious financial trouble when Ochs acquired it in 1896. He was a successful publisher in Chattanooga, Tennessee, but the *Times* appeared to be a much larger challenge. As he moved into direct competition with the two titans of yellow journalism, Ochs charted a different course. It was reflected in the slogan he placed atop the front page, where it remains today: "All the News That's Fit to Print."

He would not try to match the sensationalism of the *Journal* and the *World*. Surely he could not have outdone them. It worked, and the *Times* emerged from the yellow journalism era in better shape financially than his sensational competitors. With the guiding genius of Carr Van Anda as managing editor, the *Times* set a new standard for news coverage. A prime example was its coverage of the sinking of the *Titanic* in 1912.

Van Anda deduced that the information available in the early morning hours of April 15 meant that the *Titanic* had sunk. The *Times* was first with the story, but what was more notable was the coverage they had of the survivors, who were interviewed by dozens of *Times* reporters when they landed.

The *Times* prevailed, but sensationalism would return before long. The rise of the tabloids outdid even Hearst and Pulitzer. Hearst and Pulitzer were interested in politics partly on a personal basis, and their newspapers covered politics and government to some extent. That was not the case, though, with the tabloids, which paid little attention to politics. The *New York Daily News* was the first tabloid published, starting in 1919. With its emphasis on crime and sex, it had the second largest circulation in New York City in two years. In a decade it reached a circulation of one million, and before World War II it reached two million. The *News* was joined by Hearst's *Mirror* and by the most sensational of all, the *Graphic*. The latter well earned the nickname of the "Pornographic." The *Graphic* lasted only until 1932, and the *Mirror* survived until 1963 only because Hearst was willing to subsidize it—it never made money. The *Daily News*, on the other hand, has been successful to this day.

The rest of the New York field did not turn to sensationalism. The impact of the tabloids was to drive some of the standard papers out of business. Tabloids did not have the impact on journalism nationally that the penny press of the 1830s did, and there were few imitators.

Daily journalism has not seen another burst of sensationalism since the tabloids, but they have been replaced by the weekly "grocery store tabloids"—the *National Inquirer* and the *Star*, to name a couple. Unfortunately, this sensationalism sometimes spills over into the mainline media. Even the *New York Times* cannot ignore sensational disclosures about prominent political figures by the grocery store tabloids. In many instances, those publications really set the agenda for the major newspapers and network television news.

Wars and Political Communication in the Twentieth Century

The United States was involved in five wars in the twentieth century, and there were implications of each for political communication. In World War I, the United States was exposed mostly to the British perspective: Because the British cut the German Atlantic cable, all news about the war had to travel through London. Even what American journalists in Europe wrote about the war had to clear British censorship. It was only after the war that Americans began to think that they had been manipulated. Perhaps the prime example is that even now it is frequently said the United States entered the war because of the sinking of the RMS *Lusitania* by a German submarine. In fact, the *Lusitania* was a British ship, and it was sunk in 1915, two years before the United States entered the war.

The entry of the United States into the war brought forth something new—the Committee on Public Information headed by George Creel, a newspaper editor with experience in Denver,

Kansas City, and New York City. The committee's primary function was propaganda. Creel also instituted voluntary censorship, but said it should cover only troop movements, ship sailings, and similar military matters. Creel did not quite succeed in limiting censorship to that, but it is generally conceded that U.S. censorship was less than that of U.S. allies. The Committee issued a daily report on the war, and it reached a daily circulation of 118,000.

World War I also saw the passage of the Espionage Act in 1917, which became a means of censoring socialist and German publications. Because of this act, forty-four publishers lost their mailing privileges in the next year (Emery and Emery, 297).

As was the case in the Civil War, not all newspapers supported the entry of the United States into the World War I. Most notable among the opponents were the Hearst newspapers, although they did support the war effort once the United States entered the war.

World War II was different in that respect. The United States entered the war as a result of the Japanese attack on Pearl Harbor on 7 December 1941, and the response of the press, the politicians, and the public alike was complete support of the war. During World War II, the government wisely separated the propaganda and censorship efforts. Byron Price, executive editor of the Associated Press, was named director of the Office of Censorship. Elmer Davis, a well-known news analyst and commentator on CBS, was named head of the Office of War Information. Both were widely accepted, and while there was some criticism of censorship, it was less than it had been during World War I.

World War II brought a new perspective because it was genuinely a world war—the American people found themselves reading and hearing media accounts of foreign places. This had an impact on politicians, too, in that an international perspective was required. Isolationism had dominated American politics after World War I, but that could not and would not be the case this time. Wendell Willkie, the losing presidential candidate in 1940, wrote a book during the war with a title that turned out to be prophetic—*One World* (1943). The media responded with what many felt was the best effort at war coverage the world had ever seen, with newspaper, wire service, and radio personnel literally covering the globe. Throughout all the reporting of the war, thirty-seven media people were killed (Emery and Emery, 401).

Five years after the end of World War II, the United States was at war again—in Korea. The centrality of the war made it much easier to cover. However, General Douglas MacArthur, heavily criticized for his handling of the retreat from North Korea when the Chinese entered the war, retaliated by instituting severe censorship. MacArthur, however, was removed from his command in April 1951, and censorship was eased.

Among other things, the press was permitted at the site of truce negotiations, which went on for almost two years before the war ended. The Department of Defense also issued a new policy directive that restricted censorship to matters of national security (ibid., 414–415).

With the Korean War came a wave of anticommunism, which many politicians joined, and the media covered. Republican Senator Joseph McCarthy from Wisconsin spearheaded this drive, and while President Eisenhower and much of the Republican leadership were opposed, they could not control McCarthy.

The sixties brought the Vietnam War, and with it, conflict at home as well as abroad. As the war lingered, opposition to it on the home front increased, and by 1969 polls were indicating that the majority of Americans thought the United States should leave Vietnam. Politicians, however, were divided, with the majority opting to stay in the war.

As the war continued, criticism shifted from the policy of politicians to the performance of the military. There was limited censorship, and the military said that reporters had too much freedom in where to go and what to cover. Yet, the reporters could not get anywhere without transportation from the military. Nonetheless, the military felt the press was responsible for the public turning against the war.

But if the press had more freedom and thereby reported things not previously reported, there was another difference between Vietnam coverage and that of earlier wars. Television brought the war directly into the living rooms of common U.S. citizens. Pictures of the fighting were displayed on television screens, and that was unlike anything ever seen before in wartime. Some military leaders blamed the media for the failure of the United States to win in Vietnam and said the media caused the American people to turn against the war. Yet research has shown that the media followed public opinion more than it led it.

The response to this came after the war when the Defense Department put together new regulations for the media. The major test of these regulations came with the Persian Gulf War in 1990. The rules provided that reporters had to be accompanied by a public affairs officer wherever they went and whenever they spoke to someone. The media objected this, but the war ended quickly before any changes in policy or procedure could occur (Sohn, 106–107).

The Persian Gulf War turned into something of a television spectacular. Screens showed the American people the air raids against Baghdad as the war began. CNN maintained its operation in Baghdad. Anchor Peter Arnett broadcast live from Baghdad, at considerable personal risk. He was commended by some and attacked as being unpatriotic by others. He also broadcast a live interview with Saddam Hussein.

Another factor in the Persian Gulf War situation was that up-links permitted reporters to send stories and pictures directly to their newspaper or television station. The result was that more reporters covered this war than any other war. The Defense Department estimated that there were 1,500 reporters there at one time or another.

Sectionalism

Though the Pledge of Allegiance speaks of "one nation indivisible," sectionalism has been a factor for politics and the media for nearly two centuries. It was a problem when the Declaration of Independence and Constitution were drafted. What divided the country was slavery and that would continue to be true until the Civil War. It was sectionalism that was largely responsible for the stalemate in the 1824 presidential election. In part, it was the last hurrah of the original thirteen states. At that point the United States had seen five presidents—four from Virginia and one from Massachusetts. John Quincy Adams would make it two for Massachusetts, but the election of Jackson four years later marked a new era in American politics. Jackson was from Tennessee—the frontier. He was a farmer, a man of the people, and a military hero. As he moved into the White House, senators and representatives from the Western states began coming to Washington.

The issue pitted North against South because the Southern states had slavery and could not have survived economically without it, and the North did not have slavery. The Missouri Compromise of 1820 made part of the Louisiana territory free and part slave. As more new states entered the union, the issue of slavery came up again. As the United States moved closer to the Civil War, the slavery issue placed the Democrats against the Republicans, yet in a sense the basis was still sectionalism. That the

South had an economy based largely on cotton, while the North became industrialized as the Civil War approached was also a factor that promoted sectionalism.

Out of the Civil War and Reconstruction came the Solid South—Southern states consistently voting Democratic. From the Southern point of view, the Republicans were the source of their difficulties. The Republican Lincoln had defeated the Democrat Stephen A. Douglas for the presidency in 1860 and had emancipated the slaves. He had seen the Civil War through to its successful conclusion. And the Republicans had instituted the harsh reconstruction after the war. As a result, the Southern states voted as a block in presidential elections and elected only Democrats to the Congress. The South did not have a genuine two-party system for years.

And despite the Fourteenth and Fifteenth Amendments, which mandated equal rights and the right to vote for all citizens, the South did not comply. Its schools were segregated and blacks were prevented from voting and denied access to public facilities. Blacks could not use the same restrooms, drink from the same water fountains, or eat in the same restaurants as whites. Even public buses were segregated, with blacks forced to sit in the rear. And the Democratic Party supported this locally. Therefore, after the Civil War, the North and South still had different values, with segregation replacing slavery as the point of contention.

It was not until the 1948 election that the Solid South began to break apart. Because of Harry Truman's support of civil rights, Strom Thurmond, a Democrat from South Carolina, ran for president and received thirty-nine electoral votes from the Southern states. In a few years he would switch to the Republican Party and keep his seat in the Senate. Integration started slowly in the 1950s, with relatively little political impact. President Truman issued an executive order integrating the armed forces. The Supreme Court in *Brown v. Board of Education of Topeka* (1954) outlawed segregated schools. The job of enforcing school desegregation, however, fell first upon the Republican administration of Dwight Eisenhower. It was still the Democratic South against the Republican North.

This status changed in the 1960s. Lyndon B. Johnson from Texas became president and pushed a civil rights agenda started by John F. Kennedy. The United States had federal voting rights laws, a public accommodations law, and enforcement of school desegregation at the college and university level. The Democratic Party was no longer the party of segregation. The Republicans defined that in 1968 with their so-called Southern Strategy: a clear and simple invitation for segregationists to come over to the Republican side.

Creating a new sectional alignment, the Republicans were very successful in the South, but a Southern Republican was a Southerner first and not always in agreement with his or her fellow Republicans from the Northeast, the Midwest, or the Far West.

The Democrats still had that problem. In short, sectional labels today are at least as important as party labels in assessing political activities.

If one thinks of Republicans as conservatives and Democrats as liberals, consider these results from a national survey in 2002. Nationally, 39 percent of the respondents said they were Democrats, 37 percent aid they were Republicans, and 24 percent said they were independent. When asked about political ideology, 46 percent said they were conservatives, 28 percent said they were liberals, and 27 percent said they were middle of the road. A glance at these numbers should tell you that the notion that Republicans are conservatives and Democrats are liberals does not fit. In fact, a third of the Republicans are not conservatives and a third of the Democrats are conservatives (Unpublished survey, June 2002).

Regionally, there are clear differences in alignments. Forty-two percent of the Democrats in the West and 35 percent of the Democrats in the South are conservatives. Only 23 percent of the Democrats in the Midwest and 22 percent of the Democrats in the Northeast are conservatives. Fifty-two percent of the Democrats in the Northeast are liberals, while only 38 percent of the Democrats in the Midwest are liberals. Forty-three percent of the Democrats in the South and 41 percent of the Democrats in the West are liberals. Seventy-two percent of the Republicans in the South and 70 percent of the Republicans in the Midwest are conservatives, while only 52 percent of the Republicans in the Northwest and 61 percent of the Republicans in the West are conservatives (Unpublished survey, June 2002).

In short, party labels do not tell the whole story. A Southern Democrat is different from a Western Democrat, and a Northeastern Republican is different from a Midwestern Republican. Sectionalism remains a factor in politics. Sectionalism matters in political communication in part because most media are not national in nature. Network television news and the news magazines are exceptions, but even with television, there is local news.

Newspaper coverage basically revolves around local coverage. That local coverage reflects community values and the media are reluctant to go against those local values, as was seen in the coverage of civil rights, with many Southern media outlets holding to the values of their communities. Likewise, media in communities that are traditionally liberal or conservative will reflect those values in their coverage. This tendency means that the political agenda is shaped accordingly, and there are wide differences across the country.

Civil Rights and Political Communication

Civil rights has long been a factor in political communication. In 1831, William Lloyd Garrison started an abolitionist paper called the *Liberator*. Frederick Douglass carried the abolitionist cause for forty years before and after the Civil War. Their efforts foretold a black press that numbered more than a thousand by 1900 and more than twenty-five hundred by 1950 (Pride).

Yet the Civil Rights movement that began after World War II had a much larger impact on both politics and the media, and therefore on political communication. World War II raised consciousness about civil rights, as minorities served with distinction in World War II. Many are aware of two spectacular examples—the Tuskegee Airmen, the first blacks allowed to fly military planes, and the 442d Regimental Combat Team, a Japanese American unit that was the most decorated outfit in the war. And there were countless stories of minority group members who came home from the war and were refused service in restaurants, hotels, and other places.

The incongruity of this affected many Americans. Minorities could fight and risk their lives for their country, but they still had to sit in the back of the bus when they came home. President Truman took care of the problem in the military with an executive order in 1948 ending discrimination in the armed forces. Yet, the problem in the larger society remained.

The next major step was the Supreme Court decision in 1954 proclaiming that school segregation violated the Constitutional rights of blacks (*Brown v. Board of Education of Topeka,* 347 U.S. 483 [1964]). Yet, that did not end segregation. The next major event was the integration of schools in Little Rock, Arkansas, in 1957, and it did not happen easily. Resistance was so fierce that President Eisenhower sent federal troops to Little Rock to enforce the desegregation and stop segregationist adults from attacking black school children. Sending federal troops to deal with such a situation is rare, and to send the 101st Airborne Division, the most combat-ready unit in the U.S. Army, was significant.

At the same time, Martin Luther King began leading civil disobedience against segregation, starting with the Birmingham bus boycott in 1955. There were lunch-counter sit-ins to protest discrimination at eating places, there were protest marches, there were voter registration drives, and there were the actions of police against participants in these acts of civil disobedience, including the murder of three voter-registration activists by law-enforcement personnel in Mississippi in 1964. The police did solve those murders, but they did not solve the bombing murders of four young black girls in a church in Birmingham, Alabama, in 1963 until nearly forty years later. The media covered all of this. Northern newspapers like the *New York Times* and the *Washington Post* and the three news magazines—*Newsweek, Time,* and *U.S. News*—led the way. Southern newspapers were, for the most part, slow to catch on. But most important, network television news was national and delivered the same message in the South as in the rest of the country.

As the United States moved through the 1960s, segregation became a dirty word. Segregationists talked of states' rights until people saw through that talk. Then "law and order" became a code word for segregation and Republicans came up with their "Southern Strategy." What also has followed is "political correctness"—the use of language that is not offensive to members of minority groups. Some of what is called "political correctness" is not much more than simple courtesy, but politicians and media alike are sensitive to the feelings of minorities, something that was not always true a half century ago.

A critical event for the media in its efforts to cover the Civil Rights movement was the Supreme Court decision in *New York Times v. Sullivan,* 376 U.S. 254 (1964). L. B. Sullivan, commissioner in charge of police in Montgomery, Alabama, sued the *Times* because of an advertisement it ran that was highly critical of Southern law enforcement. The court ruled in favor of the *Times,* saying that a public official could collect damages for libel only if he or she could show actual malice or reckless disregard of the truth. Had the *Times* lost, coverage of the Civil Rights movement by major U.S. media would have been significantly subdued.

The *Times* faced a dozen other suits, all of which became moot with the Sullivan decision, and other media were also being threatened with suits over their coverage of the civil rights movement. The decision's implications went far beyond civil rights. The decision meant that any politician attempting to sue a newspaper or broadcast station for libel would have to demonstrate malice or reckless disregard of the truth. Establishing that the material in question was false would not be enough.

Although the 1960s saw significant legislation establishing rights of minorities, the issue is not resolved. Affirmative action and the rights of employees remain matters of controversy today. And while the right to vote, the right to rent or buy housing, and the right to use public accommodations are all protected by law, exercising those rights is not always easy.

Public Opinion Polling and Politics

Public opinion polling has been conducted for two centuries, but it was not until the 1930s that it really developed, and not until the 1960s that politicians became fully involved. Modern polling began with George Gallup (Lacy, 54). Gallup polled on newspaper readership for his doctoral dissertation at the University of Iowa and eventually went from there into polling as a business. His interest was not in politics, but rather in business applications of polling. However, he found he could make money polling on elections. Furthermore, this served as kind of validation; there is really no way to validate a poll about brand preferences in cereals, but with an election, there is a result known to the public. The pollster is either correct or incorrect in his or her prediction.

Others entered the field, and 1936 provided the first real test of Gallup's personal interview surveys. The *Literary Digest* did what has become perhaps the most famous presidential election poll that year. Their poll was a mail survey of names drawn from telephone directories. They predicted that Alf Landon would win. He did not. Franklin Roosevelt won all but two states and had eleven million more votes than Landon—Roosevelt had 62.5 percent of the vote.

It is widely suggested that what went wrong for *Literary Digest* was that they used telephone directories as a source of names at a time when many people did not have telephones. A bigger problem, however, is that it was a mail poll with a response rate of less than 20 percent. The poll killed the *Literary Digest*, but polling became more popular. The next crisis came in 1948 when

Gallup and most of the other pollsters incorrectly predicted that Thomas Dewey would defeat Harry Truman. With any poll, there is a margin of error that depends on the size of the sample. Most national polls uses samples of 1,000 and the margin of error is 3.2 percent. The pollsters missed by far more than that in 1948. The pollsters had to explain what, in their methods, might have caused them to be so wrong about the outcome. They survived to poll again with better luck in 1952.

The next development was the use of polls not to predict the outcome of an election but to find out how the public felt about various issues. In 1960, John F. Kennedy first made significant use of this, with Lou Harris as his pollster. It is commonplace now not only in presidential elections, but also in state and local elections. What this does is give the politician a chance to test an idea in a poll before offering it to the public; the politician thus is less likely to get criticized for a new idea or to lose an election because of it. And a politician may discover a hot issue that will affect the outcome of an election (Richard, 37).

Polling organizations are so numerous now that any politician can find one to do a survey of his electorate if he can afford it, and the cost is no longer prohibitive. Nearly all surveys are done by telephone, and with reduced long-distance rates in recent years, the actual cost is about $5 an interview. A polling company will charge more than this, but still for less than $10,000 a politician can find out how he or she really is doing, and that's not a large sum, given current levels of campaign expenditures.

Another important change is that computer-assisted interviewing generates results almost instantly. Within an hour of the time the last interview is made, results are available. This is because interviewers are keyboarding the answers into their computer that in turn sends them to the central computer. That is why is it possible for the television networks to give you results in the morning from a poll last night and for most polls to be only a few days old when you see them. There are two advantages to that: One is that the pollster can pick up on a hot issue at its peak, and the other is that it is known that public opinion shifts, sometimes dramatically, in just a few days. A poll is most accurate at the time it is taken. So the quicker poll results are made available, the better.

These current developments in polling have drawbacks. One drawback is that if a politician is not willing to put forth an idea without knowing that it will meet with public approval, then ideas are limited. Throughout history, many unpopular ideas have in time become accepted as conditions changed and the public became more informed about the idea. The other drawback is that some politicians seem to lean too heavily on poll results and lack individual thought.

Yet the reality is that polls make news, even bad polls. They make more news than most press conferences and most campaign speeches, and political communicators have to live with that reality.

The Electronic Media and Politics

The advent of electronic media in the twentieth century changed political communication. For politicians it meant new opportunities to reach people but also new challenges. At the same time, it offered new opportunities to the public to find out about politics and politicians.

Radio began in 1920 with the station 8MK, later to be WWJ, going on the air in Detroit in August, and KDKA, a Pittsburgh station, going on the air 2 November with results of the presidential election. Radio, however, was primarily used for entertainment and did not cover much news until the 1930s. It therefore was not a major factor in political communication in those years.

Franklin D. Roosevelt, the first politician to use radio effectively, changed things—nobody since has used it better. He had a great radio voice, and with his "fireside chats," he had a great presence. He averaged about three "chats" per year, but their impact was enormous. His opening line of "My fellow Americans" or "My friends" achieved an aura of intimacy. He delivered good news to his listeners and the fireside chats were morale boosters. No contemporary of his approached his effectiveness with radio (Stempel, "Franklin D. Roosevelt," 125).

Television was ready to enter the American culture by 1939, but World War II delayed its appearance until 1946. When it did begin, it took off rather slowly. In the presidential year of 1948, there were only 108 stations, and less than a fifth of the homes had television sets. Television was not a factor in that presidential election. Four years later, with a third of the homes having sets, television became a factor, with televised speeches by candidates and advertisements for the candidates on television (Baughman, 141–142).

The rest of the 1950s saw rapid growth, and by the end of the decade there were 573 stations, and more than three-fourths of the homes had television sets. Television would play a bigger role in the 1960 presidential election than it ever had before, but the reason was not the growth; it was the televised debates, something entirely new in a presidential campaign. John F. Kennedy and Richard Nixon met in four televised debates, and it is widely said that these debates decided the election because Kennedy performed much better than Nixon did. But it was not all four debates—it was the first one. Kennedy was relatively unknown, while Nixon had been in the public eye as vice president. It was assumed that he would fare the best in the first debate. He did not. He was no match for the quick-thinking Kennedy. Furthermore, Nixon looked terrible. He had a poor make-up job, and two days after the debate the *Chicago Daily News* asked in a front page story if Nixon had not been sabotaged. Whatever the explanation, Kennedy gained considerably in the polls after the first debate. The remaining three were not terribly decisive for either candidate (Kraus, 253–270, 331–340).

The debates had such impact that the assumption was that they would appear in every presidential election, but in fact did not appear again until 1976. The 1960 debates were made possible by an act of Congress that exempted them from the Federal Communication Commission's Equal Time Provision. That, however, was for 1960 only. President Lyndon Johnson, comfortably in the lead in 1964, did not want to debate, and the Democratic Congress did not renew the exemption. Between the candidates and the Congress, the exemption was blocked in 1968 and 1972.

Then in 1976, the League of Women Voters took over sponsorship of the debates, and debates were held between Gerald Ford and Jimmy Carter. Subsequently, the Federal Communications Commission (FCC) changed the Equal Time Rule so that debates between candidates were not covered, and there have been presidential debates ever since. Debates also have spread to state races, but on a rather limited basis. The idea of debating your opponent is not particularly popular among candidates for governor or U.S. senator.

Television news has become a major player in presidential campaigns. A national survey by Ohio University and the Scripps Howard News Service in 2000 showed that television news was the most widely used source of information about the presidential campaign, and by nearly a two to one margin considered the best source, with newspapers second (Unpublished survey, July 2000).

The Internet may challenge television as the main source of information about presidential campaigns, but in the 2000 presidential election, it had not yet achieved that status. The growth of Internet use in the last five years of the twentieth century was phenomenal. Daily use of the Internet went from 5 percent to 35 percent between 1995 and 1999. By the 2000 election, more than half the homes had access to the Internet. However, a national survey in 2000 by Ohio University and the Scripps Howard News Service found that only 25 percent of respondents thought the Internet was a useful source of information about the campaign and only 7 percent considered it most useful (ibid.). What the Internet offered were websites from newspapers and television stations, from the two political parties, and from nonpartisan groups like the League of Women Voters.

The newspaper and television websites merely offered abbreviated versions of what the newspapers had printed and the television stations had aired. The party websites offered somewhat limited content and were not updated regularly. They did not offer a great deal of timely information on issues. The nonpartisan groups offered mainly demographic information on candidates. In short, there is an opportunity for a great deal more content on the Internet from these three sources. It seems that the parties in particular did not fully utilize the capability of the Internet, but more utilization can be expected in the future.

What the Internet offers the parties and the candidates is the opportunity to present their message without it being changed in both content and emphasis by the media. Politicians generally like such an opportunity. They want their story, not the media's version of the story, to get to the public. The interest in doing that is indicated by another recent development. The parties have been sending out videotapes to their supporters. This may be as cost effective as television advertisements. It provides the opportunity to target an audience segment, whether that segment be contributors or independent voters, as opposed to the shotgun approach of a television ad. The parties also have achieved the same effect by using closed-circuit television.

Undoubtedly other technologies will emerge that will provide the same kind of opportunity for politicians to go directly to the voters. As this happens, the media will have to change the way they cover campaigns. This shift already has happened to a limited extent because of television advertisements. Those advertisements now are newsworthy, and media run stories about the latest television ad by a given candidate. Internet content may soon get the same kind of coverage by newspapers and television.

The ongoing expansion of electronic communication may pose another problem for political communication. The day that there are 500 television channels is not far off, and websites are virtually unlimited. Yet, as mass communication expands, the proportion of it devoted to political communication declines. That is really one of the stories of mass communication in the twentieth century, and there is no reason to suppose it will not be a trend of the current century. For voters who want information, the opportunities to get it have increased. For those who are indifferent to it, the likelihood of chance exposure to political communication has decreased.

An Expanding Electorate

We take for granted the right to vote, but one of the facts of the political history of the United States is that everyone has not always had the right to vote. In the beginning, it was only the landholders who could vote. Then the right to vote was extended to all white males. It was not, however, until 1920 that women had the right to vote. And, as already mentioned, the Civil Rights movement resulted in extending the right to vote to minorities. This, in part, was achieved by removing artificial barriers such as poll taxes and voter tests that tended to consist of obscure trick questions that most people would not be able to answer; whites did not have to answer them, but blacks or Asians might have to answer them.

Expanding the vote changed politics and political communication. When women got the right to vote, politicians had to think about issues that affected women and were of interest to women. Those issues became part of campaigns and part of the coverage of campaigns, which meant the media were dealing with issues and perspectives it had not dealt with before. Similarly, when the right of blacks to vote was established throughout the United States, politicians had to deal with issues of interest to blacks, and media ultimately reported those issues. Media coverage then moved toward discussing these issues and perhaps setting the agenda for politicians on the issues or assessing voter interest in the issues.

Politicians and the media also became aware that voter turnout varied for segments of the population. The most discussed difference in turnout has been between young people and old people—old people are much more likely to vote. This meant that politicians would pay more attention to issues of interest to older people. This certainly is one of the reasons why Social Security and Medicare have been such significant issues in recent elections.

Now, it appears that the electorate is going to have to change in a different way. The election of 2000 demonstrated that the American voting system was antiquated and obsolete. Critics wondered why, if there can be automatic teller machines by the dozens in communities, something similar could not be done for voting. Oregon experimented with voting by mail, and electronic voting may be tried soon in this country. It may be a few years, but if the United States is not already at the point that this would be both the cheapest and most accurate way to vote, it surely will be before long. When this occurs, who will vote? Will differences between age groups and income groups decrease? Will the overall turnout increase? Until it happens, one can only guess, but whatever the answers are, they will affect political communication in the years ahead.

References

Baughman, James L. "Television's Initial Handling of Politics." In *Historical Dictionary of Political Communication in the United States*, edited by Guido H. Stempel III and Jacqueline Nash Gifford. Westport, CT: Greenwood, 1999.

Brown v. Board of Education of Topeka, 347 U.S. 483 (1964).

Burriss, Larry L. "Ida Tarbell." In *Historical Dictionary of Political Communication in the United States*, edited by Guido H. Stempel III and Jacqueline Nash Gifford. Westport, CT: Greenwood, 1999.

Eberhard, Wallace B. "Zenger." In *Historical Dictionary of Political Communication in the United States*, edited by Guido H. Stempel III and Jacqueline Nash Gifford. Westport, CT: Greenwood, 1999.

Emery, Michael, and Edwin Emery. *The Press and America*. 6th ed. Englewood Cliffs, NJ: Prentice Hall, 1988.

Kraus, Sidney. *The Great Debates: Background, Perspective, Effects*. Bloomington: Indiana University Press, 1962.

Lacy, Stephen. "George Gallup." In *Historical Dictionary of Political Communication in the United States*, edited by Guido H. Stempel III and Jacqueline Nash Gifford. Westport, CT: Greenwood, 1999.

Levy, Leonard W., ed. *Freedom of the Press from Zenger to Jefferson*. Indianapolis, IN: Bobbs-Merrill, 1966.

Littlefield, Roy Everett. *William Randolph Hearst.* Lanham, MD: University Press of America, 1980.

Morley, Christopher, and Louella D. Everett, eds. *Familiar Quotations by John Bartlett.* 11th ed. Boston: Little, Brown and Company, 1939.

New York Times v. Sullivan, 376 U.S. 254 (1964).

Pride, Armistead. "Negro Newspapers: Yesterday, Today, and Tomorrow." *Journalism Quarterly* 28 (Spring 1951): 179.

Richard, Patricia. "Polling and Political Campaigns." In *The Practice of Political Communication,* edited by Guido H. Stempel III. Englewood Cliffs, NJ: Prentice Hall, 1994.

Sohn, Ardyth. "Persian Gulf War." In *Historical Dictionary of Political Communication in the United States,* edited by Guido H. Stempel III and Jacqueline Nash Gifford, 37. Westport, CT: Greenwood, 1999.

Stempel, Guido H., III. "Franklin D. Roosevelt." In *Historical Dictionary of Political Communication in the United States,* edited by Guido H. Stempel III and Jacqueline Nash Gifford. Westport, CT: Greenwood, 1999.

———, ed. *The Practice of Political Communication.* Englewood Cliffs, NJ: Prentice Hall, 1994.

Stewart, Kenneth, and John Tebbel. *Makers of Modern Journalism.* New York: Prentice Hall, 1952.

Swanberg, W. A. *Citizen Hearst.* New York: Scribner's, 1961.

———. *Pulitzer.* New York: Scribner's, 1967.

Tebbel, John W. and Sarah Miles Watts. *The Presidents and the Press.* New York: Oxford University Press, 1985.

Unpublished survey. Scripps Howard News Service and Ohio University, July 2000. Posted at http://www. newspolls.com. Accessed 10 December 2002.

———. Scripps Howard News Service and Ohio University, July 2001. Posted at http://www.newspolls.com. Accessed 10 December 2002.

Willkie, Wendell L. *One World.* New York: Simon and Schuster, 1943.

2

Problems in
Political Communication

Voter Turnout

The biggest problem in political communication today is voter turnout. It is a problem that involves politicians, the media, and voters. The record more than speaks for itself, as can be seen from Table 2.1. The turnout for presidential elections has been on a downward path for the last thirty years. The turnout in the last two presidential elections is the lowest in the last seventy years, and in 1996 less than half the adults in the United States voted for president. In 1952, 1960, 1964, and 1968, more than 60 percent of the adults voted in the presidential election, but then the decline began. It is widely said that the reason for the big drop in 1972 was that eighteen-year-olds were eligible to vote for the first time. Yet, in the next four presidential elections and six of the next seven after that, the turnout was lower than it had been in 1972. Eighteen-year-olds cannot be blamed for that. By way of comparison, it should be noted that in the spring of 2001, Great Britain had an election in which 60 percent voted, and that was by far the lowest turnout in Great Britain in forty years. In general, in the democracies of Western Europe, turnouts below 70 percent are rare.

But low as the presidential figures are, the figures for the House of Representatives vote are much worse. In the two off-year elections in the 1960s, 45.4 percent voted, but by 1974 the figure had dropped to 35.9 percent, and it has not been above 40 percent since. The most spectacular House election of recent times was in 1994 when Speaker of the House Newt Gingrich offered his "Contract with America," and the Republicans won control of the House for the first time in three decades. The victory was called a conservative revolution, but those who voted for Gin-

33

TABLE 2.1

Percentage of Adults Voting in Presidential and Off-Year Elections, 1932–2000

Year	Percent Voting	Year	Percent Voting
1932	**52.4**	1966	45.4
1934	41.4	**1968**	**60.9**
1936	**56.0**	1970	43.5
1938	44.0	**1972**	**55.2**
1940	**58.9**	1974	35.9
1942	32.5	**1976**	**53.5**
1944	**56.0**	1978	34.9
1946	37.1	**1980**	**52.6**
1948	**51.1**	1982	38.0
1950	41.1	**1984**	**53.1**
1952	**61.6**	1986	33.4
1954	41.7	**1988**	**50.1**
1956	**59.3**	1990	33.1
1958	43.0	**1992**	**55.2**
1960	**62.8**	1994	39.0
1962	45.4	**1996**	**49.0**
1964	**61.9**	1998	34.8
		2000	50.7

(Boldface years and votes are for president. Off-year figures are total voting percentage for races for U.S. House of Representatives.)
Source: Compiled from figures from the U.S. Bureau of Census, Congressional Quarterly, and Federal Election Commission published in World Almanac and American Almanac.

grich and the contract with America constituted about a fifth of the adult population. That election had the largest turnout for a congressional election in thirty years. However, the 1998 election returned to the lower levels that have prevailed in recent times.

Why is the voter turnout so low, and why has it been dropping? One reason is that elections take place on Tuesday, a working day, and for many living where the polls are open twelve hours, there is not much chance to vote. They work for eight hours, eat lunch for an hour, and perhaps commute an hour each way. If elections were moved to Sundays, as a number of countries have, that might help increase the turnout. Or, as some have suggested, Election Day could be made a national holiday.

A second reason for low voter turnout is negative advertising, which has become increasingly popular during the very period in which the decline has occurred. Conventional wisdom has it that negative advertisements win votes, but there are plenty of examples to the contrary. And negative advertisements convince some voters that there is no reason to vote. If Candidate A's ad tells you that Candidate B is a bum, and Candidate B's ad

tells you that Candidate A is a scoundrel, why vote? Some political scientists suggest that negative media coverage of politics
and politicians leads to disenchantment of voters and causes
them not to vote. Yet one has to ask: Is the coverage unfairly negative or is it a fair representation of what the politicians do? It is
the coverage or the actions that are the problem?

Another factor is the way in which presidential candidates
are chosen. Until 1972, the party conventions picked the candidates. There were primary elections, but not in all states, and in
many cases, the state results were not binding on the delegates.
Then in 1972 binding primaries became the norm in all fifty
states. What that has meant in every presidential election since
then is that the candidates were determined before the convention. Likewise, the candidates were usually determined well before all the primaries were over.

There is also some disenchantment among voters with the
candidates that are selected. A poll by the Scripps Howard News
Service and Ohio University in July of 2000, found that only a
fourth of the voters thought both parties had picked the best candidates (Unpublished survey, July 2000). With the candidates already determined, the party convention plays a much different
role than it previously did. The conventions have no say in the
selection of candidates, which turns them into pep rallies of the
party faithful. This is very different than the conventions of yes-
teryear where sometimes there was an element of suspense,
which in turn created interest.

It also should be noted that the downturn has occurred in
spite of increased voter registration. In the 1960s, Congress
passed legislation that gave blacks the right to register and therefore vote, something that they had been denied for years in the
South. And many states made efforts to make registration easier,
including in some cases allowing voters to register on the day of
the election.

Some say that the problem is the failure of the candidates to
discuss and the media to cover issues, that campaigns merely
consist of slogans and images. Certainly this is a problem, and
both the parties and the media are to blame. However, slogans
and images have always been a part of politics. There are many
well-known images from elections long ago. George Washington
could not tell a lie—remember the story of how he cut down his
father's favorite cherry tree and then confessed what he had
done to his father? In the 1840 election, William Henry Harrison
campaigned with the slogan "Tippecanoe and Tyler too."

Tippecanoe was a battle that Harrison, as general, won against the Indians. Tyler was his running mate. Abraham Lincoln was the rail-splitter. Theodore Roosevelt was "Old Rough and Ready" who led a charge of Rough Riders on horseback up San Juan Hill in Cuba during the Spanish-American War. An interesting story, but historians have fairly well established that it never happened because the horses were still in Florida. All of these are images unrelated to the issues of the time.

What is the solution? Voter turnout is an issue for the political parties, for the media, and for the voters. There is, in effect, a triangle, and the question is: In what direction does communication and influence flow? Do parties influence the media, or is it the other way around? Do the parties influence the voters, or is it the other way around? And what about the media and the voters? Of the three, which can do something to change the present pattern? It seems that the voters have little ability to influence either the parties or the media. What, then, about the media and the parties? If the parties make a concerted effort, the media probably will cooperate. If the media make a concerted effort, the politicians will pay attention. Yet, too often what is seen is a half-hearted effort. Neither the parties nor the media at the present time really see voter turnout as the most important consideration in an election. The issue may be raised, but attention soon turns to other topics. The solution is for the parties, the media, and voters to take voter turnout seriously.

Campaign Finance

It costs money to run for political office. A candidate for office in a small town may be able to run a campaign for a couple of thousand dollars, but a candidate for president will need $100 million, and a candidate for the U.S. Senate probably will need at least $20 million.

There are two ways to get that money—from individual and business contributors, and from public financing of campaigns. Public financing has by and large been rejected, although some political contributions are tax deductible and therefore are, in effect, publicly supported. However, the bulk of the millions of dollars generated in any year for the presidential candidate, 435 House of Representatives candidates, and 33 or 34 Senate candidates comes from contributions (Sorauf, 181).

Both Congress and state legislatures have limited individual contributions, and Congress passed another law limiting contributions in 2002, the intent of which is to eliminate so-called soft money—money not given directly to the candidates. It is too soon to tell what the effect will be, and there are pros and cons for it. There are two other kinds of contributions besides those to candidates. One is a contribution to the political party, not to an individual campaign. This is the soft money, which the party is supposed to use to support its regular operations, but not to support specific candidates. Many feel this restriction is frequently not met. The other kind is contribution to educational funds. Such funds presumably deal with information about issues. They are tax deductible and can be anonymous. These can be a problem because such educational campaigns are in fact frequently aimed at a particular candidate. Furthermore, the names of donors are not known. For contributions to candidates and to parties, the identity of the donor is on public record. You may have noticed in advertisements on television or newspapers that the source of funding is indicated because it is mandated by law, and this has been upheld in court tests.

The largest concerns, however, are with the amount of money donated to candidates and with how much an individual can donate to a candidate. Those who advocate no limits on contributions argue that the First Amendment gives a person a right to give as much money to a candidate as he or she wishes. They also say that the First Amendment permits no restrictions on such contributions or on communication related to campaigns. There are two kinds of restrictions that have been upheld in a number of court decisions. One is that the name of the contributor is a public record. The other is that false and misleading statements are unlawful, and a contributor could be accountable.

The U.S. Supreme Court rejected much of the First Amendment argument in a decision in June of 2001 (Clymer). The court upheld a Colorado law restricting not only the amount of money that could be given directly to a candidate but also the amount of money a party could give to a candidate.

In so ruling, the majority accepted the argument that campaign contributions are at least in part an attempt to buy influence. Justice David Souter wrote in the majority opinion that "Parties function for the benefit of donors whose object it is to place candidates under obligation, a fact that parties cannot escape" (Clymer). The court majority thus rejected the notion put forth by proponents of unlimited campaign contributions that those who contribute large sums of money expect nothing in return.

The legislation passed in 2002 will help, but it will not solve the entire problem. The issue of campaign contributions has been around for a long time, and there is little reason to suppose that it will not remain an important issue in the years ahead.

Electoral College

The presidential election of 2000 once again focused attention on the electoral college. In that election, Al Gore had 48,971,067 votes to 48,779,508 for George W. Bush. Bush, however, had 271 electoral votes to 267 for Gore, and thus was elected president. Yet this was not the first instance. In 1876 Samuel J. Tilden had 4,284,767 to 4,033,950 for Rutherford B. Hayes, but Hayes had 185 electoral votes to 184 for Tilden. There were four states in which votes were disputed, and a special commission investigated. The commission had eight Republicans and seven Democrats, and it voted 8 to 7 four times, giving all the disputed votes and the presidency to Hayes. Twelve years later Grover Cleveland had 5,540,050 votes to 5,444,337 for Benjamin Harrison, but Harrison had 233 electoral votes to 166 for Harrison (*2000 World Almanac*, 558–590).

How could this happen? It happened in the election of 2000 simply because of the way each state's number of electoral votes is determined. A state gets one elector for each seat in the House of Representatives, which is proportional to the population of the state. But in addition, each state gets an electoral vote for each seat in the U.S. Senate, which is two per state. North Dakota and South Dakota, with a total of 1.5 million people, have 6 electoral votes. So does Kansas, with 2.5 million people. Ohio has 11 million people, the same as the combined total of three of its neighbors—Indiana, Kentucky, and West Virginia. Those three states, however, have 25 electoral votes to Ohio's 21 (*2000 World Almanac*, 558–590).

What happened in the election of 2000 was that Bush won thirty states and Gore, twenty. Bush therefore got sixty votes related to the Senate seats, while Gore got forty. Take away the electoral votes for the Senate seats, and Gore wins. So, the possible reform is to give each state electoral votes based on the number of House seats, which in turn would make the number of electoral votes directly proportional to the population. However, it is not likely to happen. It will require a Constitutional amendment, and the small states would never approve. Neither would their senators. There are twenty-seven states with fewer than ten electoral votes, and a change to make the electoral college directly proportional to population would not only reduce their electoral votes significantly but reduce their political power as well.

The other problem is that the candidate who has the most votes in a given state gets all the electoral votes, whether the margin of victory was one vote or a million. It has been suggested that the electoral votes be divided proportionately to the state vote. In other words, if a candidate gets 60 percent of the vote, he or she should get 60 percent of the electoral votes, not all of them. The objection to that is that it would encourage and aid third-party candidates and possibly lead to situations in which no candidate had a majority of the electoral votes. That would, under the Constitution, put selection of the president in the hands of the House of Representatives.

The electoral college began in the first place because the intent of the founding fathers was not to have the president chosen by the general public. So they put in Article 2 of the Constitution that each state would select electors in whatever way its legislature directed, and those electors would meet and cast votes for president and vice president.

There were problems almost immediately. In 1796 John Adams, the Federalist, was selected as president, and Thomas Jefferson, the Republican, was chosen as vice president. There was significant discord with this arrangement, something the framers of the Constitution had not anticipated. In 1800, it became worse because Burr, the vice-presidential candidate, claimed that the seventy-three electoral votes he received were for president, as were the seventy-three electoral votes for Jefferson. The House of Representatives then was called on to break the deadlock and selected Jefferson. This situation led to the passage of the Twelfth Amendment in 1803. It specified that the votes for president and vice president were separate. That settled the matter at hand, but proposals to change the electoral college in some way or other arise in almost every session of Congress. Yet two centuries after the Twelfth Amendment, the electoral college remains spelled out by that amendment and Article 2.

Competent Communicators

The shortage of competent political communicators is a significant problem for political communication, for the political parties, for the media, and ultimately for the people of the United States. The shortage is in part because of a larger problem—a shortage of people who can write. That in turn is because it is not a high priority to teach people to write. Discussion is widespread about the failure to teach enough math, science, and foreign language in high schools and colleges, but more time is spent teaching those subjects than teaching writing. Many colleges and universities are not requiring as much writing as they used to, and they are not assigning their best teachers to this task. (Much is written and said about how grade school and high school students perform in math, reading, and science. Students are tested in these areas and thus there are results to discuss. Writing by grade school or high school children, however, is not always tested, and therefore their performance is not always discussed.) Political communication is not the only field that suffers from the lack of good writers. One needs only to read memos and reports of organizations and businesses to see evidence of this. Or you can look at the laws legislators write and pass or the decisions that judges write to see evidence of the problem.

The problem for political communication goes beyond writing. Another major aspect is the large number of political communicators that are needed. Take, for example, Ohio, a state with eighty-eight counties and 611 school districts. In those eighty-eight counties, there are county commissioners, the sheriff, the treasurer, and the auditor who must to some extent communicate with the public. Those 611 school districts likewise need to communicate with the public. Beyond this there are several hundred cities, towns and villages, which have mayors, councils, and police departments that need to communicate with the public. There are ninety-nine state representatives and thirty-four state senators, as well as eighteen U.S. representatives and two U.S. senators, all of whom need political communications. In short, there are a few thousand public officials who need to communicate with the public. The issue is not whether communicating can be avoided, but whether communicating can be done well enough to be effective.

The media, of course, also need people to participate in political communication by covering the activities of these offices and agencies. Their resources are limited, and the total number of media people committed full-time or part-time to political coverage by Ohio media is probably about 500. Nationally, it might run to 20,000.

Political communication thus becomes a competitive sport for those representing the various parts of the political process. If supporters want coverage of their official or candidate, they have to figure out what they can do that will make a reporter willing to cover him or her. That task requires an understanding of how the media operate, and they have to pay attention to what gets covered and what does not get covered. An additional concern is for political communicators to be knowledgeable about the changing ways of delivering news. The challenge of the moment is to use the Internet effectively, which politicians are not doing.

If political communicators decide to send a news release, they have to be aware of the requirements of the newspaper or broadcast station to which the release is sent. The first thing they should note is that the stories that get used are short, and it helps if they are interesting. Communicators also need to be aware that studies show that 90 percent of the releases sent to media are ignored. There are, in short, some winners and some losers in the game of political communication.

On the media side, there is also the problem of finding reporters and editors who understand politics well enough to write and edit intelligently. It helps if they have studied political science, and it also helps if they can communicate effectively with the political communicators. Everything in politics and government is not self-evident. The novice reporter will not believe how complicated the budget of the smallest city or smallest school district can be until he or she encounters one. It is also important that politicians and officeholders think about their political communication needs when hiring people.

College journalism majors who are interested enough in politics to get the background that they will need by taking courses in political science, sociology, history, and economics are also needed. Political writing needs to be viewed as being as much of a specialty as science writing. In short, politicians and the media must put a higher priority on informing the public.

Status of the Political Parties

The American people are not content with the way the political parties are currently performing. Evidence of this comes from a national poll conducted by the Scripps Survey Center at Ohio University and the Scripps Howard News Service in the summer of 2000. The 1,020 respondents were asked if each party was healthy, had a good agenda, and had clear issues. They were asked if the parties were doing a good job or bad job of controlling special interests. They also were asked if George W. Bush was the best candidate the Republicans could have found and whether Al Gore was the best candidate the Democrats could have found. The results were not flattering. Forty-five percent of the respondents said the Democratic Party was healthy, 49 percent said it had a good agenda, and 54 percent said it has clear issues. Forty-nine percent said the Republican Party was healthy, 47 percent said it had a good agenda, and 57 percent said it had clear issues (Unpublished survey, July 2000). Those are moderately favorable results. Nearly half the people doubted the health, the agenda, and the clarity of issues of each party. However, the responses to the other two questions are much more unfavorable.

The survey also revealed that 15 percent said the Republicans did a good job of controlling special interests, and 18 percent said the Democrats did a good job of controlling special interests. In other words, the people of America do not believe the parties when they say that campaign contributions do not affect the actions of government. They believe that big-money interests have too much influence. Forty-two percent thought George W. Bush was the best candidate the Republicans could have found, while only 35 percent thought Al Gore was the best candidate the Democrats could have found. Only 19 percent thought that both candidates were the best the parties could have found. Considering these results, it is no surprise that only half the people vote in presidential elections and less than that in state and local elections. That level of voter participation has to be considered an indication of failure on the part of the political parties.

Why the disenchantment with the parties? People tend to feel that their vote does not count and that the outcome of the election will not affect them. The survey asked how much difference it would make in respondents' lives who won. Twenty-four percent thought it would make a big difference, but 45 percent said it would make a small difference and 24 percent thought it would make no difference at all. In other words, two-thirds of the people did not really think it would matter a lot who was president.

Part of the problem may be the increasing partisanship of the parties. Voters are all urged to vote for the candidate, not the party. In turn, many do so. For example in the 2000 election there were thirty-three U.S. senators elected. In ten states, people voted for a senator from one party and a presidential candidate from the other. Do the parties realize that this is happening? Their rhetoric makes one wonder.

What can the parties do to increase public acceptance of them? Certainly it will help if they can agree on reasonable limitations to campaign contributions. It will also help if they listen to the people more than they have. New communication technology offers opportunities ranging from televised town meetings to e-mail. It also will help if the presidential primary process can be revised so that every voter has a chance to vote while the outcome is still in doubt. A solution, however, must begin with the parties recognizing that there is a problem. There is not a lot of evidence right now that they do.

Media Bias

Claims of media bias are made frequently by politicians, and there has been considerable research on the subject. The question became a major one in the election of 1948 when Harry Truman made "one-party press" one of the two main themes of his campaign, the other was the "Do Nothing" Eightieth Congress. Truman was expected to lose the election—all the polls said so—but he embarked on an extensive and vigorous whistle-stop campaign and won the election. By "one-party press" Truman meant that because most newspapers had endorsed his opponent Thomas E. Dewey editorially, their bias spilled over into the news columns.

Obviously "one-party press" had been an effective issue, and the message was not lost on other politicians. Adlai Stevenson, the Democratic candidate who lost to Dwight Eisenhower in the next election repeated the charge. There were several studies of newspaper coverage of that election, and they provided limited support for Stevenson's claim. He repeated the charge in 1956, but the only study of coverage of that campaign did not support his claim.

Still it was a viable political issue, and in 1960 both sides employed it. John F. Kennedy followed the Truman line that news coverage was affected by the fact that more than three times as many newspapers endorsed Nixon editorially. Not to be outdone, Nixon claimed that the coverage was biased against him because a poll of correspondences covering the campaign showed they favored Kennedy by a wide margin.

Studies of coverage of that campaign found that it was very even. Two years later, Nixon may have saved his political career with his claim of press bias. He ran for governor of California and was upset by Pat Browne. On the same day, Nelson Rockefeller of New York, George Romney of Michigan, and James Rhodes of Ohio scored stunning victories in races for governor. That seemed to make them the leading candidates for the Republican nomination for president in 1964 and seemed to mean the end of Nixon's political career. However, two days after the election, Nixon held a press conference ostensibly to announce his retirement from politics. The press conference, however, was an attack on the press. He told the assembled media representatives, "You won't have old Dick Nixon to kick around any more." It was front-page news all over America, and Nixon, the loser on Tuesday, had stolen the play from the three Republicans who had won.

Nixon made no claims of coverage bias in the 1968 campaign, but once he was in office his administration did. Vice President Spiro Agnew led an all-out attack on the media, claiming that the media were unfair to the Nixon administration. The attack was effective in that it reduced public confidence in the media. However, the Watergate scandal and Nixon's subsequent resignation restored public confidence in the media.

Recent campaigns have not seen the claims of biased coverage by candidates, but there have been claims of liberal bias by conservative politicians and conservative think tanks. The claims have been backed by anecdotes, not by systematic analysis of media coverage. The serious studies that have been made have not supported the claims of bias. Two recent studies add to the long list of studies that have found little bias in coverage. A Minnesota study of coverage of the 1996 presidential campaign looked at 12,215 randomly selected news stories from forty-three newspapers and television newscasts (Domke, et al.). Looking at 151,057 references to issues, they found that Bill Clinton and Bob Dole had slightly favorable coverage. Dole got favorable coverage on character while Clinton did not, but Clinton fared much better than Dole in horse-race coverage.

M. Mark Miller, Julie L. Andsager, and Bonnie P. Riechert looked at coverage of the 1996 Republican primary in the *New York Times*, the *Washington Post*, and the *Los Angeles Times* (Miller, et al.). They also looked at press releases by the candidates. They found that while newspaper coverage of issues differed from that of the press releases, each candidate still was able to get his positions represented accurately in the newspapers.

Governmental Secrecy

Although some progress has been made in recent years, secrecy in government remains a major problem in political communication. It is a problem for the media because they cannot get information about the activities of government. It is a problem for politicians because information they may need for a decision is kept from them. It is also a problem for politicians in that secrecy tends to favor the party in power. This means that it is a problem for the public, too, because the public cannot find out what the government is really doing in some instances. And though it is talked about mostly with regard to national government, it is a problem at all three levels of government—local, state, and national (Wiggins, 199–226).

At the local level, state laws mandate some degree of openness. Meetings of councils, committees, and boards must be open to the public. However, laws provide exceptions, and politicians show great imagination in applying the exceptions. The common exceptions are meetings discussing personnel matters and land transactions. The exceptions usually are called executive sessions, a misleading term because rather than being simply a closed meeting, in fact it is a means for doing public business in private.

For example, if a city decides to hire a new police chief, it may be up to the city council to make the selection. The council is permitted to interview the candidates in closed session. The council cannot vote or make the decision in closed session, but usually a consensus emerges. Then the council goes into open session, has no discussion, and votes unanimously for one of the applicants. The public has no idea why that person was chosen. Also there can be a situation in which three members of a five-person committee screen the applicants in secret and then come to the open meeting and move to hire a candidate that the other two members know nothing about. They have not even seen the candidate's application. Obviously, such actions violate the spirit of open-meeting laws.

By law, labor negotiations are considered personnel matters, and personnel matters, by law, can be discussed in closed meetings. Therefore, negotiations between a city and its employees or a school board can be discussed in secret. Though these negotiations involve public funds, the public does not learn anything until the negotiations are complete and it is presented with an accomplished fact.

State laws also mandate that general records that cities, townships, and counties are required to keep are by definition public records—every citizen has a right to know the salaries of public employees and the amounts of other expenditures made by various governmental bodies. At the state level, the problem is less severe. Legislatures meet in public, although committees sometimes meet in secret. Actions of state agencies generally become matters of public record. What is not visible to the public are the conferences and meetings between various members of the executive branch. The actions that come out of those meetings are public, but the reasons for them frequently are not known to the public.

Federal government secrecy is a different matter. Although the Freedom of Information Act provides access to documents of government agencies, there are nine exceptions, national security being by far the most important. The present national security system was set up by President Truman shortly after the end of World War II. Two things account for this action. First, the atomic bomb was to be kept classified from other countries. Second, the Cold War provided an unprecedented peacetime situation. The United States and Great Britain distrusted their World War II ally, Russia, and the feeling was mutual. While the ideological differences between Soviet Communism and democracy were a major factor, Russian expansion in Eastern Europe became the more specific concern. The result was that national security became a major concern, and that had not happened to the United States after any other previous war.

Truman's order has been modified by those who have succeeded him in office. The power to classify has been given to more than 10,000 people, and it is estimated that there are about 40 million classified documents. The problem is that the authority to classify has been greatly abused. This was most vividly demonstrated in the so-called Pentagon Papers case. In 1971, the *New York Times* received a copy of a classified study of the origins of the Vietnam War. The *Times* published it, and other papers followed their lead. Despite the government injunction to stop the publication, the case went immediately to the Supreme Court. Eight of the nine justices said they did not believe there was anything in the Pentagon Papers that endangered national security, and by a 6 to 3 vote the Court ruled that publication could be resumed. The Court's ruling meant that the fact that a document was classified did not mean that it related to national security. While the court was deliberating, the chief of Naval Security was called to testify before a House Committee. Asked how many classified documents he knew existed, he said about twenty million had been created in twenty-five years. He then was asked how many of those papers truly dealt with military secrets or national security, and he said one-half of 1 percent. The other 99.5 percent were essentially political secrets.

Perhaps the most memorable anecdote from the Pentagon Papers decision was Justice Potter Stewart's comment that "when everything is classified, nothing is classified" (*New York Times v. United States* 403 U.S. 713 [1971]). The case certainly indicated a need to revise the security system, but it has not yet happened. The result of the Pentagon Papers case was that the government was forced to permit disclosure of only one of the twenty million documents that were classified at that time.

Some people at the time viewed the Pentagon Papers as a limited decision, but thirty years later it stands in place, evidence that the security system can be challenged. The Freedom of Information Act provides a more direct means of challenge. If someone requests a document and is denied on the grounds of national security, the person making the request can appeal to the Federal District Court. The Freedom of Information Act, however, applies only to documents, and there are many secrets within the executive branch. Executive policy is made in meetings that are not open to the public.

Congress is open to the public. Some committee meetings are closed, but the sessions are open, and votes are a matter of record. The public undoubtedly knows more about the actions of Congress than it does about the actions of the executive branch. Although the U.S. government is perhaps the most open in the world, there is still a great deal of secrecy, and the public's right to know what the various parts of government are doing is by no means universally acknowledged or respected.

Public Confidence

The American people do not have a lot confidence in government. A Gallup poll in 2000 asked people if they had a great deal of confidence, quite a lot of confidence, some confidence, or very little confidence in a particular entity. Seven percent said they had a great deal of confidence and 17 percent said that they had quite a lot of confidence in Congress. Fifteen percent said that they had a great deal of confidence in the presidency and 27 percent said they had quite a lot of confidence in the presidency

(Gallup, 208, 209). Another Gallup poll asked respondents about the degree of honesty and ethical standards of various professions. Twenty-four percent rated senators high or very high, and 21 percent rated congressmen high or very high. In contrast, 79 percent rated nurses high or very high, and 62 percent rated elementary school and high school teachers very high (ibid., 388–389).

In economically prosperous times, two-thirds of the American people will say that the president is doing a good job, but often the approval rating drops below 50 percent. On the other hand, the approval ratings of Congress are on average much lower, and yet in most elections, most incumbents in Congress are reelected. Of the members of the House of Representatives who ran for reelection in 2000, 98.5 percent won (Patterson). The public response largely can be traced to media coverage, which is critical much of the time. And if the news coverage is not critical, the editorials and the columnists are. Quite often the editorial and opinion pages of a metropolitan newspaper will print criticism of government on some topic. The criticism of government and its actions easily spills over to criticism of individuals and too often degenerates into sleaze. The private lives of politicians become public, and attacks on the politician for real indiscretions may be followed by attacks for hypothetical or imaginary indiscretions.

President Bill Clinton experienced this. There was a true indiscretion with Monica Lewinsky, but as a result, both Bill and Hillary Clinton were in turn investigated for years for supposed illegal dealings in Arkansas, investigations that produced nothing but accusations. New York City Mayor Rudolph Giuliani also experienced it. His affair with Judith Nathan and his conflict with his wife were in the news for months.

Campaigns intensify the problem. It was widely reported that the reason Colin Powell did not enter the Republican presidential primary race in 1996 or 2000 was that he did not want to expose his family to the attacks that have unfortunately become routine in campaigns. Candidates for lesser offices have expressed the same concern, and it is evident that the wickedness that has become part of campaigns limits the field of candidates and deprives the country of people of talent and integrity who would serve America well.

The media bear considerable responsibility for this situation. They become the carrier for the inappropriate messages of candidates, and there is great reluctance in newsrooms to decide that such messages are not truly newsworthy. There is also a least common denominator factor operating. If a grocery store tabloid offers up a charge against a candidate, it is difficult for the television networks to ignore it.

The media often argue that the public wants this coverage, but the evidence for this is limited. In the Clinton impeachment proceedings, poll after poll showed that the public wanted less coverage, not more. Clinton's job approval rating stayed high during this period, to the amazement of both political and media people, and media credibility declined, much to the consternation of media people. Yet anyone who thinks the media learned something from this experience need look only at the Giuliani coverage or that of California Congressman Gary Condit and the disappearance of Chandra Levy, an intern who was working for him. In the latter situation, there was a long period in which there really was no fresh or genuine news, but the story stayed on television newscasts and newspaper front pages for months. CBS anchor Dan Rather, to his credit, announced that CBS would stop covering the story on a daily basis. When Levy's body was found months later, it was evident that much of the media attack on Condit had been misguided.

Television Advertising

Political advertising on television is criticized for two things—it is too brief and too negative. Few issues lend themselves to sensible discussion in thirty seconds, so little discussion of issues is provided. What is provided is as superficial as it is clever. In the absence of issues, images are given—positive images of the candidate whose advertisement it is and negative ones of his or her opponent (Jamieson, 43–63, 237–266).

Conventional wisdom says that negative television advertising is effective, and it does seem that in some instances it has been. On the other hand, there are clear instances of the failure of negative campaign advertising. One such advertisement that received national attention in 2000 was a $5 million negative campaign in Ohio against a state Supreme Court justice, Alice Robie Resnick. This was considered highly offensive, but not illegal by the state's election commission. Its net effect was that Resnick won by 14 percent, a much larger margin than she had in two earlier campaigns. Yet, there are many other examples of candidates who used negative advertising and did not win. However, the advocates of negative advertising forget about these as they recite the examples of those who won with negative advertisements. Some examples of candidates succeeding with negative advertising are actually from campaigns in which both candidates engaged in considerable negative advertising. Did the winning candidate win because of negative advertising? Did the losing candidate lose because of negative advertising? Who knows?

Some have suggested restriction on television advertisements, but almost any plan that you can think of will run into First Amendment concerns. It would be nice to eliminate thirty-second advertisements in favor of longer ones. It would be nice not to have any campaign advertisements until one month before the election. There are many other possible reforms, but it's not likely that those too would not run into problems with the First Amendment.

Media Monopoly

Consolidation has been a major trend among mass media companies as it has been in much of the American business world in recent years. Ben Bagdikian, long a critic of the concentration of ownership in the media, says in the preface to the sixth edition of *Media Monopoly*, "The country's most widespread news, commentary and daily entertainment are controlled by six firms that are among the world's largest corporations" (Bagdikian, viii). The six are AOL Time Warner, Disney, Viacom, News Corporation, Bertelsmann, and General Electric. Bagdikian goes on to say that their annual revenue is greater than that of the next twenty largest media companies.

Perhaps more telling than Bagdikian's statement is the fact that chains now own three-fourths of the daily newspapers in the United States and all but one of the VHF television stations in the top ten markets in the United States. Herbert H. Howard found that 92 percent of VHF stations and 62 percent of the UHF stations in the top 100 markets are owned by large companies (Howard). Likewise, John C. Busterna found that 43 percent of the cities with daily newspapers in 1920 had competing papers, while by 1986, only 2 percent of the cities with daily newspapers had competing dailies (Busterna).

Given that there is considerable concentration of ownership, two questions must be asked: How did such concentration of ownership arise? What are the implications of it for what the public gets from the media? The combination of the advent of radio and the depression of the late 1920s and early 1930s caused some newspapers to consolidate and others to go out of business. The trend continued after World War II as television came about. By 1960, only 4 percent of the cities with daily newspapers had competing dailies. However, it should be noted that while the number of newspapers declined, the number of media increased, so in most cities with daily newspapers, there was competition from the broadcast media. The next question is whether the Internet will hurt the other media. Audiences for newspapers and television news are down. Will the Internet become a more viable way to distribute news than newspapers or television? Perhaps, but most likely not in the immediate future. As for the implications of concentration of ownership, critics argue that it decreases the diversity of information. The argument is that the powerful corporate owners control media content and do so in ways that cause the establishment view and the conservative view to be all that is heard.

Neither research nor common sense supports this view. Time Warner can not control all the content of its media holdings. Corporate executives can not look over the shoulder of every reporter or every writer. It is also argued that this concentration of ownership and lack of competition causes the public to get less news. It certainly can, but it does not have to. Bagdikian argues that Gannett, a company that owns more than eighty newspapers as well as other media properties, has done this. On the other hand, Knight Ridder, a large Internet and newspaper publishing communications company, has substantially improved many of the newspapers it has bought. For example, it took over a newspaper in Philadelphia, the *Inquirer*, and has turned it into one of the nation's best. In Lexington, Kentucky, it bought two unsuccessful newspapers and turned them into the *Herald-Leader*, which is now capable of competing with Kentucky's best and one of the nation's best, the Louisville *Courier-Journal*.

It also is evident that media seek varied viewpoints. The opinion page of most metropolitan dailies contains writers who are very liberal and writers who are very conservative. Television panels that interview political leaders or discuss major issues likewise contain people whose viewpoints vary widely. In contrast, the Internet provides unlimited opportunity for expression of divergent viewpoints. There is limited substantial evidence that the concentration of ownership of media keeps politicians from getting their points of view out to the public. The politician who is available to the media and who is cooperative with the media is going to have the opportunity to be heard.

Negativism

It is often said that news is negative. Certainly a lot of it is, but all news is not negative. Gerald C. Stone, Barbara Hartung, and Dwight Jensen found that 43 percent of the local television news in three markets was negative and 33 percent was positive (Stone, Hartung, and Jensen, 41–43). An earlier study by Gerald C. Stone and Elinor Grusin found that 47 percent of the network television news was negative news, and only 25 percent positive news (Stone and Grusin, 520–523). A number of studies indicate that while newspapers also have bad news, it is not as much as these two studies found. However, if news is negative, part of the reason is that newsmakers are negative. Political campaigns have an appreciable amount of negative content. Some partisan politicians are constantly criticizing the opponent. Both Bill Clinton and George W. Bush ran against the federal government in Washington, D.C. As their success shows, for them, it was good politics to criticize the federal government and to say, "Vote for me; I'm not part of that."

The net result is that public perception of politics and politicians tends to be negative. At any moment in time, polls show that somewhere between one-fourth and one-half of the people think the president is not doing a good job (Patterson, 41).

A new concept called civic journalism offers some hope for decreasing negative coverage. The focus of civic journalism is on finding solutions rather than just pointing out problems. This media focus will affect politicians because they will recognize that offering solutions will get them more media coverage. Furthermore, it is obvious that the public will like this approach better, and will hold both the media and the politicians in higher regard.

Another benefit would be if the media localized stories more than they do. An example of the failure to do this has been the discussion of SAT and ACT test scores that has been going on for the past two decades. National scores do not tell people how their own schools are doing, and the media rarely report scores for individual school systems.

The same point can be made with regard to politicians. It is very hard to find out what any one U.S. senator or representative is doing. Media coverage focuses on an average of a dozen representatives and leaves citizens with the impression that the rest of the representatives are not doing anything important (Weaver and Wilhoit, 12–26).

References

Bagdikian, Ben. *Media Monopoly.* 6th ed. Boston: Beacon Press, 2000.

Busterna, John C. "Trends in Daily Newspaper Ownership." *Journalism Quarterly* 65 (Winter 1988): 831–838.

Clymer, Adam. "Justices Uphold Curbs on Coordinated Political Spending." *New York Times* (26 June 2001): A15.

Domke, David, David P. Fan, Michael Fibison, Dhavan H. Shah, Steven S. Smith, and Mark D. Watts. "News Media, Candidates and Issues, and Public Opinion in the 1996 Presidential Campaign." *Journalism & Mass Communication Quarterly* 74 (Winter 1997): 718–737.

Gallup, George, Jr. *The Gallup Poll: Public Opinion 2000.* Wilmington, DE: Scholarly Resources, Inc., 2001.

Howard, Herbert H. "TV Station Group and Cross-Media Ownership: 1995 Update." *Journalism & Mass Communication Quarterly* 72 (Summer 1995): 390–401.

Jamieson, Kathleen Hall. *Dirty Politics: Deception, Distraction, and Democracy.* New York: Oxford University Press, 1992.

Miller, M. Mark, Julie L. Andsager, and Bonnie P. Riechert. "Framing the Candidates in Presidential Primaries: Issues and Images in Press Releases and News Coverage." *Journalism & Mass Communication Quarterly* 75 (Summer 1998): 312–324.

Patterson, Thomas E. "Where Have All the Voters Gone?" *Christian Science Monitor* (4 November 2002): 41.

Patterson, Thomas. *Out of Order.* New York: Alfred A. Knopf, 1993.

Stone, Gerald C., and Elinor Grusin. "Network TV as the Bad News Bearer." *Journalism Quarterly* 61 (Autumn 1984): 517–523.

Stone, Gerald C., Barbara Hartung, and Dwight Jensen. "Local TV News and the Good-Bad Dyad." *Journalism Quarterly* 64 (Spring 1987): 37–44.

Sorauf, Frank. *Inside Campaign Finance.* New Haven: Yale University Press, 1992.

2000 World Almanac. Mahwah, NJ: World Almanac Books, 2001.

Unpublished survey. Scripps Howard News Service and Ohio University, July 2000. Posted at http://www. newspolls.com. Accessed 10 December 2002.

Weaver, David H., and G. Cleveland Wilhoit. "News Media Coverage of U.S. Senators in Four Congresses, 1953–1974." *Journalism Monographs* 67, 1980.

Wiggins, James Russell. *Freedom or Secrecy.* New York: Oxford University Press, 1964.

3

The Process of
News Communication

News communication is very uncertain because communicating news depends on decisions that are made by newspeople, news sources, and news audiences. Newspeople decide on which events to cover, which not to cover, and how prominently to play the ones that they do cover. Political news sources decide whether or not to cooperate with media and whether or not to engage in activities that are likely to get covered by the media. News audiences decide whether or not to read a newspaper, and if they decide to read one, they decide which stories they will read and how much of each story they will read. They decide whether or not to watch television news, and if they decide to watch it, they decide consciously or unconsciously whether or not to pay attention. The interaction between these three players is now being referred to as agenda setting.

Agenda setting raises the question of which of the three sets the agenda—the media, the politicians, or the public. Research has established that each does so in certain circumstances. There are six possible agenda routes for the three: (1) the media set the agenda for the politicians who set it for the public, (2) the media set the agenda for the public who set it for the politicians, (3) the politicians set the agenda for the media, which set it for the public, (4) the politicians set the agenda for the public who set it for the media, (5) the public sets the agenda for the politicians who set it for the media, and (6) the public sets the agenda for the media who set it for the public.

On any given issue any of the six agendas may be set. In health care, for example, the media, by covering problems, may alert the public who in turn may pass their concerns along to the politicians. Or the media coverage may cause politicians to think there is an issue worth exploring, and the politicians will pass that perspective along to the public. Public concern may push the issue to the media, and media coverage alerts the politicians. Public concern may cause the politicians to react and that passes the issue along to the media. Politicians may decide to take on the issue and pass it along to the media who in turn put it in front of the public. Politicians may alert the public to the issue and that in turn gets the media interested. The answer in part will be determined by choices made by the media, the politicians, and the public. The role of each will be discussed, starting with the media.

The News Media

The very fact that a given news event gets covered is the result of arbitrary decisions in the newsroom. The *New York Times* has for years carried the slogan "All the News That's Fit to Print" on the upper left of its front page; yet literally, this is not so. Some have suggested that the *Times* change it to "All the News That Fits." This is not to deny that the *Times* prints more news that any other newspaper in the United States or that it provides more news than any television station. The *Times* simply does not cover everything. There are too many things happening in the world and in a community for any medium to cover all of them.

Consider a metropolitan area of a half a million, which consists of the main city and perhaps ten suburbs. The city has a city council and a school board, as do the ten suburban communities. They also have zoning boards, a county health board, a county mental health board, a county children's services board, a county board of elections, and a county welfare board, among others. All the organizations meet once or twice a month, all are using public funds, and therefore all are doing things that are of legitimate public interest. There are at least fifty meetings per month of such public bodies. How many are read about in the newspaper in your community or heard about in local broadcast news? There is more to cover than that, however. These communities all have mayors, police departments, fire departments, water departments, and sewage departments. Beyond that is the court system with county courts, usually called common pleas courts and municipal courts.

There is other news besides that which is made by the various agencies of government. There is more news than any newspaper or any television station has the staffing to be able to cover.

How do they decide what to cover? At least three things enter into the decision. The first is presumed reader or listener interest in the story. The truth is that newspaper editors and television news directors often do not know what their readers and listeners are interested in. They tend to assume that if they are interested in a story, their readers and listeners will be also. But it is important to take into consideration that an editor is of a given sex, ethnic origin, age, religious preference, educational background, and income. All these matters affect what newspeople are interested in and what they think the public is interested in, and in today's diverse society, no one individual can be representative of the entire society. Many studies have asked readers and listeners about their interests and then asked editors or news directors to estimate the interests of the audiences they serve. Without exception, they find that editors and news directors are not very good at estimating interests of their audiences.

The second factor is the presumed importance of a story. Again, the diversity of people and diversity of interests in society makes this difficult to determine. Yet the editor of a metropolitan newspaper or the news director of a metropolitan television station surely knows that readers and listeners in the suburbs are not really affected by what the city council of the big city does or what the big city's school district does. Those readers and listeners have their own local government and local schools that are of concern and importance to them. Yet the typical pattern of coverage is that the meetings of the city council of the big city and the school board of the big city are routinely covered, while the council meetings and school board meetings of the suburbs are covered only when there is conflict or consideration of a tax increase. The stories that are routinely covered for the big city council and school board do not get covered for the suburbs much of the time. Realistically, there are relatively few stories that are important to every reader or every listener.

The third factor is the difficulty and cost of covering the story. Some stories are easy to cover. That is one reason there are so many stories off the police blotter in most newspapers. The reporter can get a lot of information that will lead to a lot of words for the paper relatively easily. That is also why newspapers and television stations cover city council meetings and school board meetings. They can be considered important, although many such meetings in fact do little of any importance on a given night. The reporter can write many words about the meeting that lasts perhaps two hours, whereas he or she cannot cover many other things in two hours that will produce as much copy. Likewise, press conferences by public officials are covered for the same reason. Some public officials have them regularly, while others have them only when there is something special to announce. Either way, a minimal investment of time will produce a substantial amount of news for the newspaper or television station. The other side of this factor is that there are stories the newspaper or television station believes are so difficult to cover that there is no point in trying to cover them. Some news sources simply will not cooperate about anything, some news sources may cooperate at least up to a point but do not have enough information, some stories are so complicated that it takes a number of sources to get them, and the media often are not willing to commit that much time to the story.

For example, suppose that a local citizen goes before city council to complain that there is too much sodium in the city's water supply—that the amount of sodium constitutes a health hazard. The council will hear him or her out, but probably do nothing. If one goes to the mayor after the meeting, the mayor probably will dismiss the complaint as unfounded and tell the person that the city's water is very healthy and perhaps the healthiest in the state. A good reporter then probably goes to the water department and asks the head of the department about the sodium. Should it be tested? How much sodium is in the water? How much is safe? It will be difficult for the reporter to get an answer from the head of the city water department to all three of those questions. Maybe the reporter should talk to the person who made the complaint. Will that person know how much there is and how much is safe, or will that person simply say, "Well, all you have to do is to taste to know what I'm talking about." Now it is time to seek some expert opinion from the state health board, from biologists, or perhaps chemists or physicians. This takes a lot of time. Will the story be worth it? Perhaps. The newsroom tendency, however, is to wait for somebody to make the next move. Let the water department initiate a response. Let the person complaining write a letter to the editor. Yet the story is important. Too much sodium is a health hazard, particularly to people with heart problems. The public is entitled to an answer, and reporters know that the best chance of getting an answer is for the media to follow up the story. Yet, often they do not.

Consider another story that has been in the media for half a century, and in that time, either covered badly or not at all. Not every child learns to read. The dominant story about this issue over the years has been that this is because phonics are not used. Though there was minimal use of phonics a half century ago, that is not the case now. Most schools use phonics in teaching reading. Some people still claim otherwise, perhaps because they simply do not know and the media has not told them.

How can one find out why some children do not learn how to read? The easy way is to go to a school board meeting where it is discussed or to talk to the superintendent of schools. Or one can find self-appointed experts. The trouble is that none of these potential sources—school board members, superintendents, or self-appointed experts—have ever taught children to read. To find the answer to this question, one has to go to reading teachers. They're harder to get to—much harder than the superintendent of schools. And one would have to talk to several reading teachers. It would take a lot of time. Examples of this problem abound, but the simple point is that there are important stories that do not get covered by the media in a given community. There are also stories that get covered so badly that the coverage is really dysfunctional.

Secrecy is another factor that reduces coverage. The executive branch, whether it be the federal government, the state government, or city government, discusses many things in secret. The need to do so is real in many cases, but the result is that the executive branch announces policies or requests for legislation without any opportunity for public discussion or any public knowledge of the reasons for the policies or requests. Public bodies from the Congress down to the city council have to meet in public, but they can discuss some things in secret. At the federal level, the major reason for secrecy is national security. The federal courts have consistently told various agencies of the executive branch that they are defining national security too broadly, but it has made little difference. For state and local agencies, this is set by state law, and there are three reasons for secrecy that are valid in most state laws—personnel matters, land transactions, and labor negotiations. Most of what the public wants to know is within those categories. If, for example, the local school board is considering firing the high school principal, the public will be interested. Yet what happens is that the board meets in secret session, perhaps for hours, and then comes out of the session and goes into regular session and votes. The public knows what the vote is, but not what the reasons are. It is often suggested that this is only fair to the principal, but this assumes information will not be leaked out of the closed session, and it often is. Furthermore, the secret session lacks the safeguards for the principal that an open session has. In a secret session, people can spread gossip and rumors, and that would be challenged in an open session. The public will in time create its own story of what happened on the basis of word-of-mouth communication in the community. The result is often more damaging than the truth.

This scenario is repeated at all levels of government. Since the media are seldom able to report the reasons for someone being fired, the public, therefore, is kept in the dark. The public, in fact, may end up being misled by statements made to the press by the person who was fired or by his attorney. Since there is no record of the closed session, there is no way of referencing the statements made by the person who was fired.

Coverage of any given story is dealt with almost on a story-by-story basis, and it should be pointed out that a significant part of coverage is organized so that certain stories routinely get covered. In many cases, certain reporters are regularly assigned to certain sources and are in touch with those sources daily.

Thus far local news coverage has been discussed. Coverage of state, national, and international news is a different matter. Most newspapers, radio stations, and television stations get their coverage of state, national, and international news from other organizations. With state news, there are a few larger newspapers that have reporters in the state capital and perhaps in one or two other major cities in the state, but most of the state news seen and heard comes from the Associated Press, a news-gathering cooperative that depends on its members for much of the news it disseminates. If a member newspaper or broadcast station has a story that it believes is of interest and importance to others in the state, it makes that story available to the Associated Press. The Associated Press in turn makes it available to its member papers in that state. The Associated Press thus benefits from the reporting efforts of its member papers and broadcast stations, and the papers and broadcast stations benefit in that they get stories it would not be possible for them to get otherwise. However, one result of this is that the papers and stations get far more state news than they can use, and they end up using less than a quarter of it.

With national and international news, the Associated Press again is a major source, but there is another large source—the *New York Times News Service*, which is used by nearly all of the newspapers of more than 100,000 circulation. More than half the newspaper readers in the country read newspapers that get the

New York Times News Service. Other newspapers and newspaper groups have services that provide some news coverage as well as columns and features, but none are in the same class as the *Times News Service.* The volume of material provided again far exceeds what newspapers can use, and many newspapers use only about a tenth of the national and international news that they get. The result of this deluge of material is that despite all that has been written about standardization of newspapers, each paper is at least somewhat unique in its selection of state, national, and international news.

Television stations have network affiliation, and there are network newscasts that cover national and international news. In addition to the newscasts, the networks provide other stories that their affiliated stations can use on the newscasts that they prepare. Television stations also have the Associated Press and perhaps other news services for national and international news.

When all this is considered, it is evident that no newspaper, radio station, or television station covers all the news. Each medium selects what news to cover and what news stories to run from wire and feature services, and no one medium can really claim that it is providing all the news or providing a mirror image of the world.

The Politicians

The second group whose decisions affect what happens in coverage are the politicians and public officeholders. Politicians want media coverage—preferably favorable coverage, and they have five ways of getting media coverage: (1) interviews with reporters from the media; (2) press conferences with reporters; (3) events such as speeches and signing of legislation that the politician creates; (4) publicity releases that they send to the media; and (5) events that happen without any effort by the politician but which involve the politician in some way or other. Each has its advantages and disadvantages from the standpoint of the politician, and politicians differ in how well they can handle each of these.

A news interview is a competitive sport. When the interview is over, one side or the other—either the reporter or the politician—has won. By won, what is meant is that they attained what they hoped to attain from the interview. An interview between a reporter and a politician is not simply a cooperative effort by two people to disclose information. One advantage for the politician is that the interview is almost certain to result in a story in a newspaper or over the air, and to result in better play than the politician would get from a press conference, a speech, or a publicity release. A second advantage is that the give-and-take between two people offers a better opportunity for the two to understand each other, and that can help coverage of other stories in the future. The big disadvantage is that to an appreciable degree the reporter determines the agenda for the interview. The reporter will decide what questions he or she wants to ask, and those may not be the questions the politician wants to answer. The politician can refuse to answer, but he or she knows that doing this runs the risk of the resulting story indicating that refusal, thus suggesting that the politician is not being candid or has something to hide on that subject.

The politician may be able to avoid this risk by making the first move in the interview—that is telling the reporter about something the politician wants to talk about and thereby encouraging the reporter to follow that lead. The politician may tell the reporter at the outset that he or she intends only to talk about a specific topic and is not interested in dealing with anything else at this time. There also can be a problem with the reporter being so forceful that the politician does not get to say fully what he or she wants to say on the topic.

Beyond that there is the problem of a slip of the tongue—of the politician saying something that he or she does not want to say and that has the possibility of being very damaging and the politician wanting to withdraw or retract something that was said in an interview. The reporter may not agree to that.

The biggest problem with a press conference is that it may not generate much coverage. If a press conference is hosted by the president of the United States, it will get covered. On the other hand, mayors have given up on press conferences because media paid little attention to them and perhaps did not come to them at all. The reporters tend to set the agenda, but the politician conducting a press conference has an easier time not answering questions than he or she would in an interview. In a press conference, it is frequently difficult for a reporter to follow up on a question to get a more complete answer. That probably works to the advantage of the politician. He or she can get away with evading a question. On the upside, the press conference may generate positive coverage on matters that might not come up in an interview. A second plus is that it gives the politician the opportunity to deal with a number of media at the same time, thus saving time. It also puts all the media on the same footing, thus eliminating charges of favoritism.

A great deal depends on the ability the politician has to handle a press conference. Some politicians are comfortable with this kind of give-and-take and some are not. The U.S. president who was best at handling a press conference was John F. Kennedy— he had a quick mind and always seemed to have a large reservoir of factual information on key topics. He also had wit, which made the press conferences more interesting and enabled him to turn aside questions he really did not want to talk about. The presidents since Kennedy have had varying degrees of discomfort with press conferences, and that has been one reason the presidential press conference has almost disappeared. The same mixed results can be found if one looks at what governors and mayors have done with press conferences. When presidential press conferences happen, they are televised. That is less likely to be the case with a governor of a state and almost never the case with a mayor.

There are times when a press conference cannot be avoided. If there is a major disaster of some kind in a city or state, then there really is a need for the politician in charge to speak up, and the press conference is the obvious way. Events created by the politician, sometimes called pseudo events, give the politician the opportunity to set the agenda and to call attention to his or her own accomplishments in a given area. The classic example of such events is the so-called photo-op, short for photo opportunity. The event may be the signing of a bill, or it may be a meeting between two politicians to discuss a current concern. It may be the appearance of a politician at a local event—the appearance of the governor, for example, at the county fair. Politicians do these things, presumably because the visibility they get from these pseudo events is considered valuable.

The problem with such events is the lack of substance. Whatever the issue is that is represented, it is dealt with rather superficially. Most bills that are signed are only a partial answer to the issue being addressed. Most conferences between politicians do not result in major policy breakthroughs. Most appearances of politicians at events like county fairs are of no real significance. Furthermore the media become weary of them, and there is the risk that the media coverage will poke fun at the photo-op, thus destroying the value of it for the politician. There is also the possibility that the media simply will not cover them at all.

Yet politicians continue to hold these events. Furthermore, they are strictly one-sided, one-way events. The politician chooses his or her spot, his or her issue, and nothing else is dealt with. It is a given that no questions will be asked or answered. But if these pseudo events are valuable to the politician, there is the considerable question as to whether or not they are valuable to the public.

Publicity releases are an easy way for a politician to get a message into the hands of the media. It is a message that the politician controls completely, and it is on a topic of his or her choosing. They are positive messages. However, two bad things can happen with publicity releases. The first is that the media will toss them in the wastebasket. It is well established that less than 10 percent of publicity releases are used by newspapers and broadcast stations. It also is evident that this is more likely to happen with big city media. The second bad thing from the politician's standpoint is that many media will rewrite the release rather than using it as it was sent. This probably means that the slant of the story will change. For example, suppose the governor sends out a glowing release about a proposed prescription drug plan for the people of his or her state that the release says will save the people millions of dollars. He or she may pick up the newspaper the next morning and find that the story begins, "After opposing every health care proposal presented in recent years, Governor Smith. . . ." The story, rather than promoting the current positive move, will focus on the unfavorable history of the governor and health care. While the publicity release gives the politician a chance to present his or her side of an issue, it may not succeed in presenting it to very many people, and the re-lease could backfire.

Finally, there are the events that the politician does not cre-ate, but that he or she cannot help being a part of. For example, if the state has a major flood, the governor has to be involved. He or she did not cause the flood, but he or she will have to respond. Suggesting waiting for the water to recede is not an acceptable response. The governor needs to develop a plan quickly, and it has to be a plan that appears plausible at the time and works in the long run. Whether it is a good plan or a bad plan, the gover-nor is in the spotlight.

Sometimes the negative event is something for which the politician is responsible. A hypothetical situation could be that a city is not prepared for snow the last week in October but gets fif-teen inches. The city can not cope with it, comes to a standstill, and the public is unhappy. At this point, what occurs is called damage control. The mayor and the safety director can not make the snow go away, but they can lead a maximum effort to deal with it and can attempt to reassure the public. They also can announce later changes that will be made in preparations for snow that will lessen the likelihood of a repetition of the recent disaster. Sometimes a policy developed with the best of intentions is a total failure. For example, a state welfare department decides to computerize the issuance of monthly checks. Somehow, the system collapses, and thousands of people not only do not get their checks on the first of the month; they do not get them at all for that month. The task of damage control is a lot more difficult.

Another factor beyond these five types of situations is the attitude of the media or the perceived attitude of the media toward the politician. Newspapers endorse candidates editorially, but the norm is that the endorsement does not influence news coverage. Yet many politicians have believed that it does affect coverage. And some politicians have simply not been able to deal with certain individual reporters because of this possibility. Politicians naturally prefer reporters who have given them what they consider to be fair coverage in the past.

Politicians have to hope these varied communication opportunities with their assorted problems will balance out favorably overall, but they know it takes a lot of skill and effort to achieve. That is why many politicians turn over much of the task of communication to an expert staff member. That staff member makes most of the contact with the media. At the White House level, it has become commonplace for a staff member to brief the media almost daily and the president to be available to the media relatively infrequently. This happens not merely at the White House but at all levels of government. There are governors and mayors who rarely talk with reporters, but instead delegate that responsibility to a staff member. That staff member has the opportunity to bring the politician and the reporter closer together by talking through differences separately from each other. However, in some cases that staff person becomes larger than the official he or she is representing, and that damages coverage.

The Public—Media Use

So far, many issues have been covered: the media cover news selectively thus presenting a picture that may be accurate as far as it goes, but may be inaccurate because it stops short. In covering state, national, and international stories, the media will exclude more stories than they include. Politicians will try to manipulate relations with the press to give themselves the best possible image. Yet, both the media and politicians will profess that they are there to serve the public. They will reject any suggestion that they do not act in the public interest overall.

Where does this leave the public—the readers and listeners? First of all, it leaves the public to some extent overwhelmed because the media and the politicians produce far more news than the public can possibly consume. The five major national network television stations, ABC, CBS, CNN, NBC, and FOX, together produce 100 hours of news each twenty-four-hour day. In a typical television market, the local stations produce another twelve to fifteen hours of local news. The radio listener can choose between at least a dozen stations for news on the hour or the half hour and in many cases has an all-news station available. In most cities, the reader can get the local daily, in addition to the *New York Times, USA Today,* and the *Wall Street Journal,* enough reading material to cover most of his or her waking hours.

It is up to each member of the public to select the medium and to select what portion of the medium to which to attend. Some of that selection is purely random, but some of it is purposive. The theory of cognitive dissonance says that people use the medium to reduce dissonance. Dissonance occurs when the individual has a difficult decision to make. One such decision is voting when the two candidates appeal nearly equal. Once the voter has made up his or her mind, he or she uses the media to reduce dissonance. How? By looking for and finding stories that tell him or her how great the candidate is for whom he or she intends to vote.

A second consideration is what gratification the individual gets from the media use. This is not to say that the reader or listener is looking for entertainment. Rather, he or she is looking for content that will be useful or reassuring. What content that is will vary with the interests of the individual. Some like stories that enable them to feel they are checking up on government, some are looking for content about people and their needs, and some are looking for information that will be useful in their daily dialogue with friends and fellow workers.

Surveys Show Public Attitudes

In this section, results from five surveys conducted by the Scripps Survey Research Center at Ohio University and the Scripps Howard News Service will be presented. These are telephone surveys done by the Ohio University campus using computer-assisted telephone interviewing equipment. In each survey a national random sample of about one thousand adults were interviewed. The sampling error in these surveys is plus or minus 3.1 percent. In other words, the results, nineteen out of twenty times, are within 3.1 percent of what would be achieved by interviewing every adult in the United States.

Since the early years of television, there has been great interest in whether people got most of their news from newspapers, radio, or television. The first time the Roper Organization asked a national sample where they got most of their news, the majority replied that they got their news from newspapers. Soon, however, television moved ahead of newspapers, and by 1970, the usual margin was about 20 percent. For many years, ABC closed their early evening newscast with, "More people get news from ABC than any other source." In actuality, most of the news that Americans get on any given day comes from the Associated Press through newspapers, radio stations, and television stations. And because so many newspapers subscribe to the *New York Times News Service*, more people get news from that source than from ABC. Furthermore, most Americans get news from more than one source, as is evident from Table 3.1. In the statement above, ABC is saying that more people watch their news than watch news on NBC, CBS, CNN, or FOX. This is simply not true. Table 3.1 shows the results of three national surveys by the Scripps Survey Center at Ohio University and the Scripps Howard News Service. Each was a national survey by telephone of slightly more than one thousand randomly selected adults. The first survey was made in July of 2000 just before the Republican convention. The second survey was made in the last two weeks of October 2001, slightly more than a month after the terrorist attacks of September 11. The third survey was made in June 2002. Respondents were asked how many days in the past week they had used each of these media. Then regular use was defined as four days a week or more. Averages were calculated from these responses, and they turned out to be almost exactly the same, so these figures in effect represent average daily use of each of these media.

All three surveys show that television is the most used news

TABLE 3.1
Percent Using Various Media Regularly

	2000	2001	2002
Television News	65.1	82.8	70.7
Daily Newspapers	49.4	55.4	52.9
Radio News	*	57.1	51.8
Internet	37.5	33.6	39.9
N	1,012	1,151	1,008

*radio news not included in 2000 survey
Source: Scripps Survey Research Center—Scripps Howard News Service, 2000, 2001, and 2002.

medium, with newspapers and radio news used about the same and the Internet well behind those two. There also is considerable variation for all the media in these three surveys. Part of this variation is because the 2001 survey was taken slightly more than a month after the terrorist attack, and media use was still abnormally high. A number of media-use surveys have been conducted over the last thirty-five years and there has never been a figure like the 82.8 percent for television news in October 2001. By June of 2002 television news had dropped back slightly more than 12 percent, but it still was higher than it had been in 2000.

Newspaper reading was 5 percent higher than it had been a year earlier, but that it dropped back more than 2 percent in the 2002 survey. Radio news listening dropped even more—it was down 5 percent from what it had been in 2001. Interestingly enough, use of the Internet was lower in October 2001 than it had been in July of 2000. It then jumped up to almost 40 percent in June of 2002. Use of the Internet had increased dramatically in the last half of the 1990s. A survey conducted in 1995 showed regular use of the Internet to be 7 percent. Four years later it was 35 percent. The growth seems to have continued, but at a much lower rate. Some people are suggesting that considerable growth of the Internet will occur in the next few years, but what the surveys have revealed in the last three years suggest growth will be modest. Table 3.1 has an important message for political communicators. There is no one news medium that everybody uses, and most people use more than one medium. So, one medium should not be counted on completely, and news, good or bad, probably will reach the average citizen through more than one medium.

Many studies show a decline in both newspaper and television news audiences in the last half of the 1990s. Many observers attributed this to the impact of the Internet. Yet, these three surveys indicate that the Internet does not drive people away from newspapers. In the 2002 survey, for example, of those who are regular users of the Internet, 57 percent read a daily newspaper regularly, while of those who are not regular users of the Internet, 50 percent are regular daily newspaper readers. This is also true of radio news listening. In the 2002 survey, of those who are regular Internet users, 54 percent are regular radio news listeners, while of those who are not regular Internet users only 49 percent are regular radio news listeners. However, the story is different for television news. Regular Internet users are less likely to be regular television news watchers. In the 2002 survey, of the regular Internet users, 68 percent are regular television news watchers, while of those who are not regular Internet users, 73 percent are regular television news viewers. Internet users thus are less likely to watch television news. The explanation for this is at least in part that one can go from a newspaper to the Internet or from the Internet to a newspaper, but while one can go from television news to the Internet, one will not really go from the Internet to television news. If you find something on the Internet that you would like to find out more about, there is no efficient way to use television news to do that because there is no way of knowing when the story of interest will appear on television news. One might have to wait hours for it.

Although television news is the most used of these media, people who watch television news also tend to use other media more than people who do not watch television news. Table 3.2 shows the relation between watching television news regularly and reading a newspaper regularly. Note that 41.9 percent used both media. Furthermore, 59.3 percent of the regular television news watchers are regular newspaper readers. Also, of those who are not regular television news watchers, only 37.4 percent are regular daily newspaper readers. There are somewhat similar results with regular radio news listening and daily newspaper reading, but not with radio news listening and television news watching.

There are important demographic differences in media use. Consider first the differences in media use between men and women, as shown in Table 3.3. The biggest gap is in the use of the Internet, with 9 percent more men than women using it regularly. A difference of about 10 percent has been true for some time. It is not known if it has to do with use in the workplace or use at home, or whether it simply has to do with fewer women being accepting of the Internet. Whatever the reason, it is important for those who communicate by means of the Internet to be aware of it. There are smaller differences for other media, with men more likely to be regular newspaper readers and radio news listeners,

TABLE 3.2
Regular Television News Watching versus Regular Daily Newspaper Reading

| | Television News | | |
	Watch Regularly	Don't Watch Regularly	Total
Newspapers			
Read Regularly	420	110	530
Do not Read Regularly	288	184	472
Total	708	294	1,002

Source: Scripps Survey Research Center—Scripps Howard News Service Survey, 2002

TABLE 3.3
Regularly Media Use by Men and Women, in Percent

	Men	Women
Television News	68.3	72.9
Daily Newspapers	57.3	48.9
Radio News	53.8	49.9
Internet	44.8	35.4
N	482	526

Source: Scripps Survey Research Center—Scripps Howard News Service Survey, 2002

and women more likely to be regular television news watchers. Some of this may have to do with the content that is selected by each of these media. Newspaper executives have wrestled for years with what to do to make their papers more attractive to women. They are aware of the problem, but not of the solution.

There are marked differences in media use by age, as Table 3.4 shows. In general, media use increases with age. For television news and daily newspapers it is almost a straight line with audiences among persons more than sixty-five years old being more than 30 percent higher than the audiences for persons eighteen to twenty-four years old. For radio, the audience size increases up to the forty-five to fifty-four-year-old group, but then drops almost back to where it was for persons eighteen to twenty-four years old. Given the emphasis that many radio stations put on contemporary music, the figure for those eighteen to twenty-four years old is surprisingly low. There is no clear pattern for the Internet, and there is not a whole lot of difference by age except for the low use by those more than sixty-five years old. Some have suggested that Internet is the medium of younger people, but these data do not really confirm that. There has been considerable talk in the television industry about the need to reach more younger viewers.

TABLE 3.4

Regular Media Use by Age, in Percent

	18–24	26–34	35–44	45–54	55–64	More than 65
Television News	57.5	62.7	69.6	70.8	80.2	88.0
Daily Newspaper	40.6	38.9	52.1	56.2	62.7	72.4
Radio News	39.1	52.7	57.8	59.3	56.8	43.0
Internet	45.1	38.9	45.3	47.2	44.1	16.0
N	153	185	232	161	111	150

Source: Scripps Survey Research Center—Scripps Howard News Service Survey, 2002.

TABLE 3.5

Regular Media Use by Education, in Percent

	High School	Some College	College Grad	Post Grad
Television News	72.2	69.3	69.7	70.7
Daily Newspaper	47.1	48.5	59.1	66.2
Radio News	52.1	47.0	55.1	54.9
Internet	19.9	41.4	52.7	59.4
N	311	266	273	133

Source: Scripps Survey Research Center—Scripps Howard News Service Survey, 2002.

The target appears to be the thirty-five to forty-four age group, which has the highest average household income, although it is not much higher than the forty-five to fifty-four age group. Newspapers, on the other hand, continue to be concerned about reaching those under thirty-five years of age. For politicians, all age groups are important, but voter turnout is one more thing that correlates directly with age. It is more important for politicians to reach those who are more than forty-five years old, because those are the people most likely to get to the polls.

Two things stand out when the relation between media use and education is examined, as Table 3.5 shows. The first is that newspaper reading and Internet use increase markedly with education. The second is that there is relatively little relation between education and use of either television news or radio news. Two reasons seem likely. One is that one reads newspapers, and basically one reads the Internet. Both have their visual aspects, and the Internet does so more than newspapers and will do so even more in the future. Secondly, education and income correlate, and as seen in Table 3.6, income correlates with use of newspapers and the Internet. For the politician, this suggests that one should not have the same message on radio and television as is

TABLE 3.6
Regular Media Use vs. Income, in Percent

	Less Than $25,000	$25,000 to $40,000	$40,000 to $60,000	$60,000 to $80,000	More Than $80,000
Television News	73.1	78.8	72.7	65.4	66.7
Daily Newspaper	45.4	47.4	54.1	54.0	62.0
Radio News	39.1	55.8	61.8	52.2	62.6
Internet	26.0	37.2	36.0	51.8	67.1
N	197	156	162	136	171

Source: Scripps Survey Research Center—Scripps Howard News Service Survey, 2002.

in newspapers and on the Internet. Newspaper and Internet audiences can be expected to comprehend more complex messages. It is evident from Table 3.5 that education is not a factor with regard to television audiences and not much of a factor with regard to radio audiences.

The relation between income and media use, shown in Table 3.6, is rather complex, with no two media showing quite the same pattern. Television news reaches the lower income brackets better than it reaches the highest income brackets. All media are in effect selling their audiences to advertisers, and the mix that television news offers is not particularly attractive to most advertisers. Television news audiences are not that different from television audiences for other programs, and that does make one wonder why certain companies advertise on television as much as they do. Newspapers, on the other hand, reach more upper-income than lower-income people, and the Internet does so even more, which is promising for the advertiser seeking the upscale audience. The pattern for radio is not very consistent. Because income tends to be related to voter turnout, these figures are important for politicians, too. Television reaches all income groups, but both newspapers and the Internet offer a pattern in terms of income of their audiences that may serve politicians better.

The most striking thing about party preference and media use in Table 3.7 is that independents tend to use media less than either Democrats or Republicans. There is one exception—Independents use the Internet slightly more than Democrats. This goes against conventional wisdom that tends to think independents are perhaps better informed and less committed to partisan considerations. That may apply to some Independents, but perhaps others are Independent out of indifference and unawareness of the political processes. The table indicates that Democrats use

TABLE 3.7

Regular Media Use by Political Party Preference, in Percent

	Democrat	Independent	Republican
Television News	75.8	67.0	71.5
Daily Newspaper	55.9	48.6	54.0
Radio News	52.7	49.1	56.7
Internet	37.0	39.3	45.7
N	355	218	336

Source: Scripps Survey Research Center—Scripps Howard News Service Survey, 2002.

TABLE 3.8

Regular Media Use by Region, in Percent

	Northeast	South	Midwest	West
Television News	71.8	73.9	69.6	65.9
Daily Newspaper	64.8	51.5	49.8	47.8
Radio News	46.9	51.8	52.0	55.0
Internet	43.9	35.7	40.5	43.0
N	196	357	227	228

Source: Scripps Survey Researchy Center—Scripps Howard News Service Survey, 2002.

television news a little more, while Republicans use radio news a little more and the Internet a good deal more. Newspaper reading is almost a standoff, with a slight margin to the Democrats.

Table 3.8 shows variations in regular media use for four regions of the country—the Northeast, the South, the Midwest, and the West. The most striking difference is in newspaper reading with the Northeast far ahead of the other three regions. Sixty-five percent of those in the Northeast read a daily newspaper regularly, which is 13 percent more than for the South, where 52 percent read a daily newspaper regularly. In the Midwest, 50 percent read a daily newspaper regularly and in the West, only 48 percent read a daily newspaper regularly. People in the Northeast also use the Internet more, but the margin is small—44 percent do in the Northeast and 42 percent do in the West. People listen to radio news the most in the West—55 percent, which is 3 percent more than in the South and Midwest. People in the Midwest and West use radio news more than the daily newspaper, which is in sharp contrast to use of those media in the Northeast, where 18 percent more use the daily newspaper regularly than listened to radio news regularly.

Table 3.9 reflects a divide between urban areas and the rest of the country. People in small cities and rural areas use television

TABLE 3.9
Regular Media Use versus Where Respondent Lives

	Big City	Small City	Suburb	Rural Area
Television News	69.5	71.7	69.5	73.3
Daily Newspaper	52.3	51.2	64.7	51.3
Radio News	49.2	52.8	54.8	50.1
Internet	44.2	35.6	55.1	28.7
N	367	250	187	195

Source: Scripps Survey Research Center—Scripps Howard News Service Survey, 2002.

news a little more even though they have less television offered to them and probably no local television. The daily newspaper does best in the suburbs, a finding that is a bit of a surprise because it is not the daily about their own community that they're reading. There are only a handful of suburban dailies in the entire country; therefore, people from the suburbs are reading the daily from the city to which their suburb is attached. It is also worth noting that use of all media except television is greater in the suburbs than in the big cities. For television the two are the same, but differences on the other media are substantial. Some of this is related to income, but whatever the reason, the message is clear—it is harder to reach people in the big cities with media. Use of the Internet in small cities and rural areas lags the use in big cities and suburbs by a large amount. Availability, or lack of it, may have a lot to do with this difference. Availability is increasing, and use of the Internet in small cities and rural areas undoubtedly will increase, but how fast it is increasing is unknown.

What this all adds up to is that while television news is pervasive in contemporary America, it is not the only answer and sometimes not the best answer. Effective political communication means recognizing the differences that gender, age, income, education, party affiliation, and where a person lives seem to influence their choices of media.

Sources of News

There are many media providing an enormous amount of coverage of politics and government, and politicians pay considerable attention to that coverage. In a survey during October of 2000, respondents were asked to indicate which sources of information were useful and to indicate which of a number of sources men-

TABLE 3.10
Useful Sources of News in 2000 Presidential Campaign, in Percent

	Useful	Most Useful
Television News	84.2	52.1
Radio News	56.3	12.4
Newspapers	53.6	16.7
News Magazines	34.0	6.7
Internet	27.0	5.9
Television Ads	25.1	0.3
Political Magazines	18.9	2.3
Grocery Store Tabloids	4.6	0
Don't Know	—	3.6
N=1,005		

Source: Scripps Survey Research Center—Scripps Howard News Service Survey, 2000.

tioned was most useful. Television news came out on top. Eighty-four percent said it was useful and 52.1 percent said it was the most useful source, as Table 3.10 shows. However, both newspapers and radio news were considered useful by more than half the respondents. News magazines were considered useful by 34 percent, but most useful by only 6.7 percent. In a way, those figures are consistent with the circulation figures for news magazines. The total circulation of *Time, Newsweek,* and *U.S. News* is slightly less than ten million. That is not quite 10 percent of the number of households in the United States.

Internet was considered useful by 27 percent, which means that about a fourth of those who were using the Internet did not consider it a useful source of information about the campaign. Furthermore, only 5.9 percent considered it most useful. When this result was published in a news article, a newspaper editor objected that the Internet's impact on younger voters was not taken into consideration. The figures for people under thirty-five years of age were taken into consideration, and the Internet did not fare particularly well there. It was the first campaign in which the Internet really was used, but the use was not extensive. One would expect the parties and candidates to use it more effectively in coming elections. In spite of the claims made for it by some, the Internet was not a major player in the 2000 election.

The results for television advertisements also are interesting. Everybody who watches television is exposed to these advertisements, but only 25.1 percent found that they provided useful information. Some will suggest that they do not provide any information at all—that they are merely emotional appeals

TABLE 3.11
How People Found Out about Terrorism Attack, in Percent

Television	49.2
Friends and Coworkers	20.9
Radio	16.8
Family Member	8.9
Other, Don't Know	4.2
N	1,131

Source: Scripps Survey Research Center—Scripps Howard News Service Survey, 2001.

largely devoid of facts. Despite the high esteem with which politicians hold television advertisements—it is television advertisements that are at stake in the debate over campaign finances—only 0.3 percent of respondents considered them the most useful source of information. Finally, only 4.6 percent of the respondents considered the grocery store tabloids a useful source of information and no respondent said they were the most useful source.

The terrorist attack of September 11 provides another look at sources of news, as seen in a survey conducted during the last two weeks of October 2001, slightly more than a month after the event. Respondents were first asked from what source they first found out about the attack. Television was the most mentioned source, as Table 3.11 shows, which is not surprising because the attack started when the morning shows were on, and television actually showed the second plane hitting the World Trade Center tower as it happened. Time is a factor. People in the Eastern time zone were already at work. People in the Central time zone were perhaps on their way to work, but people in the Mountain and Pacific time zones were still at home when the attack occurred. For major events like this, television usually turns out to be the most common first source. But for lesser events, relatively few people will report learning about it first from television.

Respondents were then asked which sources had been useful for information about terrorism in the period since September 11, 2001. As Table 3.12 shows, television was the overwhelming choice with 90 percent considering it a useful source and nearly 66 percent considering it the best source. Television news made a major attempt to cover this story. It has made efforts before on such stories as the Kennedy assassination, the Challenger disaster, and others, but never before over such a long period of time. It also indicates that a majority of people found family and

TABLE 3.12
Useful Sources of Information about Terrorism by Sex, in Percent

| | Useful | | | Most Useful | | |
	Men	Women	Total	Men	Women	Total
Television News	90.1	91.7	91.0	63.8	73.5	69.1
Family and Friends	66.1	71.4	69.0	1.6	2.0	1.8
Radio News	69.0	67.2	68.0	9.1	7.5	8.2
Daily Newspapers	64.5	68.9	66.8	12.2	8.1	10.0
Internet	41.3	32.7	36.6	7.8	4.9	6.2
News Magazines	27.9	32.7	30.5	2.9	1.1	1.9
Other, Don't Know				0.8	1.8	1.4
N	516	615	1,131			

Source: Scripps Survey Research Center—Scripps Howard News Service Survey, 2001.

friends, radio news, and newspapers useful sources. The Internet came in higher than it did in the presidential campaign of 2000, and news magazines came in lower. Yet, the Internet figure as the most useful source was lower than one might expect. There was, after all, an enormous amount of information about terrorism on the Internet, and a person could easily have made it their main source.

Gender plays a role here: one is the typical difference between people regarding the Internet as a useful source. Most striking, though, is the difference on television news as being most useful, with women using it 10 percent more. Women were more likely to say that family and friends were a useful source, and while more women than men said newspapers were a useful source, considerably fewer said it was most useful.

Comparing these results with those in Table 3.10, more people thought television news, radio, newspapers, and the Internet were useful sources of information about terrorism than thought they were useful sources about the 2000 election. Television was considerably more dominant as the best source than it had been in the election year survey, but it provided more coverage than it had during the election. These results and those for media use indicate that when they need information, people do find the media useful. That also came out in response to another question asked in the 2001 survey. Respondents were asked if media coverage had helped them cope with terrorism, made them feel worse, or had no effect. Table 3.13 shows slightly more people said it made them feel worse than said it helped them cope. And twice as many men as women said media coverage had no effect.

TABLE 3.13

Reaction to Media Coverage by Sex, in Percent

	Men	Women	All
Media coverage helped me cope	25.8	35.6	30.9
Media coverage made me feel worse	28.9	36.3	33.3
Media coverage had no effect	36.6	18.9	26.9
Don't know, no answer	8.7	8.9	8.8
N	516	615	1,131

Source: Scripps Survey Research Center—Scripps Howard News Service Survey, 2001.

When media use and reaction to coverage was examined, it was evident that the people who said media coverage helped them cope used television news, newspapers, and radio more than people who said media coverage made them feel worse and more than those who said it had no effect. On the other hand, those who said media coverage helped them cope used the Internet less than those who said media coverage made them feel worse or had no effect. Also revealed was that those who said media coverage helped them cope were more likely to feel safe and were less likely to feel they would be likely victims of terrorism than those who said media coverage made them feel worse.

How It Looks to the Public

What the public knows about politics and government is the result of what the media do, what the politicians do, and what use the public makes of the resulting information. As individuals, the political process is not experienced personally very often. The vision is formed from what is absorbed from the media. The Scripps Survey Research Center and the Scripps Howard News Service have made several studies that dealt with the public perception of various aspects of the political process. In July 2000, a series of questions about the political parties was asked as well as another series about the two presidential candidates. Table 3.14 shows how the public felt about the two parties. Slightly less than half the respondents felt the parties were healthy. Overwhelmingly, the public did not believe the parties were doing a good job of resisting special interests. This refers to the extent to which influence is acquired through contributions to the parties and candidates. One might suppose that the Democrats thought

TABLE 3.14
Public Attitudes about the Political Parties, in Percent

	Yes	No	Don't Know/NA
Is the Democratic Party healthy?	45.1	35.4	19.6
Is the Republican Party healthy?	48.8	33.6	17.6
Do the Democrats do a good job of resisting special interests?	17.5	55.8	26.7
Do the Republicans do a good job of resisting special interests?	14.7	61.7	23.8
Do the Democrats have a good agenda?	48.5	29.8	21.7
Do the Republicans have a good agenda?	46.6	31.3	22.1
Do the Democrats have clear issues?	54.6	27.2	18.2
Do the Republicans have clear issues?	57.2	26.9	15.9

N=1,020

Source: Scripps Survey Research Center—Scripps Howard News Service Survey, 2000.

their party was doing a good job of resisting special interests and the Republicans were not and vice versa, but that was not really the case. The Democrats were more critical of the Republicans and Republicans more critical of the Democrats on this issue. However, cross-tabulation by party shows that in addition, a majority of the Democrats did not think their party was doing a good job of resisting special interests, and a majority of the Republicans did not think the Republicans were doing a good job of controlling special interests. There was concern across the board about influence being bought. Party officials have insisted that campaign finance is not a problem and have resisted reform in every possible way including invoking the First Amendment, but this survey shows that they are out of touch with the majority of the American people on this issue.

Slightly less than half the respondents thought both parties had clear agendas and slightly more than half thought both parties had clear issues. Yet more than a fourth of the respondents did not think the parties had good agendas or clear issues. Is it any wonder that half the people do not vote in presidential elections and 60 percent do not vote in congressional elections?

We also asked respondents if they thought Al Gore was the best Democratic candidate and if they thought George W. Bush as the best Republican candidate. Only 34.2 percent thought Gore was the best candidate the Democrats cold have picked, and 40.6

TABLE 3.15

Reactions to Changes in Elections, in Percent

	Approve	Disapprove	Don't Know/NA
Voting by mail	47.4	47.2	5.4
Voting On Line	42.1	48.8	9.1
Having elections on Sunday	39.0	52.5	8.5
Making election a holiday	60.6	34.0	5.4
Prohibiting projections of races by media	52.1	41.0	6.9
N=1,127			

Source: Scripps Survey Research Center—Scripps Howard News Service Survey, 2001.

percent though Bush was the best candidate the Republicans could have picked. Naturally party affiliation affected the answers, but only 51.3 percent of the Democrats thought Gore was the best candidate their party could have picked, and only 57.4 percent of the Republicans thought Bush was the best candidate their party could have picked. Only 18.6 percent of respondents thought both candidates were the best candidates their parties could have picked. Some of this reaction may be fallout from the primaries, which had ended less than two months before the survey. Both primaries were vigorously contested in 2000. Nonetheless, the results on this question do not speak well for the parties or the primary process.

In the October 2000 survey, the questions posed were: which candidate is more intelligent and which candidate is more likable. Gore was the pick as most intelligent, 42 to 20, while Bush was the pick as most likable, 49 to 34. How much Bush and Gore differed on issues was also asked. The response was that 16.7 percent said they differed completely, 34.2 percent said they differed a great deal, 31 percent said they differed somewhat, and 8.5 percent said they differed hardly at all. Only 31.7 percent of respondents thought that the outcome of the presidential election would make a big difference in their lives.

The survey in October 2001 asked respondents about voting. First, respondents were asked why they thought people were not voting, and 35.8 percent said it was because people disliked politics. Another 29.7 percent said it was because people do not believe their vote really counts. Then, as Table 3.15 shows, questions were asked about some possible changes in elections, and result revealed that people did not find great eagerness for change. Voting by mail won by two-tenths of a percent. That is somewhat surprising given that most states permit absentee voting by mail, and a few states go beyond that in allowing voting

TABLE 3.16
Which Party Is Best for Various Issues, in Percent

	Democrat	Republican	Don't Know	Other
Best to Combat Terrorism	23.4	50.2	18.4	8.0
Best to Get Middle East Peace	34.6	35.2	19.0	11.2
Best to Keep Social Security Safe	45.0	30.6	17.5	6.9
Best for Good Health Care	51.3	25.1	16.3	7.3
Best for Reducing Federal Deficit	34.7	38.2	18.3	8.8
Best for the National Economy	36.4	41.0	16.3	6.2

N=1,008

Source: Scripps Survey Research Center—Scripps Howard News Service Survey, 2002.

by mail. Online voting may be the wave of the future, but judging from these results, it is the distant future.

Having elections on Sunday, something that has been done in many countries for years, was the most strongly rejected of the suggestions. The other two results were perhaps predictable: making Election Day a national holiday is popular. And the objection to projections was to be expected after the fiasco with projections in Florida in the 2000 presidential race. Gore was projected a winner at one time and Bush at another, and the race became too close to call after it had been called.

The most recent survey, conducted in June 2002, gave respondents the opportunity to react to six major issues currently before the country—terrorism, peace in the Middle East, social security, health care, the economy, and the federal deficit. Table 3.16 shows that respondents picked Republicans by a wide margin on terrorism and Democrats by a wide margin on social security and health care. The other three are reasonably close, with the Republicans having a slight edge on each. The configuration is not a surprise. National security has over the years been a Republican issue. Social security and health care have been Democratic issues. Neither party has really had a handle on the Middle East situation. Both certainly have had some success (as well as some failure) with the issues of the federal deficit and the economy.

We then asked respondents which of these issues they felt was most important. Terrorism ranked first, as Table 3.17 shows, but not by as much of a margin as might be expected given the emphasis that has been placed on the terrorism issue. Health care is second, and if the number considering health care is important is combined with the number who think Social Security is most important, there are just as many people saying terrorism is most important.

TABLE 3.17
Which Issue Respondents Feel Is Most Important by Party Preference, in Percent

	Democrats	Independents	Republicans	Total
Combating Terrorism	28.3	27.4	36.3	31.1
Health Care	25.9	18.9	14.3	20.0
National Economy	9.6	15.4	15.0	13.0
Mid-East Peace	12.0	16.4	10.8	12.6
Social Security	13.3	9.5	9.6	11.0
Cut Deficit	9.0	9.5	12.7	10.5
Don't Know	1.9	2.9	1.3	1.8
N	332	201	314	847

167 respondents who did not express party preference are not included

Source: Scripps Survey Research Center—Scripps Howard News Service Survey, 2002.

Health care and Social Security are domestic issues, while terrorism is being defined as a world issue. Furthermore, less than one-third of respondents thought that terrorism was the most important issue facing the country. Table 3.17 also shows that the perspectives of Democrats and Republicans differ substantially. Although both said combating terrorism is the most important issue, the Democrats place health care second and Social Security third. Republicans, on the other hand, put the economy second, health care third, and Social Security last. These responses indicate that Republicans are listening to the Republican Party definition of issues, and the Democrats are listening to the Democratic Party definition of issues. Independents, on the other hand, put health care second and Middle East peace third. One can predict that in future election campaigns, there will be the same emphasis by each of the parties. What will decide elections will be the relative importance of these issues at the time of the election. This tendency was demonstrated in the 1992 presidential campaign when the Democrats made the economy the issue and defeated George Bush Sr., who had looked unbeatable a year and a half earlier as he basked in the success of the Persian Gulf War. However, the economy faltered, and the Bush administration was unable to straighten it out, and that made the economy, not national security and the Persian Gulf War, the major issue in 1992.

This chapter has discussed what the role of the media and the politicians is in communicating with the public, and the public response has been revealed. It is obvious that the system is not working perfectly. The voters ignore much of the media content and express dissatisfaction with what the politicians do. The voters, incidentally, give only modest approval to what the media are doing. Politicians and political scientists blame the media for the low esteem in which the public holds politicians and government. They argue that the media go out of their way to find negative news about politicians. Certainly that has been true in some circumstances. Yet journalists will say with some justification that it is the politicians who are creating the negative coverage. In fact, some of the negative coverage has to do with what politicians say about each other.

What can be said about both the media and the politicians is that they are not particularly in touch with the public. Some of the survey results mentioned in this chapter indicate that the politicians are out of touch with the public. Some studies that have been done indicate that journalists do not really understand what the public wants in media. What worked for United States as a country of a few million no longer works very well now that it is a country of 280 million. Public opinion polls offer some insight to what the public thinks about the media and politics, and both journalists and politicians scoff at polls that produce results they do not happen to agree with.

Some feel the Internet may be the answer. It offers politicians the opportunity to go directly to the public rather than through the media. It also offers other sources, some of them nonpartisan, and that may be appealing to the public. And the Internet gives citizens more information than they can get from the media. On the other hand, the quality of some of that information is questionable, and citizens will be challenged to pick Internet sources that are truly unbiased and accurate.

The media say that one of their roles is to serve as a watchdog of government, and that is a vital function. Yet, too often this leads to a sharply adversarial relationship between the media and politicians. The blame may fall on either side. Some journalists are overly adversarial, some politicians are overly sensitive to criticism, some journalists are suspicious of everything a public official does, and some officeholders do not believe the media ever have a right to criticize them.

Improvements can be made, but not so long as the press refuses to admit its flaw, the politicians refuse to admit that they are doing anything wrong, and a sizable segment of the public uses the attitudes of the press and the politicians as an excuse for not voting or being politically active. Political communication is an imperfect process and always will be. However, that is no excuse for not trying to make it better.

4

Chronology

1620   The Mayflower Compact is signed by the pilgrims aboard the Mayflower before they leave the ship. They bind themselves together in a "civic body politic . . . to make just and equal laws." It is the first political communication in the New World.

1638   The Harvard Press becomes the first press in the New World. The university itself was established in 1636.

1690   The first newspaper, *Publick Occurrences Both Foreign and Domestic,* is established in the colonies. It lasts one issue.

1704   The first continuing newspaper, the *Boston News-Letter,* is established by John Campbell. It is published by authority of the colonial government of Massachusetts.

1721   The *New England Courant* is established by James Franklin, the older brother of Ben Franklin. It is published in spite of the colonial government. Unlike the *Boston News-Letter,* it frequently takes stands against the government, and Franklin in fact is imprisoned for his position. (Because it was independent of the government, many journalists argue that it, not the *News-Letter,* is the forerunner of today's newspapers.)

1735   John Peter Zenger, editor of the *New York Weekly Journal,* is tried for criminal libel against colonial Governor William Cosby. Andrew Hamilton, uncle of Alexander Hamilton, defends Zenger by arguing that truth is a defense and it is up to the jury to decide. This is contrary to

1735,   British law and the judge could have overturned the ver-
cont.   dict or ordered a new trial. That he did not do so indicates concern about growing dissatisfaction of colonists
with British rule. Nonetheless, the verdict is a victory for
freedom of the press.

1756–   French and Indian War affects political communication.
1763   In this instance, the effect of the war was to diminish
colonial opposition to British rule.

1765   Stamp Act. The British want the colonies to pay for the
expense of the French and Indian War; the Stamp Act is
proposed to put taxes on a wide range of goods, including paper. Since politicians oppose this because of "taxa-
tion without representation," and newspapers oppose it
because of the tax on paper, the Stamp Act brings the two
together.

1772   Committees of Correspondence, founded principally by
Samuel Adams, is a means of circulating information
among those opposed to the British.

1776   Declaration of Independence. Besides declaring the
colonies independent and providing a long list of grievances, the Declaration of Independence makes the case
for political communication by proclaiming that governments get their "just powers from the consent of the
governed."

Thomas Paine publishes *Common Sense*, which articu-
lates clearly and forcefully the reasons for the colonists to
seek independence.

1787   First daily newspaper in the United States, the *Pennsylvania Packet*, begins publication in Philadelphia.

1788   George Washington is elected president by the electoral
college with no dissenting votes. John Adams is elected
vice president. This begins an era of nonpartisan cooper-
ation, but with Thomas Jefferson as secretary of state and
Alexander Hamilton as secretary of the treasury, partisanship raises its head before long.

1791   The first ten amendments to the Constitution—the Bill of Rights—are approved. For political communication, the First Amendment is important because of its guarantee of freedom of the press, freedom of speech, and freedom of assembly.

1792   The Alien and Sedition Act passes. Triggered by concern of possible war with France, it restricts criticism of the federal government. Fourteen journalists are prosecuted and convicted for criticizing the Federalist Party and President John Adams.

1800   Thomas Jefferson defeats John Adams for president. Aaron Burr, Jefferson's running mate, has the same number of electoral votes and claims the presidency, but the House of Representatives, as provided by the Constitution, takes up the matter and rules in favor of Jefferson. With Jefferson's victory the Alien and Sedition Act, which was passed for two years, is dead.

1805   Croswell case. The New York legislature makes law the decision in the Zenger case seventy years earlier that truth was a defense in libel. The Croswell case, as it came to be known, comes about because Harry Croswell, editor of the *Hudson New York Wasp*, is convicted of criminal libel for things he wrote about Jefferson. Alexander Hamilton argues the same position that his uncle had argued in the Zenger case, but he loses the case.

1814   "Star-Spangled Banner." Francis Scott Key writes the "Star-Spangled Banner," probably the most significant political communication of the War of 1812, a poem that was published in a Baltimore newspaper and as a handbill. It is set to an English tune, "To Anacreon in Heaven." Although it was widely acclaimed, it did not officially become the U.S. national anthem until 1931.

1824   For the first time ever, the popular vote is recorded. Eighteen of the twenty-four states now provided that electors must be chosen by the public, and 352,062 votes are cast for the four candidates for president. Andrew Jackson is clear winner of the popular vote, but no candidates have majority of the electoral vote, so the election goes to the

1824, House of Representatives, which selects John Quincy
cont.   Adams. The total vote is less than 10 percent of the pop-
        ulation. Four years later, the vote total would be
        1,156,328.

1833   Penny press. Ben Day's *New York Sun* begins a new era in
        journalism—the era of the penny press. The price allows
        the paper to be aimed at the masses, not the elite. That in
        turn means that the American people are no longer de-
        pendent on the political parties and factions for informa-
        tion about politics.

1834   James Gordon Bennett begins the second penny paper,
        the *New York Herald.* Unlike Day, Bennett defines politics
        as significant news, and the *Herald* contributes consider-
        ably more in the way of political coverage, including the
        first coverage of the U.S. Senate by a paper outside
        Washington.

1840   Whig elected. The party of Jefferson, which in his day
        was the Democratic-Republican Party and which became
        simply the Democratic Party in the Jacksonian era, had
        won every presidential election between 1800 and 1836.
        William Henry Harrison, a Whig, ends that run by win-
        ning the 1840 election, only to die after being president
        for just one month.

1841   Horace Greeley starts the *New York Tribune,* which makes
        yet a different kind of contribution to the coverage of
        politics. Greeley was active in the Whig Party and would
        become one of the founders of the Republican Party. Yet
        by beginning the editorial page, he separates news and
        opinion in political coverage as well as other coverage.
        No other American journalist has mixed politics and
        journalism to the extent that he did.

1851   Henry Raymond starts the *New York Times.* He seeks to
        provide something other than the sensationalism of Ben-
        nett and the politicized coverage of Greeley.

1854   Republican Party organized. At a meeting in Ripon, Wis-
        consin, a committee composed of Whigs, Democrats, and
        Free Soilers organizes the Republican Party.

1858   Lincoln-Douglas debates. Republican Abraham Lincoln and Democrat Stephen A. Douglas are candidates for the U.S. Senate in Illinois. They engage in a series of debates throughout the state, which would be recognized as classic political communication, perhaps unmatched by any other pair of candidates. Douglas wins the election, but the debates establish Lincoln as a major figure and play a considerable part in his nomination for president in 1860.

1860   Abraham Lincoln is nominated by the Republican Party and wins the presidential election. Joseph Medill, publisher of the *Chicago Tribune*, and Horace Greeley play major roles in the nomination and election of Lincoln.

1861   Civil War. The secession of South Carolina and the attack on Fort Sumter start the Civil War between the North and South. With the war come some restrictions on media and a change in politics. The issue of slavery is no longer a subject of political debate. The North opposed it, and the South favored it, and there was nothing more to be said.

1871   Tweed ring. The *New York Times* breaks the story of Tammany Hall boss William M. Tweed and his cohorts stealing $200 million from the city of New York. Thomas Nast, of *Harper's Weekly*, adds his devastating cartoons to the documentation by the *Times*, and the Tweed ring is driven from power.

1883   Yellow journalism. Joseph Pulitzer buys the *New York World* and brings the sensationalism that had succeeded in St. Louis to New York. That sets the stage for yellow journalism, which will not reach its peak until William Randolph Hearst enters the New York market in 1895. The term gets its name from a comic strip character, the Yellow Kid.

1898   Spanish-American War. No war in U.S. history was promoted by the media the way the Spanish-American War is. The sinking of the battleship USS *Maine* in Havana Harbor is the spark that sets off the war, and the media make the most of it. Both Pulitzer's *World* and Hearst's *Journal* offer their readers spectacular front-page artists'

1898, drawings of the explosion. But the promotion of the war
cont. had begun with the sensational coverage of the Cuban
insurrection in 1895. It is a popular war and for the newspapers, a profitable one. On some days, the *World* and
the *Journal* sell three million copies between them.

1909 Presidential news conferences. William Howard Taft becomes the first president to schedule news conferences,
but he soon abandons them after misunderstandings.

1917 World War I. Two significant actions follow the United
States' entry into World War I. One is the passage of the
Sedition Act of 1917—it is used against leftist publications and not against mainstream newspaper opponents
of the war like the Hearst newspapers. The other is the
establishment of the Creel Committee on Public Information, which coordinates propaganda efforts and
draws up a voluntary censorship code. Its restriction of
the press is minimal. The difficulty of getting news back
from France is a much larger factor in limiting what the
American people know about the war.

1919 Tabloids. The first tabloid, the *New York Daily News* begins publication, thus ushering in the era of tabloid journalism. The *Daily News* is soon joined by the *Mirror* and
the *Graphic*. All are sensational. None exhibits great interest in politics, and unfortunately they drive out of
business some newspapers that did. Tabloids appear in a
few other cities, but tabloid journalism is largely a New
York City phenomenon.

Schenck case. From the Sedition Act of 1917 comes the
Schenck case, which produces perhaps the most widely
quoted statement from any Supreme Court cases. Justice
Oliver Wendell Holmes wrote, "the most stringent protection of free speech would not protect a man in falsely
shouting fire in a crowded theater." Schenck was prosecuted for distributing antidraft material. Enduring concept of the case is "clear and present danger" as a
criterion for judging such situations.

1920 Women's suffrage. Women win the right to vote, but not
many do so in this election. Nonetheless, political com-

munication changes with this major redefinition of the electorate.

First radio broadcasts. Experiments with wireless transmission had been going on for more than forty years. In 1920 it becomes available to the general public. The station to first broadcast regularly remains in dispute, but with regard to political communication, the broadcasting of returns of the presidential election by radio station KDKA in Pittsburgh is a significant first.

1927   Federal Radio Commission is established primarily to eliminate confusion on the broadcast band. With 733 stations on the air, and with some varying their frequencies, listeners faced considerable signal interference. Broadcasting and politics are thus brought together.

1931   Prior restraint. In *Near v. Minnesota,* the Supreme Court declares that prior restraint of a publication violates the First Amendment. Case involves injunction against scurrilous publication that had been found guilty of criminal libel.

1932   Newspaper-radio war. Newspapers had long been concerned about competition from radio. The American Newspaper Publishers Association (ANPA) board of directors in December 1932 recommends that press associations not sell or give away news to radio stations and that radio news be limited to brief bulletins.

1933   Roosevelt takes office. Franklin D. Roosevelt is perhaps the most effective political communicator to hold the office of president. The relationship between the press and the president changes markedly. Roosevelt was the first president to use radio effectively. With a great radio voice, he holds press conferences with a frequency never seen before or since.

1934   The Federal Communications Commission (FCC) is created, replacing the Federal Radio Commission. It is given jurisdiction over all telecommunications, including tele-

1934,   phones, and would soon include television. Today it in-
cont.   cludes the Internet.

      The Press-Radio Bureau. The radio industry's response
to the ANPA edict of 1932 is the establishment of the
Press-Radio Bureau. Although it has 245 stations sub-
scribing to it after a year, it is short-lived. Five other radio
news services spring up and then in 1935 the major press
associations end their ban on news to radio stations.

1935   Gallup Poll begins. George Gallup and Harold A. Anderson found the American Institute for Public Opinion. They offer a regular newspaper column on public
opinion poll results. In 19040, the column would be
given the name the Gallup Poll. This marks the beginning of public opinion polling as a regular part of political communication.

1936   *Literary Digest* poll. The magazine *Literary Digest* conducts a poll that predicts Alf Landon will defeat Franklin
D. Roosevelt for the presidency. Roosevelt wins in one of
the biggest landslides in U.S. history, carrying forty-six
of the forty-eight states and receiving 62 percent of the
popular vote. That is the end not only of the *Literary Digest* poll, which had correctly predicted the winner of
five previous presidential elections, but also of the magazine itself. The poll is widely criticized because it was
restricted to people who owned automobiles or had telephones, but the larger problem was that it was a mail
poll with a 23 percent return.

1941   The United States enters World War II. The United States
had in fact been aiding the British ever since the start of
the war, but the Japanese bombing of Pearl Harbor
brings the United States into the war. It is often said that
the bombing brought the country together, but along
with the bombing there was the memorable speech to
Congress by President Roosevelt the next day. There is to
be censorship at the front, and it starts with the Pearl
Harbor bombing. The American people would not be
told the full extent of the damage for more than a year.

1942   Propaganda and censorship functions are split with the establishment of the Office of War Information under Elmer Davis of CBS and the Office of Censorship under Byron Price, executive news editor of the Associated Press. Military commanders have censorship authority in their own territory, but conflict between reporters and the military is minimal.

1946   Peacetime security. World War II is over, but the Cold War has begun. Furthermore, the desire to keep the secret of the atomic bomb is a major consideration in political policy. The result is that the government institutes security measures unknown in peacetime in this country. Not only can the press not report on certain events, but also in some instances previously published material is classified as secret by the government.

1948   Truman and one-party press. President Harry Truman confounds all the experts by coming from behind to defeat Thomas E. Dewey for president. Dewey led in the polls from the start of the campaign, but Truman makes a whistle-stop campaign based on two issues—the "Do Nothing" Congress and the "one-party press." The latter refers to the fact that newspaper endorsements favor Dewey by more than 4 to 1. Truman contends the news coverage also favors Dewey. The issue obviously resonates with voters.

1949   The FCC creates the Fairness Doctrine. At first it prohibits editorializing, but the FCC changes its position on that issue. The Fairness Doctrine requires broadcasters to cover public affairs and to seek all viewpoints on controversial issues. It never works well because it assumes all issues are two-sided when in fact, with many issues, there are more than two sides.

1950   Korean War. In contrast to World War II, the Korean War is centralized with one American commander—General Douglas MacArthur. Things go well between MacArthur and the press in the military successes, but as MacArthur drives toward the Chinese border in late 1950s, the Chinese enter the war. U.S. defeats follow, and criticism of MacArthur likewise follows, and relations between the press and MacArthur's staff deteriorate. Yet part of what

1950,   is involved is conflict between MacArthur, who wants to
cont.   expand the war, and President Truman who does not.

1951   MacArthur and Truman. The conflict between MacArthur
and Truman continues until Truman relieves MacArthur
of his command on 11 April. MacArthur's return to the
United States, capped by a speech to a joint session of
Congress, is a major political communication event. Also
noteworthy is the Truman administration's decision to let
the *New York Times* have access to classified material about
the MacArthur-Truman controversy. The result is a
Pulitzer Prize–winning story.

1952   Television and the presidential campaign. Television was
born in 1948, but so few people had sets that it was not a
factor in the presidential campaign. In 1952 it is a major
factor, and Dwight Eisenhower's ability to use the
medium helps him win the election.

One-party press. Democratic candidate Adlai Stevenson
picks up where President Truman left off with the issue
of the one-party press. Newspaper endorsements once
again run better than 4 to 1 for the Republican candidate.
Sigma Delta Chi, the professional journalism society,
looks into the question and decides that a study made
after the campaign would be inconclusive.

1953   "Checkers" speech. Charges that Richard Nixon, the Republican vice-presidential candidate, has irregularities in
his campaign finances lead Nixon to make a half-hour
televised speech that has become famous as the "Checkers" speech. Checkers was Nixon's cocker spaniel, and
he was a symbol of the unpretentious life Nixon says he
and his family led. The speech saves Nixon's place on the
Republican ticket.

1954   Murrow and McCarthy. In his television program "See It
Now," on 9 March 1954, Murrow criticizes McCarthy's
smear tactics used against alleged communists. Mc-
Carthy, given time to reply, gives a confused, bumbling
reply. This broadcast is considered one of the factors in
McCarthy's downfall.

1955   Televised press conference. President Eisenhower permits televising of press conferences for delayed broadcast. They are reviewed before being aired, but this is a major step in the use of television for political coverage.

The Birmingham bus boycott is the first event in the Civil Rights movement. Media coverage is essential, and the interaction between media and politicians plays a major part.

1959   Equal Time Rule. The FCC rules that the Equal Time Rule applies to news programs. That means that any candidate is be entitled to as much time on news programs as his opponent is. However, Congress quickly passes a law exempting news and documentaries from this rule.

1960   Televised debates. Congress passes a law exempting presidential debates from the Equal Time Provision for 1960 only. This makes it possible for Democratic candidate John F. Kennedy and Republican candidate Richard Nixon to debate. They have four debates, and it is frequently said that the four debates decided the outcome of the election. Actually, the first debate is very one-sided in favor of Kennedy, but the other three are reasonably even.

1961   President John F. Kennedy begins having news conferences that are broadcast live by television and radio. Kennedy is more comfortable with live press conferences than any of his successors. His quickness and sharp wit make the press conferences both informative and entertaining.

Vietnam War. The Vietnam War began in 1954, but the first U.S. commitment of military personnel to Vietnam occurs in 1961. U.S. military personnel would be there for another thirteen years. For politicians, Vietnam is a puzzle that defies solution. For the media, it is the first chance to bring the war by television into the living rooms of the American people. The result of the actions of both politicians and the media is a seriously divided country.

1962   Cuban Missile Crisis. The Cuban Missile Crisis dispute between the United States and Russia brings the world as close as it has ever been to nuclear war. Media coverage, especially that of television, brings the American public closer to the actions in a crisis than ever before.

1963   President Kennedy is assassinated. Television brings the events of this terrible weekend live to the American people. For four days, television is free of commercials as the nation stands still.

1964   Sullivan case. The Supreme Court expands press freedom and changes the rules for coverage of politicians when it rules in *New York Times v. Sullivan* that public officials have to prove actual malice or reckless disregard of the truth to collect damages in a libel suit. The case comes out and an advertisement is run by supporters of integration that criticizes Southern law enforcement. The case may be as significant for civil rights as for media because it means that media can criticize the abuses and failures of Southern law enforcement during the Civil Rights movement.

1967   Cities in turmoil. This is a year of summer riots in major U.S. cities as blacks protest segregation and its effects on their lives. President Johnson appoints a national commission, named the Kerner Commission after its chairman, Otto Kerner, to investigate the causes.

1968   Year of turmoil. This is a year in which America sees more riots in major U.S. cities, the assassination of Martin Luther King Jr. and Robert Kennedy, and a riotous Democratic convention. Media and politicians share the spotlight. The Kerner Commission issues its report, which puts blame on both politicians for their failure to address problems and the press for their double standard in coverage of blacks.

1969   Attacks on press. The Nixon administration begins criticizing press coverage early. Heading the attack is Vice President Spiro Agnew in inflammatory speeches against the media. Media–White House relations reach an all-time low, but polls show that the attacks also hurt media credibility.

1971   Pentagon Papers. The Nixon administration gets an injunction to prevent the *New York Times* from publishing a Defense Department study of the history of the Vietnam War. The *Times* appeals, and the U.S. Supreme Court agrees to hear the case immediately. The government says an injunction is permissible because the document is classified, but eight of the nine justices say they do not believe publication would endanger national security. The court votes 6 to 3 to permit publication, thus upholding the near decision ban on prior restraint

1972   Watergate. The *Washington Post* begins what turns out to be a lengthy investigation of the break-in at Democratic headquarters in the Watergate apartments. Two young reporters, Carl Bernstein and Robert Woodward, carry out the investigative reporting, which ultimately leads to President Richard Nixon's resignation in 1974.

Eighteen-year-olds get vote. The voting age is lowered to eighteen, with disappointing results. Turnout of eighteen-year-olds is below average, and the overall average declines too.

1974   Nixon resigns. Facing the likelihood of impeachment, President Nixon resigns and Gerald Ford becomes president. Media–White House relations become reasonably cordial.

1976   Debates resume. The legislation that permitted the debates between the presidential candidates was for 1960 only. The two parties were unable to get together on terms for debates for the next three elections. In 1976, the League of Women Voters offers to sponsor the debates, and the FCC agrees. The debates are fairly even except that Gerald Ford, in answering one question, puts Poland outside the "iron curtain." He refuses to correct the statement, and this may cost him the election.

1979   Iran hostages. When Iran seizes ninety people, including sixty-three Americans at the American Embassy in

1979,   Tehran, it creates a media event as well as a political
cont.   event. For months, Walter Cronkite closes the CBS
        Evening News by saying the date and the consecutive
        day that the Americans have been held hostage. It be-
        comes an issue of the next year's presidential campaign.

1987   Fairness Doctrine. The FCC announces that it will no
        longer enforce the Fairness Doctrine. It is widely re-
        ported that the FCC has repealed it, but in fact it remains
        in the FCC regulations. The FCC could decide to resume
        enforcement but is not likely to do so.

1988   Presidential campaign. The 1988 campaign is generally
        considered the dirtiest campaign in recent times. In part,
        this reflects the fact that cable becomes a major advertis-
        ing medium, and there are advertisements that do not
        come from the campaign staffs or the parties. Most no-
        table is the infamous Willie Horton advertisement about
        a black man who had been furloughed from prison in
        Massachusetts and then committed murder. (The Demo-
        cratic candidate, Michael Dukakis, was governor of
        Massachusetts.) The advertisement is the work of a po-
        litical action committee. It appears only on cable until it
        becomes so controversial that network news programs
        run segments of it.

1992   Third-party challenge. Ross Perot runs as a third-party
        candidate and in May takes the lead in the Gallup Poll.
        He then withdraws because of concern about dirty tricks
        and reenters the campaign in September. Leaving and
        reentering costs him votes, of which he receives only 19
        percent. However, Perot spends more than $30 million of
        his own money on advertising and other communication
        and in so doing succeeds in having considerable influ-
        ence on the campaign agenda.

1996   Less than half vote. Voter participation, which has been
        declining since 1968, reaches a new low, with only 49
        percent of the adults voting in the presidential election.

1998   Clinton scandal. The effort to impeach Bill Clinton be-
        gins. It ends in early 1999 with impeachment proceed-
        ings in the Senate. Two Senate votes fall far short of the

required two-thirds majority. It is only the second time that impeachment of a president has been attempted. Media coverage is extensive and considered excessive by many.

2000   Internet a factor. The Internet becomes a major player in a presidential election, as parties and candidates create websites. However, a national survey by Scripps Howard News Service and Ohio University shows that less than one-half of the people with Internet access consider the Internet a useful source of information on the campaign. In contrast, more than one-half consider newspapers a useful source and more than three-fourths consider television news a useful source.

2001   Gary Condit. Chandra Levy, an intern working for Gary Condit, a California congressman, disappears. Media coverage is extensive, and considerable suspicion is cast upon Condit. The public again considers coverage excessive, and both newspapers and television realize that television news audiences are down, newspaper readership is down, and credibility of both media is down since the sensational coverage of the two political scandals began.

5

Biographical Sketches

his chapter presents brief biographical sketches of major figures in political communication in the United States. Some are political figures, some are journalists, and some are researchers. They are presented in alphabetical order rather than chronological order.

Samuel Adams (1722–1803)

Samuel Adams is often called the "father of the American Revolution." A graduate of Harvard, he did not enter politics until he was unsuccessful as a businessman. He was a member of the Massachusetts legislature from 1765 to 1774, he drafted a protest against the Stamp Act in 1765, and he was one of the organizers in 1767 of the nonimportation agreement that forced the British to repeal the Townshend Acts. He stirred up anti-British sentiment with what he wrote for colonial newspapers and pamphlets. He also helped to organized the Sons of Liberty and helped to foment revolt through the Committees of Correspondence, which disseminated anti-British material widely in the colonies. He was one of the organizers of the Boston Tea Party. General Thomas Gage issued a warrant for the arrest of Adams and John Hancock in 1775, but they escaped punishment. He was a member of the Continental Congress from 1774 to 1781, but after independence had been gained, his influence declined as more moderate leaders took over. He was viewed by many as an irresponsible agitator. However, he did serve as governor of Massachusetts from 1794 to 1797.

Roger Ailes (1940–)

Roger Ailes is a political consultant turned broadcaster. He began his broadcasting career on an early morning radio show while he was a student at Ohio University. After his graduation in 1962, he went to work for KYW-TV in Cleveland where he worked on the Mike Douglas Show, a television talk show. While at KYW in 1968, he met Richard Nixon. Ailes convinced Nixon that he had to learn to use television if he expected to get elected president, so Nixon hired Ailes as his media adviser. Ailes proposed a television program called "Man in the Arena." Though it appeared to be an impromptu question-and-answer session, with Nixon answering all questions, it was in fact a carefully staged program with participants screened so that unsuitable questions were not asked. Nixon won, and Ailes was in demand as a political consultant, but he stayed in television. In the 1980s, he was executive director of a show featuring Tom Snyder and Rona Barrett. And when he worked with candidates Ronald Reagan and George Bush Sr., he developed strategies to downplay Reagan's age, and he urged Bush to counterattack in an interview with Dan Rather about the Iran-Contra Affair. Ailes was the strategist for Bush's negative campaign, but he did deny any connection with the infamous Willie Horton advertisement. The advertisement was part of an effort to slam Bush's opponent, Michael Dukakis, for the furlough plan for prisoners in Massachusetts, where Dukakis was governor. The advertisement was actually done by a political action committee and by law, Ailes, a member of the Bush campaign staff, could not have been involved. And though the advertisement was shown only on cable television, it was so widely criticized that it was pulled off the air. Ailes refused to help Bush in his reelection campaign in 1992. Instead he sought to help Rush Limbaugh turn his radio talk show into a television program. He became president of CNBC in 1983 and later became president and CEO, the position he currently holds, of the FOX News network.

Jack Anderson (1922–)

Jack Anderson began covering events in Washington in 1947 and became one of the most influential Washington columnists, but he was a muckraker rather than an analyst. He began his journalistic career on the *Salt Lake City Tribune* while he was a student at the University of Utah. While there, he did an exposé of Mormon polygamy, and that piece got him in enough trouble that he left school and became a missionary. He was drafted into the Army in World War II and assigned to the *Stars and Stripes*. After the war he went to Washington and joined the staff of Drew Pearson, who wrote a syndicated column called "Washington Merry-Go-Round," and Anderson tookover the column when Pearson died in 1969. Anderson received the Pulitzer Prize in 1972 for his reporting on the Security Action Group papers, which showed that the Nixon administration favored Pakistan in its war with India.

Bess Furman Armstrong (1894–1969)

Bess Furman Armstrong was the best known of the women's press corps who covered Eleanor Roosevelt. Mrs. Roosevelt interacted with the press more than any other wife of a president did. And after she discussed the idea of having press conference with Furman, Mrs. Roosevelt became the first First Lady to have press conferences, and she permitted only women to attend her press conferences. At the time, there were very few women in newsrooms. Her father, who ran a weekly newspaper in Nebraska, introduced Furman to journalism. Furman worked on the *Omaha Bee-News* from 1920 until 1929 when the Associated Press in Washington hired her.

Peter Arnett (1934–)

Peter Arnett is a noted foreign correspondent. Born in New Zealand, he began his journalistic career at the *Southland Times*. After working for several Australian newspapers, in 1961 he became a stringer for the Associated Press. He covered Southeast Asia, including the Vietnam War, for which he received a Pulitzer Prize in 1966. He reported on discrepancies between what the U.S. government reported publicly and what he found with his own investigative reporting on the scene. Some welcomed his work, and others said he was a Vietnamese sympathizer. Arnett helped launch the Cable News Network (CNN) in its effort to cover news worldwide. He covered the Middle East, including the TWA hijacking in 1985. When the Persian Gulf War broke out, Arnett and others from CNN went to Baghdad. Iraq permitted only CNN to remain in Baghdad as the war intensified, and Arnett was criticized for his reports from Baghdad, which were censored by the Iraqi. His interview with Saddam Hussein was widely criticized, but Arnett maintained that the American people had the right to know as much as possible about the war, and the First Amendment gave him the right to report it. In 1987, Arnett became the first Western journalist to interview Osama bin Laden. In 1999 he was fired by CNN after doing a story with *Time* saying that American forces had used sarin gas in Laos. Pentagon pressure on CNN led to his termination. In 2001, he was hired by Broadcast News Network to cover Afghanistan.

James Gordon Bennett (1795–1872)

James Gordon Bennett founded the *New York Herald* in 1735. He made it clear at the outset that he intended for his paper to be politically nonpartisan. He expanded news coverage far beyond the norm when he started his paper. The *Herald* covered Wall Street, high society, politics, and sports. He took the position that he was willing to cover "anything that the Good Lord let happen." His approach to news made the *Herald* the newspaper with the largest circulation. He waged a two-month campaign in 1841 to get the U.S. Senate to allow reporters to cover Senate sessions. The Senate changed its rules to permit bona fide reporters to cover their sessions, and other newspapers joined the *Herald* in covering the Senate. During the Civil War, the *Herald* was more sympathetic to the South than most Northern newspapers. It had opposed the abolitionist movement. However, its coverage of the war was perhaps the best of any newspaper.

Hugo Black (1886–1971)

Hugo Black, a Southerner who once had ties to the Ku Klux Klan, became one of the strongest supporters of the First Amendment ever to serve on the U.S. Supreme Court. A native of Alabama, he did not have a law degree, but only a degree form a junior college. Nonetheless he was elected to the U.S. Senate twice before President Franklin D. Roosevelt nominated him for the Court, for which he served for thirty-four years. He was a strict constructionist, and that led him to the position that when the First Amendment said "no law," that meant no law. He often noted in decisions that very point, and then when acknowledging that there was a law under consideration, gave his opinion. He publicly stated that he thought libel laws were a violation of the First Amendment and should be done away with. It seemed an extreme, almost frivolous position, but he defended it with a well-reasoned argument.

Jay Blumler (1924–)

Jay Blumler is a British political communication researcher who has influenced political communication in this country as well.

After serving as director of the Centre for Television Research, as professor of sociology and political aspects of broadcasting at the University of Leeds, and as a lecturer at Oxford, he came to the University of Maryland. His major contribution to political communication is about the effects of television on political communication. He is the author of *Television in Politics: Its Uses and Influence* (1968), *The Challenge of Election Broadcasting* (1978), and a coauthored book, *The Formation of Campaign Agendas* (1991). In the later book, he analyzes British and U.S. election data to explain gatekeeping, agenda setting, and the journalist's role in political communication. From this information, he determines the relative influence of politicians and their spin doctors, the media, and the public. Blumler recently coauthored *The Crisis of Public Communication* (1995).

Louis Brandeis (1865–1941)

Louis Brandeis, a U.S. Supreme Court justice from 1916 to 1939, was a man ahead of his time. He was often in the minority on the decision of the Court, but in time the rest of the Court would come around to his way of seeing an issue. Born in Kentucky to Jewish parents, Brandeis graduated from Harvard Law School and had his own practice in Boston before joining the Court. As an attorney, he had a reputation for protecting the rights of the common man, and he carried that perspective with him to the Supreme Court. In the Schenck case in 1919, he agreed with Justice Oliver Wendell Holmes's majority opinion that speech against government should be restricted if it posed a "clear and present danger." Yet eight years later he would write in *Whitney v. California* that the remedy for falsehood was more speech, not enforced silence. He also was one of the first in the field of law to argue for the right of privacy, a right that is not specifically spelled out in the Constitution, but one that is recognized as rather basic in American society today.

William J. Brennan Jr. (1906–1997)

William J. Brennan Jr. was appointed to the U.S. Supreme Court by President Dwight Eisenhower in 1957 and served on the Court for thirty-three years. He grew up in New Jersey, and after completing law school, practiced in that state. After serving in the Army during World War II, he returned to New Jersey and served in several judicial posts there. Contrary to expectations at the time of his appointment, Brennan became one of the most liberal justices on the Court. He nearly always voted in favor of the media in First Amendment cases. He was best known as the author of the majority opinion in *New York Times v. Sullivan*. He wrote that public officials must show actual malice in order to collect damages for libel. That changed the game for public officials and specifically for Southern officials, who sought to stop unfavorable press coverage during the Civil Rights struggle. Later he applied that same principle in the majority opinion in a false-light privacy case.

David Brinkley (1920–)

David Brinkley was a newsperson for fifty-three years, which, as he put it, included eleven presidents, four wars, one moon landing, and three assassinations. He is best remembered as half of the first famous anchor team in television news—the Huntley-Brinkley team that anchored the early evening NBC news for twenty years. He began his career as a reporter for his hometown paper, the *Wilmington (North Carolina) Morning Star*, after dropping out of high school. After World War II he went to NBC in Washington. The Huntley-Brinkley team came about as a gamble by NBC as it sought to strengthen coverage of the 1956 presidential nominating conventions. The two worked together so well that they became the early evening news anchors. Brinkley stayed with NBC until 1981 when he went to ABC and had his own program "This Week with David Brinkley." He has won three Peabody Awards and ten Emmy Awards for his work in television news.

Warren Burger (1907–1995)

Warren Burger was chief justice of the U.S. Supreme Court from 1969 to 1986. He was born in St. Paul, Minnesota, and worked with a law firm there after graduation from law school. His work for Republican candidates, including Dwight Eisenhower, led to his being appointed to the U.S. Court of Appeals in the District of Columbia. He went from there to the job of chief justice. President Richard Nixon, who had pledged to make the Court more conservative than it had been under Earl Warren, appointed him. The Burger Court certainly lived up to that expectation and it was much less favorable to the media than the Warren Court had been. Yet there were two major victories for the media in the Burger era. One was the decision in *Miami Herald v. Tornillo* that rejected the idea that there was the same right of reply to print media as there was for broadcast media. The Court said the content of a newspaper was up to the editor. The other was in *Nebraska Press Association v. Stuart* in which the Court, in an 8 to 0 verdict, said the media had the right to report court cases, and gag orders could not be issued against the media. Burger was not a fan of the press, but while he kept cameras out of the Supreme Court, he voted to give states the right to allow cameras in courtrooms.

Hadley Cantril (1906–1969)

Hadley Cantril, a Princeton University researcher, is probably best known for his study of why people panicked when they listened to Orson Welles's famous "War of the Worlds" radio broadcast on Halloween in 1938. His results were the first to challenge the idea that all people respond the same way to communication. His work suggested there was selectivity based on individual differences and that critical ability affected the likelihood that a person would be manipulated by communication. He worked with George Gallup in adding psychological dimensions to the Gallup Poll. His work influenced the way researchers viewed the relation between public opinion and government policy. Media were viewed as being less politically oppressive and propagandistic in intent.

Steven H. Chaffee (1935–2001)

Steven H. Chaffee obtained his bachelor's degree at the University of Redlands, his master's degree at the University of California at Berkeley and his Ph.D. at Stanford University. In 1965 he joined the faculty at the University of Wisconsin and became director of the Institute for Communications Research. He was a political analyst for Democratic candidates from 1966 to 1984. His major research contribution was to the development with his Wisconsin colleague Jack McLeod of the theory of co-orientation. That theory deals with the extent to which any pair of individuals or groups in political communication share the same perspective on a given issue. Chaffee's book *Political Communications: Issues and Strategies for Research* (1975), deals with the role of mass media in political communication.

Walter Cronkite (1916–)

Walter Cronkite probably has had more effect on television news than anyone else. He was anchor of the CBS Evening News for thirty years. His closing line every evening, "That's the way it is," was believed by most viewers, and one poll showed that he was the most trusted person in America. He went to the University of Texas in 1933 to study economics, but soon was working for the *Houston Post* and Scripps Howard. He worked for a Kansas City radio station for a year and then went to work for the United Press for a decade. He was a correspondent in Europe during World War II—he parachuted into Holland with the 101st Airborne Division and was with the Third Army in the Battle of the Bulge. He was the United Press's chief reporter at the Nuremberg trials and then was Moscow bureau chief for two years. He became a radio reporter in the United States in 1948 and joined CBS in 1950. He went to Vietnam during the Tet Offensive in 1968, and some historians think his reporting turned many Americans against the war. He retired from CBS in 1981, but has done special assignments for CBS and public broadcasting since then.

Timothy Crouse (1947–)

Timothy Crouse is the reporter who coined the phrase "pack journalism." A Harvard graduate, he covered rock music for several East Coast newspapers and then joined *Rolling Stone* in 1971. In 1972 he had the opportunity to cover the presidential campaign. He observations about the press became a book, *The Boys on the Bus* (1990). He observed the tendency for reporters to think as a pack and write as a pack, while at the same time trying to beat the pack with the day's story. He felt that the process denied reporters the opportunity to give analysis to their stories and deprived the American public of information.

Elmer Davis (1890–1958)

Born in Aurora, Indiana, Elmer Davis graduated from Franklin College and was a Rhodes scholar. He worked on the *New York Times* for ten years beginning in 1914. Then he left the *Times* to write novels and occasional political analyses for the *Times*. He joined CBS News in 1939. He anchored live reports from Europe and presented analyses. Soon after America entered World War II, President Franklin D. Roosevelt named Davis head of the Of-

fice of War Information (OWI). The media respected him because
he was one of their own, but he encountered opposition from the
army and the navy, and received little support from the president. Everything considered, the OWI operation was successful.
When the OWI ceased operation after the end of the war, Davis
went to ABC as a commentator. He became increasingly critical
of the Soviet Union's actions, but was one of the first critics of
Senator Joseph McCarthy and his anticommunist crusades.

George A. Donohue (1924–), Clarice N. Olien (1933–), and Philip J. Tichenor (1931–)

The collaboration of this trio of Minnesota faculty members over
a period of more than thirty years is unprecedented in social science research. They were so closely linked together that the Association for Education in Journalism and Mass Communication
presented the Paul J. Deutschmann Award for Excellence in Research to all three simultaneously in 1994. Their major contribution to political communication is the concept of the knowledge
gap. They found that the media tend to widen rather than narrow
the knowledge gap because the media tend to reach those who
are already better informed. Donohue has his Ph.D. in sociology
from Washington State University, Olien has her master's in sociology from The University of Minnesota, and Tichenor has his
Ph.D. in mass communication research from Stanford University.
They have also studied such issues as what news gets published,
how news of conflict is reported, the social consequences of information, and accuracy in news.

William O. Douglas (1898–1980)

William O. Douglas was born in Yakima, Washington. After
putting himself through Columbia Law School, he worked on
Wall Street and taught at several universities. An early clerkship
with Supreme Court Justice Harlan Stone sparked his interest in
the judicial system. He was appointed to the U.S. Supreme Court
by President Franklin D. Roosevelt in 1939 and served on the
Court until 1975. He was a liberal and a strong supporter of the
First Amendment and of speech that supported unpopular be-
liefs. He voted for the media more than 80 percent of the time in
First Amendment cases. He also believed that trials should be
public events and that government should not interfere with the
reporting of judicial proceedings.

Frederick Douglass (1817–1895)

Frederick Douglass, born the son of a black woman slave and a white man, escaped slavery in 1838 and became a leading spokesman for abolition and for the rights of blacks after slavery was abolished. In 1845 he published an autobiography, *Narrative of the Life of Frederick Douglass*, which talked of the cruelty and oppression he experienced on a plantation in Maryland. Two years later he became associate editor of the *Ram's Horn*, a strong antislavery newspaper, and started his own paper, the *North Star*. He wrote a second autobiography, *My Bondage and My Freedom* (1855). After the Civil War, he started another newspaper, the *New National Era*. In his third autobiography, published in 1881, *The Life and Times of Frederick Douglass*, he tells of his efforts to keep alive the struggle for racial equality in the years after the Civil War.

Stephen Tyree Early (1889–1951)

Stephen Tyree Early was the first effective presidential press secretary. He served as Franklin D. Roosevelt's press secretary during his entire term of office. His experience made him well suited for that job. He had been a reporter for the United Press and the Associated Press and director of publicity for the U.S. Chamber of Commerce. He was Roosevelt's advance man in Roosevelt's unsuccessful bid for the vice presidency in 1920. He then returned to the Associated Press, but left in 1927 to become Washington editor of Paramount News. He became assistant secretary in charge of press relations in 1933 and presidential secretary in 1937. Early helped Roosevelt use both newsreels and radio effectively. Early made sure that photographs of Roosevelt did not show his handicap. By dealing with reporters individually, Early facilitated relationships between Roosevelt and the press even though Roosevelt became somewhat bitter toward the press in the latter years of his presidency.

Leon Festinger (1919–)

Leon Festinger, once a psychology professor at Stanford University, developed the theory of cognitive dissonance. His book of the same title was published in 1957. Cognitive dissonance explains the thinking process when a person chooses one option over another. After a person decides, he or she will have some degree of uncertainty about the choice. The more nearly equal the choices are, the more uncertainty the person will have. People experiencing uncertainty do not seek information about both options. Instead they seek information consistent with and supportive of their decision and avoid information that is not supportive. Thus a person who has decided which candidate to vote for will seek information supportive of that choice and avoid conflicting information. Equal information may be available about candidates for any office, but the average voter will not use it equally. Festinger also taught at Massachusetts Institute of Technology and the University of Michigan.

Fred Friendly (1915–1998)

Fred Friendly played a major role in the development of television news at CBS and helped create the Corporation for Public Broadcasting. His career began on radio station WEAN in Providence, Rhode Island. There he started the "Footprints in the Sand" series of biographical sketches and stories of famous historical figures. The series was so popular that it was made into a record. He did something similar at CBS News with Edward R. Murrow, a radio series called "I Can Hear It Now." Then they moved it to television with the name "See It Now." Friendly later was asked to produce a documentary program called "CBS Reports." Friendly left CBS News as a result of conflict with the management over the role of news. When they insisted on running "I Love Lucy," instead of the congressional hearings on the Vietnam War in 1966, Friendly resigned. He then went to Columbia University to work for the journalism faculty.

George Gallup (1901–1984)

George Gallup was a pioneer in public opinion research and the person most responsible for bringing it into the field of political communication. His doctoral dissertation at the University of Iowa was a readership survey. After finishing his work at Iowa, he went to work as a researcher to Young & Rubicam, a New York advertising agency. In 1935 he and Harold A. Anderson started the American Institute for Public Opinion. They started a syndicated newspaper column that reported survey results. In 1940 the column was named the Gallup Poll. In the 1936 presidential election, Gallup correctly forcasted that Franklin D. Roosevelt would be reelected. This became a defining moment for

Gallup because he was right and the *Literary Digest* was wrong. The latter had said that Alf Landon would defeat Franklin D. Roosevelt for the presidency, but Landon lost in one of the biggest landslides in American political history. That error put the *Digest* out of business, but in a sense it put Gallup in business. The Gallup Poll was number one among the polls and has remained so over the years. Gallup started Audience Research Incorporated in 1938 to do research for media companies. In 1958 all of Gallup's research organizations were consolidated into the Gallup Organization.

Herbert Gans (1927–)

Hebert Gans is a German-born sociologist who came to the United States in 1940. He received advanced degrees from the Massachusetts Institute of Technology and Columbia University. He has made major contributions in the area of gatekeeping, showing the effect of cultural bias in news selection. He identified ethnocentrism and individualism as values that influence news judgment and are reflected constantly in the news. His book *Deciding What's News* (1979) is based on observation in the news room of news decision making. Gans recently authored *Making Sense of America: Socioloical Analyses and Essays* (1999).

William Lloyd Garrison (1805–1879)

William Lloyd Garrison, an abolitionist, was world famous for his newspaper the *Liberator*. He started publishing it in 1831, and it increased awareness of slavery and affected the political dialogue on the issue. Although abolition was the main emphasis, he addressed other issues as well. He strongly favored women's rights, including the right to vote. He said he had been called "a women's rights man," but added that "I claim to be a human rights man, and wherever there is a human being, I see God-given rights inherent in that being." He also supported the Chinese during the decision surrounding the Chinese Exclusion Act of 1882 and denounced the national policy of excluding them. He gave lectures as well as produced his paper and was one of the strongest voices for ending slavery. Leo Tolstoy called Garrison "one of the greatest reformers and promoters of true human progress."

George Gerbner (1919–)

George Gerbner has done a great deal to document the extent of violence on television. Born in Hungary, he came to this country to escape World War II. He worked as a reporter for the *San Francisco Chronicle* before joining the Office of Strategic Services. He got his master's and Ph.D. at the University of Southern California and then joined the faculty at the University of Illinois. He became dean of the Annenberg School of Communication at the University of Pennsylvania in 1964. He directed a series of annual studies of violence on prime-time network programs. He hypothesizes that viewers might identify with the victims of violence rather than imitating the violence. This led him to develop his "cultivation theory," which said that heavy television viewers believe the real world is as the world is depicted on the television screen. Gerbner was editor of the *Journal of Communication* where much of his work on cultivation appeared as well as the response to it from scholars who disagreed.

Edwin Lawrence Godkin (1831–1902)

Edwin Lawrence Godkin founded the *Nation* in 1865 and was editor until 1899. He also owned the *New York Evening Post*, for which he was associate editor from 1881 to 1899. Godkin's political views were liberal, and his publications reached a limited but elite readership. He was a harsh critic of journalism, which he described as "a moral and intellectual dunghill." He, in particular, was critical of Horace Greeley, whom he believed exemplified what was wrong with journalism. One of his attorneys said the *Post* was a "pessimistic, malignant, and malevolent sheet, which no good citizen should go to bed without reading."

Doris Graber (1923–)

Doris Graber, a native of St. Louis, received her M.A. in political science at the age of eighteen. She received her Ph.D. from Columbia University in international law and relations and began teaching at several Chicago-area schools, settling at the University of Illinois at Chicago in 1963. Her research has focused on how people process political information. She believes that people evaluate new information according to their preexisting belief structures. Her 1984 book, *Processing Information: How People Tame the Information Tide,* deals with this. She also is the author of

Mass Media and American Politics (1989), a compendium of information on media and politics, now in its fifth edition. She became the first editor of the journal *Political Communication* when it was founded in 1992.

Horace Greeley (1811–1872)

Horace Greeley was a legend in his own time. Born to a large, poor family in New Hampshire, he was self-educated. With assets of $3,000 he started what became the best-known newspaper in this country and was a major figure in national politics. He went to New York in 1830 to be a reporter and three years later he and a friend started the *Morning Post*, which lasted only three weeks. Then in 1841, at age thirty, he started the *New York Tribune*. It was a success from the start, and from it sprang the *Weekly Tribune*, which reached a circulation of 200,000 and was a genuinely national newspaper. He was an idealist and a reformer. He was for labor unions and against capital punishment and had some success on both issues. He was a strong abolitionist. He was a supporter of the Whig Party and became one of the founders of the Republican Party. Yet in 1872, disillusioned with the Republican Party and President Grant, he ran for president on the Democratic ticket. Grant won easily, and Greeley, crushed by that defeat and by the death of his wife just before the election, died later that month.

James Campbell Haggerty (1909–1981)

James Haggerty was press secretary for President Dwight Eisenhower from 1953 to 1961. He set a precedent that would be followed with other presidents when he disclosed complete details of Eisenhower's heart attack in 1955. He also broke precedence in allowing the president to be quoted directly at press conferences. He also opened press conferences to television cameras for delayed broadcast. His experience as a reporter for the *New York Times* and as an assistant to New York Governor Thomas E. Dewey, who ran for president twice, prepared him well for the job of press secretary. He was a graduate of Columbia University, and his father was chief political reporter for the *New York Times*.

William Randolph Hearst (1863–1951)

William Randolph Hearst was a media tycoon who was active in politics for nearly half a century. He got into journalism because his father, a U.S. senator, bought the *San Francisco Examiner* for political reasons. Hearst, who had seen Pulitzer's *World* while he was a student at Harvard University, was eager to imitate Pulitzer with the *Examiner* and persuaded his father to let him run the paper. He was successful there and pushed to get into the New York market. His father had been a highly successful miner and owned controlling stock in Anaconda. His mother agreed to sell that stock to finance the purchase of the *New York Journal* in 1895. That set the stage for yellow journalism, the name given to the competition between Pulitzer and Hearst, which climaxed with the Spanish-American War. Legend has it that Hearst sent the famous artist Frederic Remington to draw pictures of the war. Remington told Hearst he found no war, but Hearst wired back, "You furnish the pictures, and I'll furnish the war." When the battleship USS *Maine* was sunk, both the *Journal* and the *World* offered their readers front pages that consisted largely of artists' drawing of the sinking. The two papers continued to give heavy play to the war, and at one point they sold three million copies of their papers daily between them. Hearst was elected to Congress in 1902 and unsuccessfully sought the Democratic nomination for president in 1904. He ran against Charles Evan Hughes for governor of New York and lost in 1906. His loss was in part attributed to his unwillingness to deal with Tammany Hall. Had he won, he could have been a serious contender for the Democratic nomination for president in 1912. However, after two more unsuccessful attempts to win office, he gave up his political ambitions. He was a major factor in the nomination of Franklin D. Roosevelt in 1932, but within two years had a parting of the ways with Roosevelt. He became increasingly conservative the rest of his life and moved far away from the policies of the Democratic Party.

Roy Wilson Howard (1883–1964)

Roy Howard was a newspaper journalists and executive. Born in Gano, Ohio, he grew up in Indianapolis. In 1912, at the age of twenty-nine, he became United Press's first president and general manager in charge of both editorial and business operations. It was Howard who broke the story of the Armistice on 7 November 1918, four days before it was officially announced. Howard left United Press and went to Scripps newspapers. In 1922, E. W. Scripps changed the company's name to Scripps-Howard Newspapers, and Howard became chairman of the board. Despite his executive positions, Howard remained interested in reporting. He obtained exclusive interviews with a number of world leaders including Japanese Emperor Hirohito and Russian Premier Joseph Stalin. The *New York Times* credited Howard with being a major influence in the election of Franklin D. Roosevelt in 1932. He retired officially in 1953, but remained chairman of the Executive Committee of Scripps-Howard Newspapers until his death.

Kathleen Hall Jamieson (1946–)

Kathleen Hall Jamieson, an expert on political advertising, is dean of the Annenberg School of Communication at the University of Pennsylvania. She has studied advertising in presidential campaigns for two decades, and her approach to campaign advertising is not merely to criticize it, but to suggest solutions. In her book *Dirty Politics* (1992), she outlines specific strategies that newspeople can and should use to verify and critique political advertisements. In her book *Eloquence in an Electronic Age* (1988), she explains the impact of the glaring lights and compressed editing of television news on political coverage. Jamieson is still an active researcher.

Thomas Jefferson (1743–1826)

Thomas Jefferson provided the basis for political communication when he wrote in the Declaration of Independence that governments are created to secure God-given rights and that governments get "their just powers from the Consent of the Governed," meaning that the people had to have an informed electorate. To achieve that level of education, political communication is required, and for this process to work there must be freedom of the press. Jefferson is also important to political communication because he won the presidential election of 1800, and with that, the victory of the Alien and Sedition Act of 1798 would not be renewed. Jefferson is also remembered for saying, "Were it left to me to decide whether we should have a government without newspapers or newspapers without a government, I should not hesitate a moment to prefer the latter." However, during his presidency he became highly critical of the press, and many scholars have criticized him for this. Yet, it is frequently overlooked that after his two terms as president he was very supportive of the press. It also should be recognized that the press of Jefferson's time was partisan, and Jefferson took a lot of abuse from the press of his political opponents.

Elihu Katz (1926–)

Elihu Katz was founder of the communication program at He-brew University in Jerusalem and also professor of communication and director of the Annenberg Scholars Program at the University of Pennsylvania. His research has dealt with the effects of mass media in different social systems and with public opinion. Katz and Paul Lazarsfeld in the book *Personal Influence: The Part Played by People in the Flow of Communication* (1955) developed the concept of two-step flow of communication. They found that more people engaged in discussions with other people than were exposed to media coverage of political campaigns. Katz also did research dealing with uses and gratifications. In the book *The Uses of Mass Communication: Current Perspectives on Gratifications Research* (1974) Katz, Jay G. Blumler, and Michael Gurevitch deal with social and psychological factors of need that lead to different patterns of media use that result in gratification of needs. This puts emphasis on initiative and activity by the individual that leads the individual to select certain messages that the individual believes will fulfill his or her needs.

John F. Kennedy (1917–1963)

John F. Kennedy was really the first president of the television era. Television existed in the 1950s, but relatively few people had television sets. When Dwight Eisenhower took office in 1953, only six million American homes had television, but by the time Kennedy took office, forty million homes had it. Kennedy was up to the challenge of the new medium. He was effective when he made televised speeches and perhaps even more effective when he conducted televised press conferences, something that no previous president had done. He gave quick, precise, and specific answers to the questions. To this, he added quick wit that made his press conferences an effective combination of information and entertainment. He had shown this in the debates with Richard Nixon in the 1960 presidential campaign. His television presence was exceptional: he was young, handsome, and had an excellent speaking voice.

Martin Luther King Jr. (1929–1968)

Martin Luther King Jr.'s success as a civil rights leader was because he was an extremely effective political communicator. Born in Atlanta, he graduated from Morehouse College in 1948 and received his B.D. from Crozer Theological Seminary in 1951 and his Ph.D. from Boston University in 1955. He was ordained in 1947 and became minister of a Baptist church in Montgomery, Alabama, in 1954. Civil rights is not necessarily a political issue, but it was by the time King became involved. Segregation was the top item on the platform of most Southern politicians. King's leadership led to significant victories for blacks over the segregationists. His most famous single effort at political communication was his speech before 200,000 who took part in the March on Washington that King organized in the summer of 1963. The segment that begins "I have a dream" has been played on radio and television thousands of times, and it has not lost its power in the nearly four decades since he spoke it. He led the boycott against the segregated bus line in Montgomery in 1955–1956; he advocated passive resistance rather than the use of force, and he was able to keep his followers to that; and he organized the Southern Christian Leadership Conference (SCLC). More militant blacks challenged his leadership, but he remained the leader of SCLC and of the Civil Rights movement until his assassination in 1968 in Memphis where he had gone to support striking sanitation workers.

Ted Koppel (1940–)

Ted Koppel brought a new dimension to television news, due in part to the Iran hostage crisis, which began on 4 November 1979. Until then, network news was over by early evening, but Roone Arledge, the new head of ABC, decided to start a late-night news program, "Nightline," devoted to covering the Iran hostage crisis. Frank Reynolds was the first anchor, but Koppel began to share the anchor spot and in 1980 became the sole anchor. It was Koppel that made this news innovation work. Koppel received his B.A. in speech from Syracuse University and his master's in journalism from Stanford University. After failing the Associated Press broadcasters' test, he went to work as a copy boy for radio station WMCA. In 1963 he went to WABC where he soon began doing news. He began his television career in 1967 as an ABC correspondent in Vietnam. In 1971 he became the chief diplomatic correspondent for ABC News and covered the Department of State for eight years.

Arthur Krock (1886–1974)

Arthur Krock spent most of his sixty-year career with the *New York Times*. He joined the *Times* in 1927, and from 1932 until his retirement in 1974 was the paper's Washington Bureau chief, chief Washington correspondent, and columnist. He won three Pulitzer Prizes and suggested that a fourth not be awarded to him even though the majority of the Pulitzer committee had decided to do so. He was afraid this would show favoritism. The award would have been for an exclusive interview with President Harry S. Truman in 1950. One of his three Pulitzer Prizes was for an exclusive interview with Franklin D. Roosevelt in 1937. Krock was a confidant and consultant to all the presidents he covered and to many congressional leaders as well. Born in Glasgow, Kentucky, Krock went to Princeton University for a semester, but dropped out for financial reasons. He earned a two-year degree from Lewis Institute in Chicago and then returned to Louisville to begin his journalistic career.

Harold Lasswell (1902–1978)

Harold Lasswell was an expert in propaganda and one of the main figures in the development of content analysis. His book *Language of Politics* (1949) remains one of the definitive works on content analysis. This came out of his work as director of War Communication Research at the Library of Congress during World War II. He had also studied the propaganda techniques of World War I, and out of that came his book *Propaganda Technique in the World War* (1927). He was convinced that individuals were extremely vulnerable to messages delivered by the mass media. Lasswell also developed two important research models. He said the study of communication involves determining "who said what to whom through what channel with what effect." He also said that the study of politics involved "who gets what, when, how."

Paul F. Lazarsfeld (1901–1976)

Paul Lazarsfeld was probably the most significant communication scholar during the 1940s and 1950s. He headed the Bureau of

Social Research at Columbia University and in that role led two major studies of election campaigns. The first was in 1940 in Erie County, Ohio, and led to the book *The People's Choice* (1948), with Hazel Gaudet and Bernard Berelson as coauthors. The second was of the 1948 in Elmira, New York, which he did with Berelson and William Mcphee. That led to the book *Voting: A Study of Opinion Formation in a Presidential Campaign* (1954). Then he worked with Elihu Katz on the book *Personal Influence: The Part Played by People in the Flow of Mass Communication* (1955), which offered the two-step flow concept. This work showed that effective messages often go from the media to opinion leaders to opinion followers rather than directly from the media to the general public. A native of Austria, Lazarsfled fled Nazi Germany in 1933 and joined the Columbia University faculty in 1939.

Walter Lippmann (1889–1974)

Walter Lippmann, a Harvard University graduate, went to work for Lincoln Steffins on a Boston newspaper. In 1914 he became editor of the *New Republic*. During World War I, as assistant to the secretary of war, he wrote propaganda. He was at Versailles, France, for the treaty talks, and his experiences tin World War I led him to write *Public Opinion* (1922), which is still regarded as one of the major books in public opinion and political communication. In *Public Opinion* he talked about the pictures in people's heads and said that people do not believe what they see; they see what they believe. Lippmann became editor of the *New York World* in 1921 and in 1931 became editor of the *New York Herald Tribune*. It was at the *Herald Tribune* that he began writing a column, "Today and Tomorrow," which became syndicated.

Robert C. Maynard (1937–1993)

Robert Maynard was the first African American publisher of a major metropolitan newspaper, the *Oakland Tribune*. The sixth child of immigrants from Barbados, Maynard dropped out of school when he was sixteen and went to work for the *York (Pennsylvania) Gazette and Daily*. In 1967 he became the first black national correspondent for the *Washington Post*. In 1972 he and Earl Caldwell of the *New York Times* established a summer program for minorities at Columbia University. They guaranteed jobs on newspapers or in television newsrooms for graduates. In that same year he became ombudsman for the *Washington Post*. In

1977 he founded the Institute for Journalism at Berkeley, then in 1979 he became editor of the *Oakland Tribune,* which was owned by Gannett. Two years later, Gannett financed the sale of the paper to Maynard. He sold the paper to the Alameda Newspaper Group in 1992. The following year he died of prostate cancer.

Joseph McCarthy (1908–1957)

Joseph McCarthy has a place in the history of political communication for all the wrong reasons. He became famous and infamous for his crusade against communists in government in the early 1950s. His crusade had enormous impact on politics. One prominent example is that Dwight Eisenhower refused to take any action against McCarthy even though McCarthy had slandered one of Eisenhower's closest friends and a true American patriot George C. Marshall. McCarthy began his attack in a speech in Wheeling, West Virginia, on 9 February 1950. He claimed he had a list of 205 communists working in the Department of State, a charge that he repeated many times, and the number of communists always changed. McCarthy provided little evidence of his charges, and the media shared some of the blame for the results of McCarthy's tactics because few in the media ever challenged him on his facts and figures. His charges led to witch hunts, which spread far beyond the original target— the Department of State. Guilt by association became epidemic. In the end, McCarthy was a failure, censured by the Senate on 2 December 1954, yet his tactics worked politically. He was reelected to the Senate in 1952 despite a lackluster record in representing the real interests of the people of Wisconsin. He demonstrated how a politician can take advantage of the superficiality of much media coverage and thus taught an important lesson in political communication.

Maxwell McCombs (1938–)

Maxwell McCombs was coauthor with Donald Shaw of the first agenda-setting study, done in the 1968 presidential campaign. When it was published in *Public Opinion Quarterly,* it touched off a flurry of agenda-setting studies by other scholars. More than 200 have been published. Agenda setting says that the media do not tell people what to think—they tell people what to think about. Correlation between the media agenda and the public agenda has been well demonstrated, but causation has not. It is clear that in some instances the public sets the media agenda. A graduate of Tulane University, McCombs received his Ph.D. from Stanford University and taught for a year at the University of California at Los Angeles before going to North Carolina where he and Shaw teamed up in the first agenda-setting study. He then went to Syracuse University where he was the Jon Ben Snow Professor of Research and headed the American Newspaper Association News Research Center. The center funded and published studies of newspapers, and many dealt with political topics. From there he went to Texas University in 1985 as chair of the Department of Journalism.

Jack M. McLeod (1930–)

Jack McLeod is Maier-Bascom Professor of Journalism Emeritus at the University of Wisconsin. He joined the faculty at Wisconsin in 1962 after completing his Ph.D. in social psychology from the University of Michigan. He has become a leading authority on the role of the media in broadening democratic participation. McLeod has served for more than thirty years as the director of the Mass Communication Research Center at Wisconsin and a mentor for countless students specializing in political communication. He and Steve Chaffee developed the co-orientation concept in mass communication. The International Communication for Excellence in Research Association awarded him the Fisher Mentorship Award in 1991 in recognition of his service to students. He was the 1997 recipient of the Paul J. Deutschmann Award for Excellence in Research from the Association for Education in Journalism and Mass Communication.

Bill Moyers (1934–)

Bill Moyers was born in Texas to a blue-collar family. His first job in political communication was as a summer employee for Senator Lyndon Johnson's reelection campaign. After completing his degree in journalism at the University of Texas he became Johnson's special assistant and then director of public affairs for the Peace Corps. When Johnson became president as a result of the assassination of President John F. Kennedy, Moyers left the Peace Corps position to become an adviser to Johnson. Later he became White House Chief of Staff. In 1966, Moyers left the White House and went to *Newsday*, and under his direction, *Newsday* won three Pulitzer Prizes. In 1970 he joined CBS as a special correspondent and also joined the staff of WNET-TV, a public station in New York. That led to the creation of "Bill Moyers' Journal," in which he interviewed well-know citizens and scholars on social and political issues. His television specials have covered such varied topics as the funding of education, *Genesis*, the connection between mind and body, and drug rehabilitation.

Edward R. Murrow (1908–1965)

Edward R. Murrow was one of the pioneers in television news and he set a standard that has rarely, if ever, been equaled. Like most of the television news pioneers, he was on radio first, and it was there that he first came to the attention of the American public. During the Munich crisis in 1938, he arranged for the first multiple, live news pickup ever attempted. He came even more to the attention of the Americana public with his broadcasts from London during the German aerial blitz of 1940. Those who heard Murrow come on the air with "This is London" will not forget what it sounded like. His full introduction into television came in 1951 with the program "See It Now." For the next seven years Murrow provided excellent political coverage. One widely acclaimed program was entitled "Christmas in Korea." Reported and shot in Korea, it provided a vivid portrayal of that stalemated war. In 1954 he took on Senator Joseph McCarthy. He simply showed McCarthy in action and let the facts speak for themselves. McCarthy was given the opportunity to reply. He made a poor showing, appearing disorganized and confused. Murrow also did "Person to Person" on CBS beginning in 1953. In this program, he did informal interviews with celebrities. He left CBS in 1961 to take charge of the United States Information Agency. Illness forced his retirement in 1963.

Ralph O. Nafziger (1896–1973)

Ralph Nafziger was one of the pioneers in communication research. His legacy includes the Minnesota Poll, which he started when he was a faculty member at the University of Minnesota in 1940 and the Mass Communication Research Center at the University of Wisconsin, which he created when he was director of the School of Journalism there. The Minnesota Poll was one of the first state polls. It was later taken over by a commercial research firm. During World War II, he was part of the group of researchers who analyzed propaganda for the Office of War

Information. He was coeditor of the first research methods book in mass communication, *Introduction to Journalism Research* (1949), and of the second research methods book in mass communication, *Introduction to Mass Communications Research* (1958, 1963). He also established the doctoral program in mass communication at Wisconsin. He received his bachelor's, master's, and doctoral degree from Wisconsin and returned there from Minnesota in 1949 to become director of the School of Journalism. He served as director until 1966 and then served as executive director of the Association for Education in Journalism for six years.

Dan Nimmo (1933–)

Dan Nimmo, a very prolific author on political communication, has made a major contribution in synthesizing the knowledge of the field. A native of Springfield, Missouri, he received his bachelor's in journalism from Missouri University and then did his master's and doctoral degrees at Vanderbilt University. His first book, *American Political Patterns: Conflict and Consensus* (1964), dealt with the relationship between public relations and officials and the press in Washington. In his book, *The Political Persuaders: The Techniques of Modern Election Campaigns* (1970) he told how the political consulting industry descended from the public relations industry of the 1920s and became perhaps the mainstay of American politics. His most recent book, *The Comedy of Democracy* (1996), coauthored with James E. Combs, takes a light-hearted look at the U.S. political system. He has written extensively on how symbols are created and used to persuade the public.

Richard M. Nixon (1913–1994)

Richard Nixon was at odds with the media from the start of his political career. He was criticized for his actions in the Alger Hiss Senate committee hearings. When he was a candidate for vice president in 1952, the media exposed irregularities by him with political contributions. In 1954 he had the task of floating a trial balloon on using American troops in Indochina. He did so before the American Newspaper Editors Society, and few trial balloons have popped so loudly. In the 1960 presidential campaign he felt the press was unfair to him and made much of the fact that one poll showed that by a wide majority reporters covering the campaign favored Kennedy. In 1962, he ran for governor of California and lost in a major upset. His response was to announce two days later that he was leaving politics and the press would not be able to kick him around any longer. He had learned that attacking the press was good politics, and certainly this attack got him a lot of coverage. When he became president in 1969, he turned over the job of attacking the press to Vice President Spiro Agnew. The Nixon administration was hostile to the media and did in fact cause media credibility to drop. He left office in 1974 bitter about the Watergate exposé by the *Washington Post* that led to his resignation.

Thomas Paine (1737–1809)

Thomas Paine was known as "the poet of the American Revolution" because of such works as *Common Sense* (1776) and *Crisis Papers* (1776–1783). In the latter he offered these ringing words: "These are the times that try men's souls," and, "Tyranny, like hell, is not easily conquered." Other important works of his are *The Rights of Man* (1791), a response to Edmund Burke's *Reflections on the French Revolution* (1970), and *The Age of Reason* (1794). Although Paine was a giant among pamphleteers and journalists promoting the cause of liberty, he was among the most tragic victims of the abuse of free expression and of ungrateful political enemies. He spent almost a year in prison in France and came close to being guillotined because of the indifference of the American minister to France, Gouveneur Morris. He was scorned in America because of his criticism of organized religion in *The Age of Reason*. He died in poverty. Carl Sagan summed up Paine in saying he was one who "courageously opposed monarchy, aristocracy, racism, slavery, superstition, and Seism when all those constituted conventional wisdom."

Ross Perot (1930–)

Ross Perot is the most successful third-party candidate since Theodore Roosevelt in the 1912 election. He ran for president twice—in 1992 and 1996. In 1992, he actually took the lead in the Gallup Poll in May. Then in the summer, he withdrew as a candidate because of concern about what his opponents would say about his family. He then came back into the campaign in September and did participate in the debates with George H. W. Bush and Bill Clinton. However, his withdrawal from the race caused many of his supporters to leave him, and in the election he got only 19 percent of the vote. In 1996, he ran again, but this time got only 8 percent of the vote. He put more than thirty million dollars of his own money into his 1992 campaign and thus was not dependent on the news media to get his message to the people. It was not the traditional style of political communication. Perot spoke more directly to the issues than most presidential candidates have, and he forced his two opponents to do so to some extent. When George Bush Sr. was asked about the federal deficit in the 1988 campaign, his own response was "Read my lips: no new taxes." Perot forced him to get more specific than that in 1992. His appeal was to some extent populist in that he emphasized the government's obligation to the people. He also said he would create a new tax system that would be fair and that the public could understand. His trade policy was "buy America." Perot graduated from the Naval Academy in 1953. He was class president and chairman of the Honor Committee. In 1962, with a loan of $1,000 from his wife, who was a school teacher, Perot started Electronic Data Systems, which has become a multibillion dollar corporation employing more than 70,000 people. He received the Medal for Distinguished Public Service from the Department of Defense for his work in improving conditions for prisoners in the Vietnam War. He also has received the Horatio Alger Award, given to people who overcome obstacles and achieve significant success. He was the first recipient of the Patrick Henry Award for service to his country.

Joseph Pulitzer (1847–1911)

Joseph Pulitzer set in motion the yellow journalism of the late nineteenth and early twentieth century. Born in Hungary, he came to this country a military recruit during the Civil War. Under the Civil War draft system, a draftee could hire a substitute, and that is how Pulitzer got the chance to come to this country. After a year in the army he went to St. Louis. Legend has it that he chose St. Louis because a practical joker told him it would be the best place to learn English. It was, in fact, highly populated by German immigrants. He bought the *St. Louis Dispatch* in 1878 and then combined it with another failing newspaper, the *St. Louis Post* to form the *St. Louis Post-Dispatch*. He was also active in politics. He worked hard for the liberal Republican movement and helped nominate Horace Greeley for president in 1872. Both Greeley and the party failed, and Pulitzer turned to the Democratic Party. He bought the *New York World*. In 1882 and turned it into a vehicle to promote the Democratic Party. The *World* was something of a paradox with sensational news coverage and a serious editorial page. Pulitzer's tactics were soon imitated by William Randolph Hearst and the *New York Journal*. The name "yellow journalism" came from a cartoon called "The Yellow Kid" in the *World*. Hearst hired the cartoonist, Richard F. Outcault, but Pulitzer simply hired another artist to draw a "yellow kid." Part of yellow journalism was the sensational reporting of events in Cuba and of the Spanish-American War. Both papers gained circulation, but the *World* lost prestige. The Pulitzer legacy includes the Graduate School of Journalism at Columbia University and the prizes that bear his name. His will provided the funding that made both possible.

Ronald Reagan (1911–)

Ronald Reagan, the fortieth U.S. president, was nicknamed "the Great Communicator." The nickname reflected his effectiveness as a political communicator, not the amount of information he divulged. He was also known as the "Teflon president" because nothing stuck to him. The mistakes the government made during his administration never were blamed on him. During his presidency, he held outdoor press briefings at the White House, and many of them ended with Reagan getting on a helicopter, his answer to the last question drowned out by the noise of the helicopter's engine. Reagan grew up in Illinois in a working-class family. He became a movie actor and president of Screen Actors Guild during the McCarthy era. He cooperated fully with the House Un-American Activities Committee in investigating Communists in the film industry. He became host of the television program "General Electric Theater," and came to the attention of business interests. That led to his making motivational speeches and to his political career. He ran for governor of California in 1970 and won, and was reelected. He was a candidate for the Republican nomination for president in 1976, but Gerald Ford, the incumbent president, won the nomination. In 1980 he was nominated and elected president. His experience as an actor gave him a great television presence, and he had an excellent speaking voice. He was a convincing and credible speaker.

Pat Robertson (1930–)

Pat Robertson has successfully mixed religion and politics and led the movement of conservative Christians into the political arena. A graduate of the Yale Law School, Robertson failed the

New York bar exam and decided to work in financial and communication industries. He is the founder of the Christian Broadcasting Network (CBN), which went on the air in 1961 with religious music and programming. To keep it on the air, Robertson asked for pledges of $10 a month from 700 people, and the "700 Club" was born. CBN used the airwaves not only to promote Christianity, but also to comment on political, social, and economic issues from a Christian perspective. Through the network Robertson formed the Committee for Freedom, which gives money to political candidates who express ideas in line with conservative Christianity. Robertson ran for the Republican nomination for president in 1988, but withdrew amid scandal about his marriage. Nonetheless, he still provides leadership for Americans who seek to put their version of Christian morality into government.

Anna Eleanor Roosevelt (1884–1962)

Eleanor Roosevelt was the first wife of a U.S. president to engage in mass communication extensively. She made a role for herself as first lady separate and distinct from the presidency. She urged women to become politically active and helped to humanize the New Deal during the Depression. She reached out to the public through weekly White House press conferences for women only and through a syndicated newspaper column entitled "My Day." She made numerous speaking appearances, gave sponsored radio broadcasts and wrote for magazines. She also was the author of six books, including her autobiography. She remained in public life after her husband's death. From 1945 to 1953 and again in 1961 she was a U.S. delegate to the United Nations. In 1946 she became chair of the United Nations Commission on Human Rights.

Franklin D. Roosevelt (1882–1945)

Franklin D. Roosevelt was probably the most effective political communicator ever to occupy the White House. He presided at times of great national crisis, first from the Depression and then from World War II. He was very effective at reducing political issues to something the public could understand. He held more press conferences than any other president—998 total—in slightly more than twelve years. That's more than all of his successors combined. That was one reason he had good relations

with reporters, even though a majority of the newspapers the reporters represented opposed him. Despite the frequency of his
press conferences, they almost always yielded real news. His
"fireside chats" were inspirational, and few have had a better
radio voice. When he started by saying "My fellow Americans,"
listeners felt a part of the event. Historians differ in their esti-
mates of how many fireside chats there were. The range is
twenty-seven to thirty-one, which is to say less than three a year,
but they created a lasting impression. He also had the ability to
coin memorable quotes such as "we have nothing to fear but fear
itself" in the Depression Era and "a day that will live in infamy "
to describe the Japanese attack on Pearl Harbor.

Elmo Roper (1900–1971)

Elmo Roper was one of the pioneers in political polling. He was
educated at the University of Minnesota and the University of
Edinburgh. He established Roper Research Associates in 1933
and was one of those who correctly predicted the outcome of the
1936 presidential election. For fifteen years he wrote a public
opinion column for *Fortune* magazine. He is best known for the
work he did with the Television Information Office in 1959.
Those polls concluded that "most Americans get most of their
news from television," and that was probably the most widely
quoted poll finding of that era. The Roper organization continued to do those polls for three decades. Roper had done similar
studies earlier for the radio industry.

William Safire (1929–)

William Safire, a speechwriter in the Nixon White House, is currently a columnist for the *New York Times*. His effectiveness as a
columnist is due partly to his ability to wedge sources and thus
piece together coherent accounts on closed policy meetings. Yet he
is perhaps the only citizen of the Beltway who will admit that
"sometimes everybody can be wrong." He also is a self-styled "language maven." His columns on language and his books *The New
Language of Politics* (1968), *Political Dictionary* (1978), and *Safire's
New Political Dictionary* (1993) provide lucid and often humorous
insights into the way politicians and political writers use the language. He also was an early creator of the "for the camera pseudo
event." He staged and managed the "kitchen debate" between Vice
President Richard Nixon and Russian Premier Nikita Khrushchev.

Wilbur Schramm (1907–1987)

Wilbur Schramm was a leading pioneer in mass communication research. He played a major role in the development of research and doctoral programs at the University of Illinois and Stanford University. He was the first director of the Institute of Communication Research at the University of Illinois and later director of Stanford's Institute of Communication Research. He also taught at the University of Iowa and the East-West Institute in Hawaii. He devised communication models that looked at how human communication differed from technical communication. His models looked at the experiences of the encoder and decoder and how those experiences affected what was actually communicated. He played an important role in disseminating findings of research and the development of the field through books that he coauthored and edited.

Donald L. Shaw (1936–)

Donald Shaw was coauthor with Max McCombs of the first agenda-setting study, which dealt with the 1968 presidential election and was published in *Public Opinion Quarterly*. That study stimulated interest to such an extent that there have been more than 200 agenda-setting studies since. Agenda setting says that the media do not tell people what to think, but rather tell people what to think about. In other words the media set the agenda. However, agenda-setting research shows that it is not always the media that set the agenda. Shaw received his bachelor's and master's degrees at the University of North Carolina and returned there as a faculty member after completing his doctorate at the University of Wisconsin. He was associate editor of *Journalism Quarterly* from 1983 to 1987, and then editor from 1989–1992. He was also coeditor with Robert L. Stevenson of *Foreign News and the New World Information Order* (1984), an important assessment of foreign coverage published in 1984.

Upton Sinclair (1878–1968)

Upton Sinclair is best remembered for his book *The Jungle,* an exposé of the meatpacking industry published in 1906. He also wrote *Oil!* (1927), an exposé of the Teapot Dome scandal, *The Brass Check* (1919), a press criticism, and *Boston* (1928), about the Sacco-Vanzetti case. He was one of the journalists to whom

Theodore Roosevelt gave the name "muckrakers." Muckrakers were a force for change and reform that had an impact on politics. They were really the forerunners of the investigative reporters of today. In 1934, Sinclair ran for governor in California in what was described at the dirtiest campaign in American history. The Republicans used his muckraking career against him to suggest that he would turn California into a Siberia with palms. The press of the state opposed him. He lost the election by 200,000 votes. He then wrote a book about how he lost the campaign and sold excerpts for substantial sums to the very papers that had opposed him.

Gloria Steinem (1934–)

Gloria Steinem was cofounder of *Ms.* magazine in 1972. *Ms.* brought a feminist perspective to contemporary issues and provided a public forum on feminist issues. A 1956 graduate of Smith College, Steinem worked as a freelance writer. In the 1960s she was active in the women's liberation movement, and in the early 1970s she founded the National Women's Political Caucus, which encouraged women to run for office. She was widely sought as a spokesperson on women's issues, and Steinem and *Ms.* had a great deal to do with the increased attention politicians gave to women's issues.

Ida Tarbell (1857–1944)

Ida Tarbell was one of the muckrakers of the early twentieth century. She is best known for her nineteen-part series on Standard Oil's monopolistic practices, which appeared in *McClure's* between 1902 and 1904. The series was later published as a book entitled *The History of the Standard Oil Company* (1904). The book was an example of the watchdog function of the press because it incensed the public and probably led to the Supreme Court later breaking up the Standard Oil monopoly. Tarbell, who never married, advocated that women stay home and take care of their families. However, she also defended the notion of equal pay for women. Standard Oil was not her only topic. She also wrote about mining safety, child rearing, and women inventors. She also wrote eight books on Lincoln and one on Napoleon as well as her own autobiography, *All in a Day's Work*, which was published in 1939.

Helen Thomas (1920–)

Helen Thomas has covered the White House for United Press International for more than forty years. She was a pioneer among women journalists in Washington, and her work paved the way for other women journalists who were to follow her. She was born in Kentucky to Lebanese parents. They moved to Detroit, and she got her college education at Wayne State University. Her first job was with the *Washington Daily News,* but she lost that job. That turned out to be fortunate because she then landed a job as a writer with the United Press Radio wire. She built a reputation for asking tough, fair questions of government officials in Washington. She has covered nine presidents.

Hunter S. Thompson (1937–)

Hunter Thompson originated gonzo journalism, which rejected objectivity in favor of putting the reporter in the center of the story as a participant in the story. He influenced some political writers, but the long-term effect of his style on political communication has been minimal. Most political reporters are not ready to abandon objectivity entirely. His theme is the meaninglessness of American life, especially insofar as politics is concerned. After working for several newspapers, including the *New York Herald Tribune* and the *National Observer,* he went to *Rolling Stone* magazine in 1970, where he stayed for five years. He has written eight books, the best known of which is *Fear and Loathing: On the Campaign Trail '72* (1983). His articles have appeared in a number of magazines.

David H. Weaver (1946–)

David Weaver is the Roy W. Howard professor of journalism at Indiana University, where he has been since 1974. A graduate of Indiana University, he received his master's and doctorate degrees from the University of North Carolina. His work on agenda setting has helped expand knowledge of that process beyond the initial findings of media setting the agenda. Weaver and his Indiana colleague G. C. Wilhoit coauthored *Newsroom Guide to Polls and Surveys* (1990), which provides newspeople expert advice in how to deal with survey results. They also have done the definitive study of newspeople in the United States, *The American Journalist* (1986, 1996), which has been revised twice. It provides extensive demographic information and well as information on political attitudes. He is also coauthor and coeditor of *Mass Communication Research and Theory*, published in 2002.

Bruce H. Westley (1915–1990)

Bruce Westley was coauthor of the Westley-MacLean model, which probably is the most widely used model of mass communication. It first appeared in the Winter 1957 issue of *Journalism Quarterly*. It emphasizes purposive communication, which means that communicators make choices for a reason. Newsroom decisions are not a matter of chance. Westley played a major part of the two leading communication research textbooks. He wrote a chapter and did much of the copyediting for *Introduction to Mass Communications Research* (1958), edited by Ralph O. Nafziger and David Manning White. He was coeditor and coauthor of *Research Methods in Mass Communication* (1981). He as the founding editor of *Journalism Monographs*, which first appeared in 1963. He served as associate editor of *Journalism Quarterly*, with responsibility for theory and methodology articles from 1963 to 1973. Part of his contribution to all these publications was his copyediting skill. He maintained that research articles should be well written and readable, and he made that happen. He also was author of the most successful editing textbook of his era. He was a faculty member at the University of Wisconsin from 1946 to 1969 and chair of the Department of Journalism at the University of Kentucky from 1969 to 1983. He received the Paul J. Deutschmann Award for contributions to research from the Association for Education in Journalism in 1985.

Theodore H. White (1915–1986)

Theodore White provided the American public an insider's view of presidential campaigns with his four books entitled *The Making of the President* (1961), with the campaign year added. The first was done in 1960, and it was a best-seller. It was such an original approach to describing a presidential campaign that it was enthusiastically received. He then did the same thing for the next three presidential elections, but the consensus of reviewers was that none of the other books equaled the first one. He did not do a book on the 1976 election, but instead wrote his autobiography, *In Search of History* (1978). In it he recalls his humble beginnings in Boston as well as his journalistic career that included coverage of China during World War II and Europe in the post-war era. His last book, *America in Search of Itself: The Making of the President, 1956–1980* (1982), examined campaigns from the second Eisenhower campaign to the first Reagan campaign.

Robert Woodward (1943–) and Carl Bernstein (1943–)

These two relatively unknown young reporters on the *Washington Post* became perhaps the best known newspaper people in America in the early 1970s as a result of their reporting of Watergate. Woodward, a Yale University graduate, had turned to newspaper work after five years in the Navy. Bernstein dropped out of the University of Maryland to begin his reporting career. They teamed up in a persistent effort to get the full Watergate story. They made few mistakes and took the story of a break-in at Democratic headquarters further than anyone suspected when they started. They wrote a book entitled *All the President's Men* (1974) about their work on the story, and that title indicated how wide the Watergate conspiracy turned out to be. It involved virtually everybody in the upper levels of the administration, as the title suggests. The book was made into a movie, thus increasing public awareness of them. They were viewed as role models, and it was even suggested that increases in enrollment in college and university journalism programs was because of them, yet that enrollment boom started before Watergate. Woodward and Bernstein wrote another book about Watergate titled *The Final Days* (1976). Woodward is now assistant managing editor of the *Washington Post*. After leaving the *Washington Post* in 1977, Bernstein has worked for ABC News and *Time*.

6

Legal Documents and Court Cases

This chapter focuses on legal aspects of media and politics, mainly dealing with important documents and court cases that constitute the rules of political communication. The chapter begins with the Declaration of Independence, which stands alone as the unchanged statement of political philosophy of this country. The bulk of this chapter is about Supreme Court cases, though other important documents are discussed as well. The legal status of media and politics in the year 2002 is discussed, which will not remain unchanged, and the reader must be alert to the changes that occur by actions of the government.

Declaration of Independence (1776)

The Declaration of Independence, written by Thomas Jefferson, was proclaimed on 4 July 1776. It begins with a general statement of purpose:

> When in the Course of human Events, it becomes necessary for one People to dissolve the Political Bands which have connected them with another, and to assume among the Powers of the Earth, the separate and equal Station to which the laws of Nature and of Nature's God entitle them, a decent Respect of the Opinions of Mankind requires that they should declare the causes which impel them to the Separation

It is the second paragraph that is crucial for understanding political communication:

> We hold these Truths to be self-evident, that all Men are created equal, that they are endowed by their Creator with certain unalienable Rights, that among these rights are Life, Liberty, and the Pursuit of Happiness—That to secure these rights, Governments are instituted among men, deriving their just Powers from the Consent of the Governed.

In other words, man has God-given rights, and the function of government is not to grant these rights, but to protect them. Governments get their just powers not from divine rights, but from the consent of the governed. The people are sovereign. But if the just powers come from the consent of the governed, then the governed must be informed. That must ultimately mean that man has freedom of expression and freedom of the press. If the government controls expression and the press, then the people will not be fully informed. These words are the simple, direct expression of the political philosophy on which the United States is based. They mandate political communication.

The Declaration of Independence goes on to list the grievances the colonists have with the British and concludes:

> We, therefore, the Representatives of the United States of America, in General Congress, Assembled, appealing to the Supreme Judge of the World for the Rectitude of our Intentions, do, in the Name, and by the Authority of the good People of these Colonies, solemnly Publish and Declare, That these United Colonies are, and of Right ought to be Free and Independent States; that they are absolved from all Allegiance to the British Crown, and that all political Connection between them and the State of Great Britain, is and ought to be totally dissolved; and that as Free and Independent States, they have the full Power to levy War, conclude Peace, contract Alliances, establish Commerce, and to do all other Acts and Things which Independent States may of right do. And for the support of This declaration, with a firm Reliance on the Protection of Divine Providence, we mutually pledge to each other our lives, our Fortunes, and our sacred Honor.

Jefferson and those who signed the Declaration of Independence were indicating their total commitment and making this the official policy statement of the new government. The Declaration was not created merely for the benefit of the Continental Congress, but rather as a document to be disseminated to the people of the colonies and the world at large.

First Amendment (1791)

The First Amendment to the Constitution makes Thomas Jefferson's vision the law. It is only forty-four words long, but those few words have large implications for political communication.

> Congress shall make no law respecting an establishment of religion, or prohibiting the free exercise thereof; or abridging freedom of

speech, or of the press; or the right of the people peaceably to assemble, and to petition the Government for a redress of grievances.

The broad intent is clear, but learned people have debated the specific meaning ever since 1791. The Alien and Sedition Acts of 1798 abridged freedom of speech and of the press. Fortunately, or perhaps unfortunately, they lapsed because Congress did not renew them and there was no Supreme Court test of their constitutionality. What is an establishment of religion? Mainline denominations obviously qualify, but how far beyond does one go? What is the press? That includes the *New York Times* and television networks, but what about underground newspapers? That question was raised but not settled a generation ago. And now what of the Internet?

Nonetheless, the First Amendment is the cornerstone of political communication. If it has not been understood completely still it has been understood enough to sustain the dialogue of a democracy. America is beyond the point of cherishing freedom of expression—it is taken for granted because it is known that by and large it is protected by the First Amendment.

Schenck v. United States, 249 U.S. 47 (1919)

This World War I sedition case produced one of the most widely quoted (and misquoted) statements of any Supreme Court case. Justice Oliver Wendell Holmes wrote, "The most stringent protection of free speech would not protect a man in falsely shouting fire in a theatre and causing a panic." Those who quote this frequently omit the word "falsely." Although the quote is memorable, it really did not fit the situation. The case involved distribution of an antidraft pamphlet by the Socialist Party, of which Charles Schenck was secretary. The government presented no evidence that the pamphlet was false or had any effect on recruiting, but Holmes said the intent of the pamphlet obviously was to interfere with the draft. This endangered national security and thus constituted what Holmes termed "a clear and present danger." Yet Holmes also said that in peacetime, such a pamphlet would be protected by the First Amendment.

Whitney v. California, 274 U.S. 357 (1927)

This case is significant because Oliver Wendell Holmes joins Justice Louis Brandeis in a dissenting opinion and in so doing accepts a position that is to some extent the opposite of the one he took in *Schenck v. United States*. Anita Whitney was convicted under a California statute that outlawed membership in the Communist Party, and the court majority upheld that conviction. However, Brandeis wrote in a dissenting opinion:

> Those who won our independence be revolution were not cowards. They did not fear political change. They did not exalt order at the cost of liberty. To courageous, self-reliant men, with confidence in the power of free and fearless reasoning applied through the processes of popular government, no danger flowing from speech can be deemed clear and present unless, the incidence of the evil apprehended is so imminent that it may befall before there is opportunity for full discussion. If there be time to expose through discussion the falsehood and fallacies, to avert the evil by the processes of education, the remedy to be applied is more speech, not enforced silence.

As was often the case, Justice Brandeis was ahead of his time. The Supreme Court would come to the same position, but not for another thirty years. This case is important because it signals the beginning of a shift in the court's position on a major concern.

Near v. Minnesota, 283 U.S. 697 (1931)

This case is the first time that the U.S. Supreme Court ruled that prior restraint violates the First Amendment. Jay M. Near was copublisher of the *Saturday Press,* a newspaper that viciously attacked Jewish people, blacks, religious groups, and others. Near was convicted of criminal libel, and the court issued an injunction forbidding the paper to publish until it could demonstrate to the court that it had changed its ways. The case was appealed and worked its way to the Supreme Court, which by a 5 to 4 vote ruled that the injunction violated the First Amendment. The Court was less divided than the 5 to 4 vote might indicate. All the justices agreed that Near was guilty of criminal libel and should be punished. They differed on what an acceptable punishment would be, with four justices willing to accept the injunction as a reasonable punishment while five justices thought it violated the First Amendment. The majority view has stood the test of time, and repeatedly the Court has ruled that prior restraint of any kind for any reason raises serious First Amendment questions.

Equal Time Provision (1934)

Section 315 of the Communication Act of 1934, as amended, reads:

If any licensee shall permit any person who is a legally qualified candidate for any public office to use a broadcasting station, he shall afford equal opportunities to all other such candidates for that office in the use of such broadcasting station: *Provided,* That such licensee shall have no power of censorship over the material broadcast under the provisions of this section. No obligation is hereby imposed under this subsection upon any licensee to allow the use of its station by any such candidate. Appearance by a legally qualified candidate on any
    (1) bona fide newscast,
    (2) bona fide news interview,
    (3) bona fide news documentary (if the appearance of the candidate is incidental to the presentation of the subject or ubjects covered by the news documentary), or
    (4) on-the-spot coverage of bona fide news events (including but not limited to political conventions and activities incidental thereto), shall not be deemed use of a broadcasting station within the meaning of this subsection. Nothing in the foregoing sentence shall be construed as relieving broadcasters, in connection with the presentation of newscasts, news interviews, news documentaries, and on-the-spot coverage of news events, from the obligation imposed upon them under this chapter to operate in the public interest and to afford reasonable opportunity for the discussion of conflicting views on issues of public importance.

Section 315 posed few problems in the years of radio, but when television came on the scene, difficulties arose. In 1956, the Federal Communications Commission (FCC) ruled that stations broadcasting a three-minute spot by President Dwight Eisenhower for the United Appeal would be obligated to give equal time to other candidates for president. Then in 1959, a third-party candidate for mayor of Chicago, Lar Daly, complained that he had received less time than the other candidates in newscasts. The FCC agreed, in a 2 to 1 vote. It was at that point that Section 315 was amended to exclude newscasts. In 1960, the first televised debates of presidential candidates were aired only because Congress passed a law excluding such debates from the provisions of Section 315. That allowed John F. Kennedy and Richard Nixon to debate on national television without including third-party candidates. That law was for the 1960 election only, and it was not renewed. Then were debates between the major part presidential candidates in 1976 under the sponsorship of the League of Women Voters. This continued for two more elections until the FCC finally decided that such debates were permissible under Section 315. It would seem they might qualify as bona fide news events and therefore be covered by Point 4. Section 315:

> (b)The charges made for the use of any broadcast station by any person who is a legally qualified candidate for any public office in connection with his campaign for nomination for reelection, or electionto such office shall not exceed—
> (1) During the 45 days preceding the data of a primary or primary runoff election and during the 60 days preceeding the data of a general or a special election in which such a person is a candidate, the lowest unit charge of the station for the same class and amount of time for the same period; and
> (2) At any other time, the charges made for comparable use of such stations by other users thereof.

This means first of all that if a station gives free time to a candidate, it must give free to all candidates for the same office. However, that almost never happens. That leaves the main impact of Section 315 on political advertising. It means not only that stations must have the same rates for all candidates, but that they must give candidates their most favorable rates. So, if a station has a volume discount for regular advertisers, that may mean that preferred rate must be given to political candidates. Station managers are unsure about this, but no station wants to test the FCC on such a matter.

Lovell v. Griffin, 303 U.S. 44 (1938)

Alma Lovell was a Jehovah's Witness who was arrested for distributing literature without a permit in the city of Griffin, Georgia. She had made no attempt to seek a permit, but she argued that she did not seek one because she knew it would be denied. Rather remarkably, the Court unanimously accepted that argument, with Chief Justice Charles Evans Hughes writing that the problem with the statute was that it prohibited the distribution "of any kind, at any time, at any place, and in any manner without a permit from the City Manager." Its significance for political communication is that it assures politicians and political communicators that they cannot be censored through the use of arbitrary local ordinances or state statutes, even if they are promoting an unpopular cause, as Lovell was.

Mayflower Broadcasting Corporation, 8 FCC 333 (1941)

When Mayflower Broadcasting sought a license renewal, the FCC raised serious objections to the station's editorializing. The commission objected because the editorials were not objective and were designed to persuade listeners to support the points of view of the station. The FCC said that "the broadcaster cannot be an advocate" and went on to say:

> Freedom of speech on the radio must be broad enough to provide full and equal opportunity for the presentation to the public of all sides of public issues. Indeed, as one licensed to operate in the public domain the licensee has assumed the obligation of presenting all sides of important public questions, fairly, objectively and without bias.

Broadcasters were unsure as to what limits were intended for editorializing, and most stations responded by simply not editorializing at all. Six years later the FCC began a serious review of this matter, and the result was the Fairness Doctrine.

Fairness Doctrine, 13 FCC 1246 (1949)

What began as a review of FCC policy on editorializing became the Fairness Doctrine. It went beyond the Equal Time Provision in that it dealt not only with fairness in how issues were covered but with the obligation of the station to deal with issues of public concern. A station could avoid difficulty with the Equal Time Provision by not doing anything, but it could not meet the requirements of the Fairness Doctrine in that fashion. Furthermore, the requirement was not equal time, but providing "a sufficient amount of broadcast time" to all sides of an issue. Furthermore, the requirement was not to provide time on the same basis for all sides, as the Equal Time Provision provides. The Fairness Doctrine in some instances obligated stations to provide free time for response to paid programs. The FCC, in what became known as the "Fairness Primer," issued in 1964, went on to say that a station "is called upon to make reasonable judgments in good faith on the facts of each situation—as to whether a controversial issue of public importance is involved, as to what viewpoints have been or should be presented, as to the format and spokesmen to present the viewpoints." Although the intent was to encourage discussion of important public issues, broadcast journalists felt it had the opposite effect. For a two-sided issue, there was no problem, but if one considers an issue such as pollution in a given region, it is fairly easy to come up with a dozen or more viewpoints. The Fairness Doctrine seemed to say all had to be represented. The FCC stopped enforcing the Fairness Doctrine in 1987, but Congress voted to make it statutory law. However, President Ronald Reagan vetoed it. Congress considered it again during George Bush Sr.'s presidency, but backed down when the president made it clear he would veto it. The legislation was supported by Democrats and opposed by Republicans, and when the Republicans gained control of Congress in 1994, that ended attempts to enact it. In part the rationale for the Fairness Doctrine was that the scarcity of broadcast outlets required each one to present balanced coverage of issues. However, the number of broadcast outlets has multiplied enormously as a result of various technologies, and part of the reason the FCC stopped enforcing the Fairness Doctrine was that scarcity was no longer an issue.

Yates v. United States, 354 U.S. 298 (1957)

The *Yates* case is the final answer to the issues raised in *Schenck v. United States*. Clear and present danger remains the concept, but the danger must be really clear and present, not hypothetical as Holmes argued it could be in Schenck. The *Yates* case involved fourteen mid-level officials in the Communist Party of America. They were convicted under the Smith Act. The Supreme Court majority, however, made the distinction between talking in the abstract about overthrowing the government and actually forming conspiracy to do that. The Court found that the Yates defendants were not really conspiring to overthrow the government and thus did not constitute a clear and present danger. The implications of this became clear during the Vietnam War when the government made no attempt to prosecute protesters. Proving that antiwar protesters constituted a clear and present danger would have been nearly impossible legally and might have created serious political problems. In an earlier case, *Dennis v. United States* (1951), the Court had upheld conviction of a more important group of communist leaders. However, the Court majority in Yates saw the two situations as different, believing that the Dennis group was doing more than just talking about overthrow of the government. Yet, despite Dennis and despite the much better known Schenck case, it is the Yates case that is the governing precedent.

New York Times v. *Sullivan,* 376 U.S. 254 (1964)

This is one of the most important, if not the most important, U.S. Supreme Court decision for political communication. It was the first libel case ever heard by the Supreme Court, but in a sense it was as much a civil rights case as a libel case. L. B. Sullivan, one of three commissioners in Montgomery, Alabama, sued the *Times* because of a full-page advertisement criticizing Southern law enforcement during the Civil Rights era. It said in part that "the Southern violators have answered Dr. [Martin Luther] King's peaceful protests with intimidation and violence. They have bombed his home, almost killing his wife and child. They have assaulted his person . . ." Sullivan claimed that "Southern violators" identified him because as a commissioner he was responsible for the police. The trial court in Alabama awarded Sullivan $500,000, and the Alabama Supreme Court upheld that verdict. Sullivan's claim that he had been identified was certainly questionable, but the Supreme Court did not address that. Had they overruled the verdict on that ground, the case would have been little noted. However, the Court saw a larger issue and chose to handle the case in a way that had major impact. At stake was the right of the media to criticize Southern law enforcement specifically and public officials in general. A number of other lawsuits against the *Times* and other northern media were pending. Had the decision against the *Times* stood, coverage of the Civil Rights movement obviously would have been curtailed. The Court ruled that a public official could collect damages for libel only if he or she could show that there was actual malice or reckless disregard of the truth. The Court did not believe that the Sullivan advertisement met that test. This was a national ruling, which created a single standard for all fifty states. About a dozen states already had a similar provision. Subsequent cases would deal with what became a difficult issue—what is a public official? The outcome of this case in effect ended the suits that had been filed by others against the *Times* and other media and assured continued coverage of the Civil Rights movement.

Garrison v. *Louisiana,* 379 U.S. 64 (1964)

New Orleans prosecutor Jim Garrison criticized New Orleans judges, saying they were sympathetic to "racketeer influences" and were "vacation minded." He was prosecuted under a Louisiana law that made it a crime to defame public officials. The Louisiana court said that Garrison's statement was not criticism of the official conduct of the judges but rather an attack on their personal integrity. The U.S. Supreme Court rejected that interpretation and applied the precedent of New York Times *v. Sullivan* to this case, saying that such a prosecution could be upheld only if it could be shown that Garrison knew the statements were false or was guilty of reckless disregard of whether or not they were false. This decision made the criterion the same for civil and criminal libel. The Sullivan decision meant that public officials could not win a civil libel case unless they could show malice or reckless disregard, and this decision said public officials had to meet the same test if they used criminal libel statutes to prosecute those who criticized them.

Estes v. Texas, 381 U.S. 532 (1965)

This was the first of two major cases on televising court trials. Billie Sol Estes, a Texas grain dealer, was convicted of swindling investors. Because of his political connections that led indirectly at least to President Lyndon Johnson, the case attracted a lot of attention. It was televised, and Estes, who was convicted, appealed on the grounds that the televising had deprived him of a fair trial. The presence of bright lights, bulky cameras, and cables undoubtedly was distracting, and the Supreme Court agreed with Estes that the presence of television had made his trial unfair. However, the vote was 5 to 4, and while four justices agreed that the presence of television would make any trial unfair, Justice John Marshall Harlan disagreed. He thought in some cases it might be possible for a trial to be televised without depriving the defendant of a fair trial. That opened the door for courtroom experiments with televising, and that ultimately led to another case, *Chandler v. Florida* (1981).

Freedom of Information Act (1966)

Secrecy in the federal government became a concern in the years following World War II. In part, it was because of secrecy brought on by the Cold War and in part secrecy that reflected the growing size and complexity of the federal government. Congress addressed this with the Freedom of Information Act in 1966. Basically the legislation intended to open all records of the federal government to the public. However, there were nine exceptions in the law, and several were very large. They were: (1) documents classified for national security reasons, (2) documents relating to "internal personnel rules and practices" of agencies, (3) matters that are exempted from public disclosure by law, (4) trade secrets and other financial information gathered by government, (5) interagency and intra-agency memos involving internal decision making, (6) personnel and medical files, (7) investigatory files for law enforcement agencies, (8) documents for regulation of banks and financial institutions, and (9) oil and gas exploration data. A person who wants a record asks the agency for it. If the request is refused, he or she then appeals to the head of the agency. If the request is still turned down, then the person making the request can appeal to the Federal District Court. If the process goes that far, it typically takes a year and a half to two years. The law has opened up the federal government to the public to some extent, but some government agencies have resisted strongly. Exceptions 1, 5, and 9 have been major barriers. And Congress had to revise the law because some agencies were using Exceptions 2 and 6 to refuse requests by employees to see their own personnel files.

Curtis Publishing v. Butts, 388 U.S. 130 (1967) and Associated Press v. Walker, 388 U.S. 130 (1967)

These two cases, coming three years after New York Times *v. Sullivan*, were joined in a single opinion by the Supreme Court. Each contributes to a further definition of "public official" and "actual malice or reckless disregard of truth," the criteria mentioned in the Sullivan case. However, each contributes something different and taken together they contribute more than they would separately. The meaning of public official arose in both cases, but was not ultimately decisive in *Curtis Publishing v. Butts*. Wally Butts was an athletic director at the University of Georgia. Did that make him a public official or if not that, a public figure? Or, given that the Georgia Athletic Association was a separate entity from the university and arguably private, was he a private figure? The case arose from an article in the *Saturday Evening Post*, which charged that Butts and Alabama football coach Bear Bryant conspired to fix an Alabama-Georgia football game. The charge was based largely on a telephone conversation between Butts and Bryant supposedly overheard by an insurance salesman who was on probation for having passed bad checks. Little evidence was presented for the claim, and Justice Harlan in the majority opinion was highly critical of the way the *Post* handled the story. He pointed out that the writer was not a football expert and wondered why the *Post* did not view the game films to see if it could verify the claims. He also pointed out that nobody from the *Post* had viewed the notes from the telephone conversation. He further pointed out that there was plenty of time to check the story because it ran in February, not in football season. In short, this was reckless disregard of the truth.

The Walker case arose from an Associated Press story about protest activities on the University of Mississippi campus when the first black student, James Meredith, entered the University. The story said that Edwin Walker, a retired general, had led a charge of the violent crowd against federal marshals. Walker was in fact well known. He had been the general in charge of American troops in Germany until four years earlier when he was removed from his command. The reason for his removal was that he had been using material from the ultraconservative John Birch Society in troop orientation programs and when ordered to stop, he refused. He thus became one of the best known American generals, and the Court could have decided he was a public figure because of this. The Court, however, did something much more useful. It ruled that he was a public figure because he had thrust himself into the "vortex of a controversy" with his actions in Mississippi. The Court also ruled that allowance had to be given because this was a breaking news story, in contrast to the story about Wally Butts, and the reporter was reporting on deadline.

Time, Inc. v. Hill, 385 U.S. 374 (1967)

In 1952, three escaped convicts took hostage the James J. Hill family in their own home. The family survived, but two of the convicts were killed in a shootout with police. Joseph Hays wrote a novel, *The Desperate Hours,* which resembled the Hills' story to some extent, but not completely. The novel was made into a Broadway play, and *Life* magazine published a review of the play. The Hills sued *Life* for invasion of privacy. Their complaint was that there was more sex and violence in the play and the review than there had been in the real situation. Justice William Brennan, who wrote the majority opinion in New York Times *v. Sullivan,* applied the same principle here. A plaintiff involved in a matter of public interest could collect damages for false-light invasion of privacy only if he or she could show that there was reckless disregard of the truth. Brennan indicated that media accounts can be expected to vary in details from the real event and in effect indicated that it was not surprising that a Broadway play would exaggerate the amount of sex and violence in an event. Perhaps the main significance of the case for politicians and the media lies in its application in situations involving novels in which political figures are identified, even if their names are changed. In such situations, factual discrepancies will not be a basis for successful invasion of privacy suits. It also means that reckless disregard of the truth is the test that must be met by a politician suing an opponent or the media for distortions that frequently occur in political campaigns.

New York Times v. United States, 406 U.S. 713 (1971)

This case is better known as the Pentagon Papers case. The Pentagon Papers was a special report on the origins and history of the Vietnam War. Daniel Ellsberg, one of the thirty-six authors of the report, leaked it to the *New York Times*. It was classified secret, but the *Times* decided to publish it. *The Washington Post* also obtained a copy, and both papers began publishing it in a series of installments in June 1971. The Nixon administration sought an injunction prohibiting further publication because the report had been classified secret. The injunction against the *Times* was denied by Judge Murray Gurfein of the Federal District Court for the southern district of New York, but this decision was reversed by the United States Court of Appeals for the Second Circuit, and the injunction was granted. The effort to get an injunction against the *Washington Post* failed in both the Federal District Court and the United States Court of Appeals for the District of Columbia. At this point the U.S. Supreme Court agreed to hear the case immediately, a highly unusual step. Since there was no injunction in force against the *Washington Post*, it was technically the *Times's* case that was heard. The *Times* argued that *Near v. Minnesota* was a clear precedent that forbade prior restraint. The government acknowledged that *Near* was a precedent, but argued that the sense of the majority opinion was that prior restraint would be permitted to protect national security. Since the Pentagon Papers was a classified document, publication of it would endanger national security. The outcome of the case hinged on the meanings of the classification system, which had been put in place by President Harry S. Truman in 1946 and modified by subsequent presidents. It was not the result of a congressional act.

This led each of the justices to make his own assessment of whether or not publication would endanger national security. Only Justice Harry Blackmun thought so. It is worth noting that while the Supreme Court was deliberating, the chief of naval security testified before a congressional committee. He was asked how many classified documents there were. He said there were twenty million (created in only twenty-five years). He was then asked how many actually dealt with national security. He said about one-half of 1 percent. It was Justice Potter Stewart who said in his opinion, "when everything is classified nothing is classified." Justice Stewart was simply saying that with twenty million documents classified, it was impossible to tell what really was a matter of national security; there could not realistically be twenty million national security secrets. In effect, other justices agreed that the classification system was meaningless, any by a 6 to 3 vote the Supreme Court lifted the injunction.

Much has been made over the fact that two of the justices in the majority, Justice Stewart and Justice Byron White, said in their opinions that prosecution after publication might be possible. Careful reading of their opinions makes it clear that they were not advocating prosecution. But if one is to consider the Stewart and White votes soft, one could also say the same of the votes of Chief Justice Warren Burger and Justice John Harlan. The chief justice deplored the haste with which the case was decided (thirteen days) and said he had not had time to review the Pentagon Papers sufficiently. Justice Harlan said there were simply too many unresolved issues and in effect said he was not ready to vote. So, if one wants to speculate that Stewart and White might go to the other side in another case, making a 5 to 4 vote for upholding an injunction, one should also allow that if the Court had had more time to consider the case, the vote could have been 8 to 1 for lifting the injunction. The other members of the six-person majority were Justices Hugo Black, William Douglas, William J. Brennan, and Thurgood Marshall.

Branzburg v. Hayes, 408 U.S. 665 (1972)

This is a case in which the dissenting opinion turned out to carry more weight than the majority opinion. It is actually three cases rolled into one to determine whether or not the First Amendment gives journalists the right of confidential privilege—that is the right to refuse to testify about what sources have given them in confidence. The *Branzburg* case involved Paul Branzburg, a reporter for the *Louisville Courier-Journal* who observed two men making hashish. He was subpoenaed by a grand jury. The second case involved Paul Pappas, a television journalist who was subpoenaed by a grand jury after he had visited Black Panther headquarters in Massachusetts. The third involved Earl Caldwell, a *New York Times* reporter who was subpoenaed by a federal grand jury after he had interviewed Black Panther leaders in California. All three refused to testify. In a 5 to 4 verdict, the Supreme Court ruled that a grand jury is entitled to everyone's testimony. That is not literally true because privilege not to testify has been routinely granted to doctors, lawyers, and others for years. It has been, however, Justice Potter Stewart's dissenting opinion that has been more widely followed. He said that to justify subpoenaing a journalist, the government should have to show that the journalist had information about a specific crime, that the information could not be obtained in a way that infringed less on the First Amendment and that the case could not be won without that information. It was the four appointees of President Richard Nixon who joined Justice White in the majority opinion, yet within a month Nixon's attorney general, John Mitchell and the Justice Department had adopted Stewart's position as their policy.

Gertz v. Robert Welch, 418 U.S. 323 (1974)

This case revolves around whether a lawyer in a celebrated court case is a public figure. Elmer Gertz, a prominent Chicago attorney, represented the family of a young man shot and killed by a Chicago policeman. The policeman was convicted of second-degree murder, so the family then filed a civil suit against the policeman. Robert Welch was the editor of *American Opinion*, a magazine published by the John Birch society. An article in the magazine attacked Gertz as someone who was trying to undermine law enforcement and as a Leninist and communist activist. Gertz won and the jury awarded him $50,000 in damages. However, a federal appeals judge threw out the verdict on the grounds that Gertz was a public figure. Gertz appealed to the U.S. Supreme Court, and that court decided, in a 5 to 4 vote, that he was not a public figure. The Court said Gertz was not a public figure but merely an attorney serving a client. The *Walker* criterion fits here—Gertz was not in the center of the controversy, and he was not the one who created it. The controversy was created by the event itself and the criminal trial, and Gertz had nothing to do with that. Gertz then filed suit again and won $400,000 in damages. As a private figure he had only to prove negligence, not actual malice.

Miami Herald v. Tornillo, 418 U.S. 241 (1974)

Florida had a right-of-reply law that gave political candidates the right of reply to newspaper editorials attacking them. Though the law had been seldom, if ever, used, Pat Tornillo, a candidate for the Florida legislature, used the law when the *Miami Herald* attacked him twice editorially. He argued that not only was this Florida law, but that the FCC's Fairness Doctrine required this of broadcasters and that this was reason enough to require it of newspapers. Tornillo's claim was upheld in court, and the Florida Supreme Court ultimately upheld decision. The U.S. Supreme Court, however, in a unanimous decision, ruled that the Florida statute violated the First Amendment. The Court ruled that the First Amendment gave editors, not legislators, the right to determine the content of their newspapers. It further said that telling a newspaper that it had to publish something was simply the other side of the coin of telling it could not publish something. The Court said that the cost of complying with this might be prohibitive and that such a provision might drive other content out of the newspaper.

Buckley v. Valeo, 424 U.S. 1 (1975)

This was the fist Supreme Court test of the Federal Election Campaign Act of 1971, which limited campaign contributions by individuals, political committees, and political parties in campaigns for federal office. It also required record keeping including names, addresses, and occupations of contributors, and provided funding for presidential candidates. The plaintiff argued that these provisions violated the First Amendment, but the Supreme Court upheld everything except that it said restrictions on contributions by committees and parties were unrealistically low and might therefore be restrictive of the First Amendment.

Virginia State Board of Pharmacy v. Virginia Citizens Consumer Council, 425 U.S. 809 (1975)

For years the "Doctrine of Commercial Speech" meant simply that advertising was not protected by the First Amendment. *New York Times v. Sullivan* was about an advertisement, and part of the plaintiff's argument was that advertisements were not protected by the First Amendment. The Supreme Court ruled, however, that ideas expressed in an advertisement were entitled to just as much First Amendment protection as idea in a news story or editorial. That seemed to say that advertising was protected by the First Amendment, but product advertising was not. The *Virginia Pharmacy* case changed that. What was involved was a Virginia law that prohibited advertising the price of drugs. The Supreme Court ruled that this violated the First Amendment on two grounds. First, the seller had a First Amendment right to advertise and to mention prices, and second, the public had a right to know what the prices were. This did not mean that advertising could not be regulated or false advertising prosecuted, but rather that any consideration of control of advertising must start from the presumption that there is a First Amendment right to advertise.

Nebraska Press Association v. Stuart, 427 U.S. 53 (1976)

Erwin Charles Simants, an unemployed handyman, borrowed his brother-in-law's rifle, went next door, and murdered six members of the James Henry Kellie family. Lincoln County, Nebraska, Judge Ronald Ruff issued an order prohibiting the media from reporting any of the testimony. That order was appealed, and the appeals court judge, Hugh Stuart, issued his own gag order. Stuart's order not only prohibited coverage of the hearing but also prohibited any mention of Simants's confession. The Nebraska Supreme Court modified but upheld the ruling, and the case was appealed to the U.S. Supreme Court. Because of some recent Supreme Court decisions unfavorable to the press, there was some apprehension about this case. The 8 to 0 vote against the gag order therefore came as something of a surprise. The primary concern of the Supreme Court turned out to be the prior restraint aspect. Chief Justice Warren Burger in the majority opinion noted that "the events disclosed by the record took place in a community of 850 people" and seemed to be suggesting that the contents of the hearing would become common knowledge by word of mouth despite the gag order. Although the decision banned gag orders on the media, it did not ban gag orders on judges, attorneys, and trial participants. Some in the media argued that gagging all the possible sources would have the same effect as gagging the media.

Time v. Firestone, 424 U.S. 448 (1976)

Russell Firestone, an heir to the rubber company's fortune, sued his wife, Mary Firestone, for divorce in Florida on the grounds of adultery and extreme cruelty. Because of the prominence of the Firestone name, the case attracted considerable attention. When the divorce was granted, *Time* ran a story about it saying the grounds for the divorce was adultery. However, that was not what the judge had said, and Florida law would have prohibited Mrs. Firestone from receiving alimony if that had been the court's finding. Mrs. Firestone sued *Time*, and *Time* defended on the grounds that Mrs. Firestone was a public figure and that they had not been guilty of malice. The Supreme Court disagreed, ruling that Mrs. Firestone had not voluntarily thrust herself into a public controversy. It was pointed out that Mrs. Firestone held two press conferences and that there had been forty-five articles about the trial in a local newspaper. However, the question was not whether Mrs. Firestone was a public figure for the purposes of the local paper, but rather whether she was a public figure for the purposes of a national magazine. She may well have been a public figure in Palm Beach, Florida, but that was not the issue.

United States v. Progressive, 467 Fsupp. 990 (1979)

The Progressive, a magazine, was preparing to publish an article entitled "The H-Bomb Secret: How We Got It, Why We're Telling It." They sought to verify it by having some experts read it, and one of them thought it was his duty to let the government know about the article. The government then filed an injunction against *The Progressive* to prevent publication. The author, Howard Morland, said that none of the material in his article was classified and that the material was available to the public. One reason he wrote the article was to show how poorly the security system was working. It was argued that publication of the article would lead to proliferation of the H-bomb, and Federal District Judge Robert Warren agreed. However, while the case was being considered, a small daily paper in Madison, Wisconsin, published a letter with a diagram and a list of key components of the H-bomb. That seemed to make the case moot, and the government immediately dropped its court action. *The Progressive* then went ahead with publishing the article, and eventually the judge dismissed the case. It should be noted that the proliferation of the H-bomb that the government was concerned about did not happen. Had the injunction been upheld, the case probably would have gone to the U.S. Supreme Court. Then the Court, which had decided publication of the Pentagon Papers did not violate national security even though they were classified, would have had to decide whether the publication of material that was not classified could violate national security.

Hutchinson v. Proxmire, 443 U.S. 111 (1979)

This case is important simply because it establishes that everyone who is on a public payroll is not a public figure. Ronald Hutchinson, director of research at the Kalamazoo State Hospital in Michigan, had received a federal grant for a study of how monkeys clench their teeth. William Proxmire, senator from Wisconsin, frequently gave Golden Fleece Awards to people he thought were wasting taxpayers' money. He gave one of those awards to Hutchinson, and Hutchinson sued for libel. Proxmire argued that Hutchinson was a public figure because he was receiving public funds, but the Supreme Court rejected that argument. It pointed out that the only controversy involved was the one created by Proxmire and that Hutchinson had not sought to be in the public eye. For public employees everywhere this is an important conclusion. Even an elected official may not be a public figure if he conducts himself and his office in a way that avoids controversy.

Gannett v. DePasquale, 443 U.S. 368 (1979)

The issue of this case was whether or not a judge could close a pretrial hearing to the press and the public. The hearing involved was for two men who had confessed to killing a former New York policeman. The judge closed the hearing because there had been so much publicity and he felt that having an open hearing would jeopardize the defendants' chances of getting a fair trial. The case was appealed to the Supreme Court, which ruled, 5 to 4, to uphold the closing of the hearing. In the majority opinion, Justice Potter Stewart said that the Sixth Amendment right of public trial was the defendant's right, not the public's right. Furthermore, the defendant could waive that right, which is what had happened in this case. So, pretrial hearings could be closed, but seven years later in *Press Enterprise v. Superior Court* (1984), the court would rule that pretrial hearings should be open unless there is a substantial probability that such a hearing would threaten the defendant's right to a fair trial.

Richmond Newspapers v. Virginia, 448 U.S. 555 (1980)

A year to the day after the Gannett v. DePasquale decision, the Supreme Court ruled, 7 to 1, that trials could not be closed. Furthermore, the majority opinion written by Chief Justice Warren Burger abandoned the notion that the Sixth Amendment was solely the right of the defendant and said it was the public's right as well. The trial involved was the fourth trail for a man charged with murder. The first trial had been invalidated on a technicality, and the next two resulted in mistrials. The judge then closed the fourth trial because a Virginia statute said a judge could remove anyone whose presence "would impair the conduct of a fair trial." The Supreme Court, while ruling that this trial should not have been closed, did not flatly forbid closed trials. It said it would be permissible under extraordinary circumstances. The Supreme Court did not specify what those conditions might be, and it took two more cases to make it clear that the Court really meant extraordinary, or one time in a million.

Chandler v. Florida, 449 U.S. 560 (1981)

The issue of televised trials came back to the Supreme Court sixteen years after the Billy Sol Estes case. The case involved two Miami Beach policemen, Noel Chandler and Robert Granger, who were arrested for burglary. Florida was experimenting with cameras in the courtroom at the time, and the trial was televised. Less than three minutes of the videotape was aired, but Chandler and Granger argued that their rights were violated by the mere presence of television cameras. The Supreme Court disagreed and said that the issue was federalism—that it was up to the states to regulate courtroom procedures. The reality was that so many states had experimented with courtroom photography and some had granted permanent use of television cameras and so many trials had been televised that if the court had found this trial unfair it would have created chaos in the court system. It took four years for the case to work its way from the trial court to the Supreme Court, and in that period twenty-three states had initiated experimental rules for televising trials. Events simply had moved too fast for the Supreme Court. Now forty-seven states permit cameras in the courtroom, but usually with some restrictions such as not photographing the defendant without his or her permission or not photographing the jury. The Chandler decision, left it up to each state to do its own thing.

Pring v. Penthouse, 695 F2d 438 (1983)

Penthouse magazine ran a fiction article about a Miss Wyoming who could levitate people by performing oral sex. Kelly Pring, who had been Miss Wyoming several years earlier, sued *Penthouse* for libel. Since there is a new Miss Wyoming every year, how could Pring establish that she was the one identified in the article? The answer was that the Miss Wyoming in the article wore a purple bathing suit in the swimsuit competition of the Miss America Contest and did baton twirling in the talent competition. Both were true of Kelly Pring. A friendly jury in her home state of Wyoming awarded Pring $26.5 million. The verdict was overturned by an appeals court that found the story too improbable to be taken literally. However, the case dramatically makes the point that fiction can be libelous and that people can be adequately identified for libel purposes by actions and characteristics without using their correct name. The point applies to both fiction and nonfiction.

Posadas de Puerto Rico Associates v. Tourism Company of Puerto Rico, 478 U.S. 328 (1986)

This is a major case in regard to the right to advertise. Puerto Rico legalized casino gambling, but prohibited casinos from advertising locally. However, casinos could and did advertise in the media in the United States in an effort to attract tourists. The U.S. Supreme Court, in a 5 to 4 verdict, ruled that the restrictions on advertising in Puerto Rico did not violate the First Amendment. Justice William Rehnquist, in the majority opinion indicated that advertising for products "deemed harmful" could be prohibited without violating the First Amendment. Justice Rehnquist mentioned specifically cigarettes, alcoholic beverages, and prostitution. Justice Rehnquist did not see a First Amendment issue in the fact that casinos could advertise in publications outside Puerto Rico but not in publications in Puerto Rico.

Hustler Magazine v. Falwell, 45 U.S. 46 (1988)

Larry Flynt's *Hustler Magazine* published a satirical purported advertisement saying that Jerry Falwell, founder of the Moral Majority had his first sexual experience in an outhouse with his mother. It was a take-off on a liquor campaign that used double entendres about the "first time" as a theme. Falwell sued *Hustler* for libel and emotional distress. The jury found for Falwell on emotional distress and awarded him $200,000 damages, but did not find that he was libeled. As a public figure, Falwell would have had to prove reckless disregard of truth or actual malice. Because the advertisement was satirical, the reader was not supposed to take it literally, and that made it difficult to prove malice. However, the U.S. Supreme Court voted unanimously to overturn the emotional distress verdict. In the Court's opinion, Chief Justice William Rehnquist said that public figures would have to prove actual malice to win damages for emotional distress. Rehnquist likened what Flint had done to political cartoons that exaggerate physical traits and events involving the subject of the cartoon, thus suggesting that literal truth is not required in satire.

Masson v. New Yorker Magazine, 501 U.S. 496 (1991)

Is misquoting someone libelous? This case answers that question. Janet Malcolm, a freelance writer, wrote an article about Jeffrey Masson, a psychoanalyst. Masson sued because he said he was misquoted. Specific issues were two quotes—one in which Masson called himself an "intellectual gigolo" and one in which he said he was "the greatest analyst who ever lived." Those two quotes were not included in the forty hours of tape-recorded interviews that Malcolm had, but she insisted he had said those things and that she had taken notes on interviews that were not tape-recorded. Masson said she had not taken notes of any of their interviews and that he had never said those things. Malcolm was unable to produce the notes at that time. Masson said that the misquotations damaged his reputation. A lower federal court dismissed the case, saying that the statements in question were "reasonable interpretations" of things that were on the tape. The cased went to the Supreme Court and in the majority opinion, Justice Anthony M. Kennedy Jr. said that journalists could not be expected to be absolutely precise in every quote. Kennedy also said that Masson was entitled to a jury trial to determine whether Malcolm knowingly misquoted him or was guilty of reckless disregard of truth. Masson then sued in Federal District Court, and the jury found that he had been libeled, but could not agree on damages, so a mistrial was declared. A second trial found that Masson had not been libeled. He appealed, and in 1996 a federal appellate court upheld the verdict of the second trial. By this time, Malcolm had found the missing notes, and they did include the statements Masson insisted he had not made. The conclusion of all this is that misquoting in and of itself is not libelous unless the meaning is changed to something defamatory and unless the writer deliberately falsified the quote or was reckless.

Rubin v. Coors Brewing Co., 514 U.S. 476 (1995)

In this case, the Supreme Court overturned beer-labeling rules enforced by the Bureau of Alcohol, Tobacco, and Firearms. Those rules prohibited beer companies from indicating the alcohol content on the label. Writing for a unanimous court, Judge Clarence Thomas conceded that the government had a legitimate interest in curbing competition among brewers over whose beer had the most alcohol. However, Justice Thomas said there were other ways the government could keep brewers from emphasizing high alcohol content. He said that Coors sought only to disclose truthful, factual information and that it had a First Amendment right to do that. This may not have been a reversal of the Puerto Rican tourism case, but it certainly went in a different direction.

44 Liquormart v. Rhode Island, 517 U.S. 484 (1996)

Rhode Island banned price advertising for liquor. The Supreme Court said that such a ban violated the First Amendment. The decision was unanimous, but the nine justices offered different reasons. They did agree that while the Twenty-first Amendment allows individual states to ban alcoholic beverages, it does not allow them to legalize alcoholic beverages and forbid advertising of them. In the plurality opinion, Justice John Paul Stevens drew the distinction between regulation advertising and banning it. This ruling seems inconsistent with the Puerto Rican tourism decision, but seven justices indicated that that case did not apply to this one, rather than saying that they wanted to reverse it.

Jeremiah W. Nixon v. Shrink Missouri Government Political Action Committee, 528 U.S. 377 (2000)

The Missouri legislature passed a law restricting campaign contributions in state elections. It was similar to the Federal Election Campaign Act, which regulates contributions in campaigns for federal offices. A political action committee sued, claiming that the law violated the First Amendment. The political action committee lost in the trial court, but won in federal court of appeals. However, the U.S. Supreme Court ruled, 6 to 3, that the Missouri law did not violate the First Amendment. In the majority opinion, Justice John Paul Stevens wrote that money did not equal ideas and that restricting contributions did not restrict expression of ideas.

Federal Elections Commission v. Colorado Republican Federal Campaign Committee, 533 U.S. 431 (2001)

The Federal Election Campaign Act of 1971 established limits on campaign contributions by individuals, political committees, and political parties. Almost from the start, it was argued that this law violated the First Amendment because it limited expression in political campaigns. After all, most money raised by politicians goes for communication ranging from television advertisements to direct mail pieces. The Colorado Republican Party was prosecuted for exceeding the limit. The party argued that this decision violated their First Amendment rights. The U.S. Supreme Court ultimately agreed that in the specific instance the party's First Amendment rights had been violated. However, the Supreme Court did not rule on whether or not the law was unconstitutional and in violation of the First Amendment in every instances, but sent the case back to the District Court to deal with that. This case then arose of that violation of the Federal Election Campaign Act a quarter of a century earlier. The Supreme Court ruled, 5 to 4, that the act did not violate the First Amendment. The majority said the government had a legitimate interest in controlling campaign contributions and that this regulation did not interfere with political parties and their relation to candidates. The minority argued that there was no proof that campaign contributions contribute to corruption and that therefore there was no justification in limiting contributions.

New York Times *v. Jonathan Tasini,*
533 U.S. 483 (2001)

Tasini is one of six authors who brought suit against the *New York Times* because articles they had written were copied into a computer database without their consent. They argued that this violated their copyright, but *Times* argued that such action was covered by the agreement they had signed with the *Times*. The authors lost in the trial court, but won in the Federal Appeals Court. The U.S. Supreme Court ruled, 7 to 2, in favor of the authors. At issue here is whether agreements between an author and a publisher extend to CD-ROMs and the Internet. The conclusion would seem to be that such things need to be spelled out in specific terms in the contract. The larger issue is that politicians and media, when they use material from CD-ROMS or the Internet or other new technologies, need to be aware of copyright considerations.

7

Associations and Organizations

This is a directory of groups that are active in political communication and thus are useful sources of information about various aspects of political communication.

Accrediting Council on Education in Journalism and Mass Communication
Suzanne Shaw, Executive Director
Stauffer/Flint Hall
University of Kansas
Lawrence, KS 66045
(785) 864-3986
Website: http://www.ku.edu/~acejmc/

This is the accrediting agency for college and university journalism programs. It was established in 1939 under the name National Council on Professional Education in Journalism. The council represents both media and academic organizations. The Council for Higher Education recognizes it. It accredits both undergraduate and graduate programs. There are about 100 accredited programs, almost a third of the journalism programs in the country.

Accuracy in Media
Reed Irvine, Chairman
4455 Connecticut Avenue, NW, Suite 330
Washington, DC 20008
(202) 364-4401
E-mail: ar1@aim.org
Website: http://aim.org

Founded in 1972, this is a media watchdog. It publishes a twice-monthly newsletter, broadcasts a daily radio commentary, promotes a speaker's bureau, and syndicates a weekly newspaper column, all devoted to setting the records straight on stories the media have not reported accurately and on media bias.

American Academy of Political and Social Science
Jaroslav Pelikan, President
3937 Chestnut Street
Philadelphia, PA 19104
(215) 386-4594
E-mail: aapss@netaxs.com
Website: http://www.asc.upenn.edu/aapss/

This is an association for professionals and lay persons interested in political and social sciences. Founded in 1889, it promotes political and social science through publications and meetings. It does not take sides on controversial issues.

American Conservative Union
David Keene, Chair
1007 Cameron Street
Alexandria, VA 22314
(703) 836-8602
E-mail: acu@conservative.org
Website: http://www.conservative.org

Founded in 1964, this is the largest and oldest grassroots conservative organization. It makes and publishes annual ratings of congress members on the basis of their voting records. It publishes *Battle Line,* a quarterly newsletter, and legislative guides on major issues. It hosts the Conservative Political Action Conference annually.

American Enterprise Institute
Christopher DeMuth, President
1150 Seventeenth Street, NW
Washington, DC 20036
(202) 862-7177
E-mail: webmaster@aei.org
Website: http://www.aei.org

Founded in 1943, American Enterprise Institute is one of America's largest and most respected think tanks. It believes in limited government, private enterprise, vital cultural and political institutions, a strong foreign policy, national defense, and supports research to these ends. It has fifty resident scholars and fellows.

The scholars testify before congressional committees, provide expert consultation to all branches of government, and are cited and quoted frequently in the media.

American Jewish Press Association
L. Malcolm Rodman, Executive Director
1828 L Street, NW, Suite 402
Washington, DC 20036
(202) 785-2282
E-mail: toby@dershowitz.com
Website: http://www.ajpa.org

This organization, founded in 1943, seeks to raise and maintain the standards of Jewish professional journalism and create instruments of information for the American Jewish community. It serves as a forum for exchange of ideas among Jewish publications and journalists. It has an annual convention and a bimonthly publication. It makes two annual awards—the Joseph Polakoff Award for integrity in Jewish journalism and the Simon Rockower Memorial Award for excellence in Jewish journalism.

American Journalism Historians Association
Carol Sue Humphrey, Secretary
OBU Box 61201
500 West University
Shawnee, OK 74804-2590
(405) 878-2221
E-mail: carolhumphrey@mail.okbu.edu
Website: http://www.ajha.org

Academics, researchers, and business professionals belong to this organization, which was founded in 1981. It focuses on the study of American and international media history. It maintains a speakers' bureau and an archive.

American News Women's Club
Donna Kaulkin, President
1607 Twenty-second Street, NW
Washington, DC 20008
(202) 332-6770
E-mail: anwc@anwc.org
Website: http://www.anwc.org

A professional organization of newswomen founded in 1932. It promotes professional pursuits, helps provide access to newsmakers, and provides help and encouragement in professional development of members. It publishes an annual directory and honors a Newsperson of the Year Award.

American Political Science Association
Catherine E. Rudder, Executive Director
1527 New Hampshire Avenue, NW
Washington, DC 20036-1206
(202) 483-2512
E-mail: apsa@apsanet.org
Website: http://www.apsanet.org

Members of this organization founded in 1903 are professors of political science, public officials, researchers, and businesspeople. The organization encourages impartial study and promotes the development of the art and science of government. It develops research projects and educational programs for political scientists and journalists and seeks to increase citizen participation in politics and government. It serves as an employment clearinghouse in its field and conducts a Congressional Fellowship Program, which enables political scientists and journalists to spend a year working with members of Congress and congressional committees. It conducts the Committee on Professional Ethics, Rights, and Freedom and gives cash awards for outstanding books and theses in political science at its annual convention.

American Press Institute
William L. Winter, Executive Director and President
11690 Sunrise Valley Drive
Reston, VA 22091-1498
(703) 620-3611
E-mail: info@americanpressinstitute.org
Website: http://www.americanpressinstitute.org

This is a center for continuing education and management training of newspaper personnel in the United States and Canada. It has fellowships for persons actively involved in the newspaper industry.

American Society of Newspaper Editors
Scott Bosley, Executive Director
11690B Sunrise Valley Drive
Reston, VA 20191-1409
(703) 453-1122
E-mail: asne@asne.org

Website: http://www.asne.org

Members are editors who determine editorial and news policies of daily newspapers. The organization, founded in 1922, has an annual convention and publishes *The American Editor*, a magazine that covers major issues in the field. Proceedings of the annual convention also are published.

Associated Collegiate Press
Tom E. Rolnicki, Executive Director
2221 University Avenue, SE, Suite 121
Minneapolis, MN 55414
(612) 625-8335
E-mail: info@studentpress.org
Website: http://www.studentpress.org

This organization, formed in 1921, conducts annual critiques of college and university newspapers and magazines, as well as an annual convention, and publishes the quarterly, *Trends in College Media*.

Associated Press Managing Editors
Chris Peck, President
50 Rockefeller Plaza
New York, NY 10020
(212) 621-1500
E-mail: apme@ap.org
Website: http://www.apme.com

This is an organization of managing editors and other news executives of Associated Press member newspapers. Founded in 1933, its purpose is to examine the news and other services of the Associated Press to help it provide the best possible services for the members. It grants an annual Freedom of Information Award and an annual Public Service Award. It publishes monthly *APME News* and has an annual convention.

Association for Communication Administration
James L. Gaudino, Director
1765 N Street, NW
Washington, DC 20036
(202) 464-4622
Website: http://www.natcom.org

Members are chairpersons of schools, divisions or departments of communication, radio and television, humanities journalism, telecommunications, theatre, or English. It is a forum for discussion of issues related to speech communication in higher education. It publishes *JACA—the Journal of the ACA* and has an annual convention.

**Association for Education in Journalism
and Mass Communication**
Jennifer H. McGill, Executive Director
234 Outlet Pointe Boulevard, Suite A
Columbia, SC 29210-5667
(803) 798-0271
E-mail: aejmc@aejmc.org
Website: http://www.aejmc.org

Founded in 1912 as the American Association of Teachers of Journalism, this organization became the Association for Education in Journalism in 1951 and the Association for Education in Journalism and Mass Communication in 1983. It is the major organization of college and university journalism teachers. It publishes two journals—*Journalism & Mass Communication Quarterly* and *Journalism and Mass Communication Educator*. It also publishes *Journalism & Mass Communication Abstracts, Journalism & Mass Communication Newsletter*, and *Journalism & Mass Communication Monographs*. It has an annual national convention and various regional conferences. It has seventeen divisions representing various specific interests in the field of journalism.

Association for Women in Communication
Patricia H. Troy, Executive Director
780 Ritchie Highway, State Route 28-S
Severna Park, MD 21146
(410) 544-7442
E-mail: pat@womcom.org
Website: http://www.womcom.org

This is a professional association for women in journalism and communication, both in the profession and in college. It was founded in 1909 as Theta Sigma Phi. It grants the Clarion Award annually and publishes *The Matrix* quarterly and an annual directory, *Communicator's Connection*. It has an annual convention.

Association of Alternative Newsweeklies
Richard Karpel, Executive Director
1020 Sixteenth Street, NW, Fourth floor

Washington, DC 20036-5702
(202) 822-2955
E-mail: aan@aan.org
Website: http://www.aan.org

Founded in 1978, this organization provides members with information about publishing an alternative newspaper. It has an annual convention and annual editorial awards contest, and publishes an annual directory.

Brookings Institution
Michael Armacost, President
1775 Massachusetts Avenue, NW
Washington, DC 20036
(202) 797-6000
E-mail: communications@brookings.edu
Website: http://www.brookings.edu

This is a nonpartisan, nonprofit organization devoted to research, education, and publication in economic, government, and foreign policy. Founded in 1916, it conducts numerous conferences, forums, and seminars. It publishes *Brookings Papers on Economics* semiannually and *Brookings Review* quarterly.

Carol Burnett Fund for Responsible Journalism
Tom Brislin, Administrator
Journalism Department
2550 Campus Road, Crawford 208
University of Hawaii
Honolulu, HI 96822
(808) 956-8881
E-mail: tbrislin@hawaii.edu
Website: http://www2.soc.hawaii.edu/css/journ/cbfund.html

This fund was established by an endowment by actress Carol Burnett after she won a libel suit against the *National Enquirer*. It supports teaching and student research aimed at furthering ethics and professionalism in journalism. Annual awards are made to students at the University of Hawaii for outstanding papers on ethical issues. The fund also sponsors an annual lecture on ethics and a workshop on journalistic ethics.

Caucus for a New Political Science
Laura Olson, Chair
c/o Carl Swidorski

History/Political Science
The College of St. Rose
Albany, NY 12202
(518) 458-5325
E-mail: swindorsc@mail.strose.edu

This is an organization of students, teachers, researchers, and organizers committed to creating a democratic, egalitarian society.
Founded in 1967, it maintains a speaker's bureau and gives the
annual Christian Bay Award for the best section paper and the
Michael Harrington Book Award for the best book. It meets annually in conjunction with the American Political Science Association. It publishes a newsletter three times a year.

College Media Advisers
Ronald E. Spielberger, Executive Director
University of Memphis
MJ-300
Memphis, TN 38152-6661
(901) 678-2403
E-mail: vsplbrgr@memphis.edu
Website: http://www.collegemedia.org

This is a professional association of advisers and others involved
in administration of college newspapers, magazines, yearbooks,
handbooks, directories, and broadcast stations. Founded in 1954,
it also encourages high school journalism. It conducts annual
surveys of student media. It maintains a placement service and
speakers' bureau. It gives an annual award for the outstanding
newspaper adviser, outstanding yearbook adviser, outstanding
magazine advisers, and outstanding broadcast adviser. It publishes *College Media Adviser*, a quarterly magazine devoted to
publications issues, a newsletter, and an annual directory.

Community College Journalism Association
Steven Ames, Executive Secretary-Treasurer
3376 Canyon Avenue
Thousand Oaks, CA 91360-1119
(805) 492-4440
E-mail: docames@gte.net
Website: http://ccjaonline.org

This is an organization of two-year college journalism educators.
Founded in 1968, its goals is to have two-year journalism programs certified through self-study and visitation so that their

courses and programs are equivalent to those at four-year colleges and universities. It seeks to make it easier for students to transfer to four-year programs and to help two-year program teachers improve. It has an annual meeting in conjunction with the convention of the Association for Education in Journalism and Mass Communication. It publishes the *Community College Journalist,* a quarterly magazine.

Conference for the Study of Political Thought
Marilyn Thompson, Chair
c/o Professor Sharon Snowiss
Department of Political Science
1050 North Mills Avenue
Claremont, CA 91711
(909) 621-8218
E-mail: ssnowiss@pitzer.edu

Founded in 1968, this is an organization of professors and graduate students of political philosophy. It has an annual conference in April and a regional meeting, both designed to provide a continuous forum for discussion of theory. The Kelly Prize and the Spitz Prize recognize outstanding work in the field.

Dow Jones Newspaper Fund
Richard S. Holden, Executive Director
P.O. Box 300
4300 Route 1, N
Princeton, NJ 08543-0300
(609) 452-2820
E-mail: newsfund@wsj.dowjones.com
Website: http://www.dowjones.com/newsfund

The Dow Jones and Company, publishers of the *Wall Street Journal,* established this fund in 1958 to encourage careers in journalism. It operates an editing internship program for juniors, seniors, and graduate students in journalism. It also offers a business reporting intern program for minority college sophomores and juniors. It gives a Teacher-of-the-Year Award and publishes *Adviser Update* quarterly. It also publishes information on careers in journalism.

Education and Research Institute
Stanton Evans, Chairman
800 Maryland Avenue, NE

Washington, DC 20002
(202) 546-1710
E-mail: mal@eri-mjc.org

Founded in 1973, this organization is dedicated to advancing awareness and understanding of America's traditional values and free-enterprise system. It publishes studies on major public policy issues and conducts educational programs for youths. Its National Journalism Center trains college students in journalism. It sponsors an internship program that includes research projects and weekly seminars with professional journalists. It operates a job bank for media-related jobs. It publishes a newsletter three times a year and has an annual meeting.

Foundation for American Communications
John E. Cox Jr., President
75–85 South Grand Avenue
Pasadena, CA 91105-1602
(626) 584-0010
Website: http://www.facnet.org

This organization, founded in 1976, seeks to improve understanding between major American institutions and news media. It sponsors short-term professional education programs for working journalists on important issues in economics, business, energy, the environment, ethics, corporate and governmental practices, technology, and foreign affairs. It conducts conferences that bring together business executives and journalists and organizes communications programs for individual corporations. It publishes reports and a media resources guide.

Heritage Foundation
Edwin J. Feulner, President
21 Massachusetts Avenue, NE
Washington, DC 20002-4999
(202) 546-8328
E-mail: staff@heritage.org
Website: http://www.heritage.org

Founded in 1973, the Heritage Foundation is a research and educational institute whose mission is to promote conservative public policies based on free enterprise, limited government, individual freedom, traditional American values, and a strong national defense. Resident scholars consult with governmental leaders. The foundation produces books on major public policy issues.

International Center for Journalists
Patrick Butler, Program Director
1616 H Street, NW, Third floor
Washington, DC 20006
(202) 737-3700
E-mail: editor@jcfj.org
Website: http://www.icfj.org

Founded in 1985, this organization conducts training programs for journalists from developing nations, operates information and referral services for foreign journalists, and offers fellowships and exchange programs for foreign and American journalists. It publishes a newsletter, *The International Journalist*, three times a year and conducts seminars and workshops periodically. It offers the Arthur F. Burns Fellowship and the Knight International Press Fellowship.

International Society of Weekly Newspaper Editors
Chad Stebbins, Director
Missouri Southern State College
3950 South Newman Road
Joplin, MO 64801-1595
(417) 625-9736
E-mail: stebbins@mail.mssc.edu
Website: http://www.mssc.edu/iswne/

This organization of weekly editors, founded in 1954, grants two annual awards—the Eugene Cervi Award for aggressive local reporting and community service and the Golden Quill Editorial Award, for outstanding editorials. It has an annual convention and publishes a quarterly journal, *Grassroots Editor*. It also has periodic seminars on such topics as investigative reporting and computer-assisted reporting.

Inter-University Consortium for Political and Social Research
Mary Vardigan, Executive Editor
P.O. Box 1248
University of Michigan Institute for Social Research
Ann Arbor, MI 48106-1248
(734) 998-9900
E-mail: netmail@icpsr.umich.edu
Website: http://www.icpsr.umich.edu

This is a cooperative partnership of college and university libraries, and departments of political science, history, sociology, and related disciplines. It has a major data repository of survey, election, census, and roll call data representing nations throughout the world. It conducts courses in methodology, research techniques, and substantive fields for advanced graduate students and faculty. It publishes an annual report, a quarterly bulletin, code books, and summaries about content of data collections.

Investigative Reporters and Editors
Brant Houston, Executive Director
School of Journalism
Neff Annex
University of Missouri
Columbia, MO 65202
(573) 882-2042
E-mail: info@ire.org
Website: http://www.ire.org

Members are journalists and students who report or edit in-depth journalism. The organization provides educational services including computer-assisted reporting. It has an annual FOI Award for open-records reporting, an annual IRE Award for investigative newspaper reporting, and the Tom Renner Award for reporting of organized crime. It publishes a quarterly, *Beat Book Series*, a handbook, and books on various reporting topics. It was founded in 1975.

Joint Center for Political and Economic Studies
Eddie N. Williams, President
1090 Vermont Avenue, NW, Suite 1100
Washington, DC 20005
(202) 789-3500
E-mail: athompson@jointcenter.org
Website: http://www.jointcenter.org

This center provides nonpartisan information research, public policy analysis, and information programs for black and other minority elected and appointed public officials. Collects data on all aspects of black political participation. It monitors elections and collects and disseminates data on black voting patterns and political participation. Provides public policy forums on issues. It publishes three newsletters—*CPRJ News, NPI News, and Quarterly Alert* and also publishes a magazine, *Focus*, an annual national roster, an annual report, analyses of public policy issues and statistical studies. It was founded in 1970.

Journalism Association of Community Colleges
Rich Camaron, Executive Secretary
Santa Monica College
1900 Pico Boulevard
Santa Monica, CA 90405
(310) 434-4542
E-mail: richCamron@aol.com
Website: http://www.collegepublisher.com/jacc/

An organization of journalism departments of two-year colleges in Arizona and California, it promotes exchange of ideas and development of curricula. It awards scholarships to students nominated by their student publications and advisers and publishes an annual directory, a quarterly newsletter, and a handbook. It has an annual faculty conference in February and a regional conference in the fall. It was founded in 1957.

Journalism Education Association
Linda S. Puntney, Executive Director
Kansas State University, 103 Kedzie Hall
Manhattan, KS 66506
(785) 532-5532
E-mail: jea@spub.ksu.edu
Website: http://www.jea.org

This is an organization of high school journalism teachers and advisers and college and university teachers interested in high-school journalism. It gives the Carl Towley Award for exemplary service to JEA annually and the Lifetime Achievement Award for lifetime achievement in scholastic journalism. It also awards medals of merit, media citations, and the Student Journalist Impact Award. It publishes a quarterly, *Journalism Education Today*, and has a semiannual conference. It was founded in 1924.

Kappa Tau Alpha
Keith P. Sanders, Executive Director
University of Missouri
School of Journalism
Columbia, MO 65211-1200
(573) 882-7685
E-mail: klahq@showme.missouri.edu
Website: http://www.missouri.edu/~ktahq/

This is a national honor society for college students majoring in journalism or mass communication. Founded in 1910, it grants the Frank Luther Mott Award annually for the best researched book in journalism and mass communication. It also gives an annual award to the best chapter adviser and top scholar awards to the student at each member school with the highest grade point average. It publishes a semiannual newsletters. Its annual meeting is held in conjunction with the convention of the Association for Education in Journalism and Mass Communication.

The Media Institute
Patrick D. Maines, President
1000 Potomac Avenue
Washington, DC 20007
(202) 298-751
E-mail: tmi@clark.net
Website: http://www.mediainst.org

This research foundation that specializes in media and communication policy issues seeks to foster freedom of speech, competition, and excellence in journalism. It grants two awards annually, the Horizon Award and the Freedom of Speech Award. Founded in 1976, it publishes a quarterly, the *Commercial Speech Digest*.

National Academy of Television Journalists
Neil F. Bayne, Executive Director
P.O. Box 31
Salisbury, MD 21803
(410) 543-5343
E-mail: nbayne@shoreintercom.net
Website: http://www.angelfire.com/md/NATJ/

This organization promotes professional advancement of members through employment services, educational programs, and competitions. It gives the annual Golden Viddy Award and has an annual convention.

National Association of Black Journalists
Tangle Newborn, Executive Director
8701 Adelphi Road
Adelphi, MD 20783-1716
(301) 445-7100
E-mail: nabj@nabj.org
Website: http://www.nabj.org

This is an organization for employees of news media. Its goal is to strengthen ties between blacks in black media and blacks in white media, sensitize white media to racism, and expand white media's coverage of the black community. Founded in 1975, it works with high schools to identify potential journalists and awards scholarships to journalism schools that support minorities. It acts as a national clearinghouse for jobs. It publishes *NABJ Journal*, a newsletter, ten times per year and has an annual conference.

National Association of Hispanic Journalists
Michael Reyes, Membership Chair
1193 National Press Building
Washington, DC 20045-2100
(202) 662-7145
E-mail: nahj@nahj.org
Website: http://www.nahj.org

This association's purpose is to organize and support Hispanics in journalism. It encourages Hispanics to enter the field and seeks recognition of Hispanics in the field, promotes fair treatment of Hispanics and opposes discrimination and stereotypes, and offers placement services and a writing contest to Hispanic students. Founded in 1984, it conducts an annual national census of Hispanics in media, grants annual awards, offers scholarships from the Reuben Salazar Scholarship Fund, and has an annual convention.

National Association of Hispanic Publications
Andres Tobar, Executive Director and CEO
941 National Press Building
Washington, DC 20045
(202) 662-7250
E-mail: info@nahp.org
Website: http://www.nahponline.org

Founded in 1982, this organization promotes high standards of ethics and professionalism among Spanish or bilingual publications. It provides technical assistance to members in all aspects of print media operations. Annual awards include the Amigo Award, the Corporate Recognition Awards, and the Hispanic Print Awards. It publishes *The Hispanic Press,* a quarterly newsletter. It has an annual convention.

National Conference of Editorial Writers
Fred Fiske, President
6223 Executive Boulevard
Rockville, MD 20852

(301) 984-3015
E-mail: ncewhqs@erols.com
Website: http://www.ncew.org

This is an organization of editorialists for newspapers, radio, and television and journalism educators. Founded in 1947, it gives the Ida B. Wells Award annually for minorities in journalism. It publishes *Beyond Argument,* a handbook, and *The Masthead,* a quarterly journal, *NCEW News,* a quarterly newsletter, and an annual membership directory. It has an annual convention.

National Newspaper Association
Kenneth B. Allen, Executive Vice President and CEO
1010 Glebe Road, No. 450
Arlington, VA 22201-5761
(703) 907-7900
E-mail: info@nna.org
Website: http://www.nna.org

Members are representatives of community newspapers. Founded in 1885, it sponsors an annual Better Newspapers Contest and sponsors an annual government affairs conference. It publishes *Publishers Auxiliary,* the oldest trade journal in the newspaper industry.

National Press Club
John Bloom, General Manager
National Press Building
529 Fourteenth Street, NW
Washington, DC 20045
(202) 662-7500
E-mail: info@npcpress.org
Website: http://www.press.org

Members are newspeople, former newspeople, and associates of newspeople. Founded in 1908, this organization sponsors sports, travel, and cultural events as well as talks with news figures and authors, and newsmaker breakfasts and luncheons. It publishes an annual directory of members and a weekly newsletter. It sponsors a regular seminar on Washington reporting and an annual WebFest trade show.

National Press Foundation
Bob Meyers, President
1211 Connecticut Avenue, NW, Suite 310

Washington, DC 20036
(202) 721-9100
E-mail: npf@natpress.org
Website: http://www.natpress.org

This organization promotes excellence in American journalism. It administers the Washington Journalism Center and funds the National Press Club. Founded in 1975, it gives the Berryman Award for editorial cartooning, the Distinguished Contributors to Journalism Award, the Editor of the Year Award, and the Sol Taishoff Award for excellence in broadcast journalism. It publishes a quarterly newsletter, *Update Newsletter,* and an annual report. It has a annual award dinner, the Washington Center Journalism Conference, and a workshop for reporters.

Nieman Foundation
Susan Goldstein, Program Assistant
Harvard University
1 Francis Avenue
Cambridge, MA 02138
(617) 495-2237
E-mail: nieman@harvard.edu
Website: http://www.nieman.harvard.edu

This is a midcareer program for journalists founded in 1938 and awards fellowships to journalist for a year of study at Harvard. Fellows may study in any department or school at Harvard. The organization gives the annual Louis M. Lyons Award for Conscience and Integrity in Journalism and publishes *Nieman Reports,* a quarterly journal dealing with contemporary media issues.

Pi Sigma Alpha
James I. Lengle, Executive Director
1527 New Hampshire Avenue, NW
Washington, DC 20036
(202) 483-2512
E-mail: pisigma@erols.com
Website: http://www.pisigmaalpha.org

This honor society for students and faculty interested in government and politics was founded in 1920 at the University of Texas. There are more than 460 chapters with 160,000 members. The organization gives annual awards for chapter activity, best undergraduate and graduate papers, best chapter adviser, and best chapter. It also grants three graduate scholarships each year. It gives the Franklin L. Burdette Award for the best paper at the American Political Science Association annual meeting and best paper awards at regional Political Science Association meetings. It publishes a semiannual newsletter.

Project Censored
Peter Phillips, Director
Sonoma State University
Rohnert Park, CA 94928
(707) 664-2500
E-mail: projectcensored@sonoma.edu
Website: http://www.sonoma.edu/projectcensored

Founded in 1976, this organization annually reports on censorship in America. It makes awards for the Most Censored News Stories and reports about them in an annual publication entitled *Censored ([Year]): The News That Didn't Make the News.*

Public Choice Society
Bernard Grofman, President
c/o Carol M. Robert
1D3 Carow Hall, Buchanan Center
George Mason University
Fairfax, VA 22030
(615)259-2000
E-mail: bgrofman@uci.edu
Website: http://www.pubchoicesoc.org

Members are academicians in economics and political science. The group promotes application of economic ideas, concepts, and methods in political science. Founded in 1963, it gives the Duncan Black Prize annually for the best article in its publication, *Public Choice,* which it publishes three times a year. It has an annual meeting and an annual European Public Choice meeting.

Society of Environmental Journalists
Beth Parke, Executive Director
P.O. Box 2492
Jenkintown, PA 19046
(215) 884-8174
E-mail: sej@sej.org
Website: http://www.sej.org

This organization of working journalists, founded in 1990, seeks to improve environmental reporting. It publishes a quarterly journal, *SEJournal*, and has an annual national convention.

Society of Professional Journalists
James L. Gray, Executive Director
3909 Meridian Street
Indianapolis, IN 46208-4011
(317) 927-8000
E-mail: spj@spj.org
Website: http://www.spj.org

This is the major organization of professional journalists. Founded in 1909, it includes both journalism students and working professionals. It sponsors the Pulliam/Kilgore Freedom of Information Internships in Washington and the Eugene C. Pulliam Editorial Writing Fellowship. It grants a distinguished teaching award and the Sigma Delta Chi Distinguished Service Awards annually. It publishes both the magazine *Quill* and *Jobs for Journalists* ten times a year, a quarterly, *SPJ Leader*, and annual reports on journalistic ethics and freedom of information. It has an annual Mark of Excellence Contest for collegiate journalists and has an annual national convention and regional conventions.

United Nations Correspondents Association
Noberto Suarzman, President
Press Secretary, Room C-327
United Nations Secretariat
New York, NY 10017
(212) 963-7130
E-mail: unca@unca.com
Website: Website: http://unca.com

An organization of accredited United Nations press, radio, and television correspondents. Founded in 1948, it seeks to protect rights of correspondents and maintain freedom of correspondents. It publishes an annual directory and has an annual meeting. It awards the Dag Hammarskjold Memorial Scholarship for journalists in developing countries and the UNCA Prize for UN Coverage.

United Press International
Arnaud DeBorchgrave, CEO
1510 H Street, NW

Washington, DC 20005
(202) 898-8000
E-mail: information@upi.com
Website: http://www.upi.com

Founded in 1958 by the merger of United Press and the International News Service, this press association gathers news and photographs for distribution to media throughout the world. It has 204 local bureaus in seventy-nine countries.

Vote Smart
Richard F. Kimball, President
One Common Ground
Philipsburg, MT 59858
(406) 859-8683
(888) 868-3762 (Voters' Research Hotline)
E-mail: membership@vote-smart.org (for membership inquiries)
Website: http://www.vote-smart.org

This organization conducts research on candidates for public office and makes results available on their hot line and website. Vote Smart makes available voting records, contributions received, positions statements, and background and biographical information about candidates.

Washington Journalism Center
Bob Meyers, President
1282 National Press Building
Washington, DC 20045
(202) 662-7352
E-mail: washjo@bu.edu
Website: http://www.bu.edu/com/jo/washjocenter/

Founded in 1965, this is an educational institution with new approaches to training people for public affairs reporting. It gives the Thomas L. Stokes Award annually for best reporting, analysis, or commentary on energy.

White House Correspondents' Association
Steve Holland, President
1067 National Press Building
Washington, DC 20045
(202) 737-2934
Website: http://www.medill.edu/whca/wcha.html

This is an organization of journalists who cover the White House. It has an annual dinner and annually gives three awards for White House coverage—the Aldo Beckman Award, the Edgar A. Poe Award, and the Merriam Smith Award.

Women's Caucus for Political Science
Martha Ackelsberg, President
Department of Government
Smith College
Northampton, MA 01063
(413) 585-3533
E-mail: mackelsb@smith.edu

This organization of women professionally trained in political science was established in 1969. Its purposes are to upgrade the status of women in the profession and promote equal opportunity for female political scientists in graduate programs and in employment. It awards the Alice Paul Award for the best dissertation proposal, the Mary Lepper Award for a nonacademic political scientists, and Mentor Awards for outstanding mentoring of women in political science. It publishes a quarterly newsletter and a membership directory.

8

Print and Nonprint Resources

This chapter deals with sources of information about political communication, which has been the primary focus of the book. This chapter contains an annotated list of books about various facets of political communication. Next is a list of journal articles. In political communication, as in most fields, journals are on the cutting edge of new information as research findings appear in journals before they make their way to other media. Standard references are listed, most of which are reissued periodically; websites of political parties, nonpartisan political groups, and political think tanks are listed; and the last section is a list of videotapes.

Books

Bagdikian, Ben. *Media Monopoly*. 6th ed. Boston: Beacon Press, 2000. 288 pages.

The author makes a strong case for the negative impact of concentration of ownership of the media. The first edition of this book came out in 1980 and though the statistics have changed somewhat, the arguments have not. Bagdikian cites anecdotally numerous examples of abuses resulting from media monopoly. A particular focus is Gannett, and he has valid criticisms. Yet, he does not acknowledge the considerable progress Gannett has made in not only employing women and minorities but placing them in management positions. He also does not have room to discuss the success Knight Ridder has had in improving newspapers they have acquired. It is, in short, a one-sided view of the monopoly issue.

Baumgartner, Frank R., and Bryan D. Jones. *Agendas and Instability in American Politics.* Chicago: University of Chicago Press, 1993. 298 pages.

This book looks at agenda-setting from a political science perspective. The emphasis is on the relation between power groups rather than the press. The authors explore the spread of big issues like drugs and smoking and concluded that the press follows more than it leads. They also suggest that the press focuses on a problem for a short time and leaves the issue long before it is resolved.

Bennett, W. Lance, and Robert M. Entman. *Mediated Politics: Communication in the Future of Democracy.* New York: Cambridge University Press, 2001. 489 pages.

This book treats political communication as a discipline of its own rather than two disciplines that happen to share common ground. Political communication does incorporate findings from sociology, mass communication, and political science, but it does not belong to any one of those areas. The book addresses the pressures facing news organizations, mediated political communication, public opinion, and the role of communication in election campaigns. The book provides a balanced overview of current thinking in political communication.

Bernstein, Carl, and Bob Woodward. *All the President's Men.* New York: Simon and Schuster, 1974. 349 pages.

The two men who did most of the reporting of the Watergate scandal that led to the resignation of Richard Nixon as president describe the process of reporting that story. They tell the reader everything except the identity of Deep Throat, the confidential source whose help made the story possible. They show how they dealt with confidential information and how they went about the process of verifying everything from at least two sources. They also describe the frustrations and the concerns that they might not be able to get the whole story and the support they got from *Washington Post* publisher Katharine Graham and executive editor Ben Bradlee.

Bugeja, Michael J. *Living Ethics: Developing Values in Mass Communication.* Boston: Allyn and Bacon, 1995. 344 pages.

This is a text on media ethics that puts ethics first. Rather than dealing with ethical codes, the author deals with such issues as responsibility, truth, lies, manipulation, bias, fairness, and power as they apply to what media do. The book includes forty-five detailed anecdotes that raise ethical issues from working journalists and journalism educators. Taken together they make a point that is central to the book—ethical issues occur constantly for the media.

Carpini, Michael X. Delli, and Scott Keeter. *What Americans Know about Politics and Why It Matters.* New Haven, CT: Yale University Press, 1996. 397 pages.

Surveys find that public knowledge about politics is very low. Although many have argued that this does not really matter, these authors make the case that an informed citizenry is required in a democracy. But they also find that total knowledge of politics is normally distributed, which means that a substantial proportion of the population is well enough informed to be able to function politically. They also conclude that aggregate levels of political knowledge are about the same as they were fifty years ago.

Christians, Clifford G., Kim B. Rotzoll, and Mark Fackler. *Media Ethics: Cases and Moral Reasoning.* 6th ed. New York: Longman, 2001. 333 pages.

This is perhaps the leading textbook for media ethics courses. It covers media ethics by grouping news issues, advertising issues, and entertainment issues separately. The authors begin by offering a basis for moral reasoning—the Potter Box, devised by Dr. Ralph Potter of the Harvard Divinity School. The authors also use principles from Aristotle, Immanuel Kant, and John Stuart Mill. They also discuss more than eighty cases, some real and some constructed from real situations.

Clarke, Peter, and Susan H. Evans. *Covering Campaigns: Journalism in Congressional Elections.* Stanford, CA: Stanford University Press, 1983. 143 pages.

This is the most extensive study of coverage of congressional campaigns ever completed. The authors randomly selected one-fourth of the 108 total congressional districts and then studied the coverage in the eighty-six of those districts that had a contested race. The study was of the coverage by the largest newspaper in each of those districts. It included content analysis and interviews with the reporters. They found that incumbents and candidates with financial support got substantially more coverage. They also found that close races got more coverage than other races, and that the advantage of incumbents was greater in those races.

Commission on Freedom of the Press. *A Free and Responsible Press.* Chicago: University of Chicago Press, 1947. 139 pages.

This is the summary report of the Commission on Freedom of the Press. The commission was suggested by Henry R. Luce, publisher of *Time,* and funded by Time Inc. and the *Encyclopedia Britannica.* The commission, consisting of thirteen American academicians, was headed by Robert M. Hutchins, chancellor of the University of Chicago. The report puts emphasis on responsibility of the press. It offers five recommendations for government, five for the press, and three for the public. Some of those recommendations have come to pass in the years since the book was written. Press response to the book was highly negative at the outset, but over the years the press and others interested in the press have viewed it more favorably. There has not been a comparable study of the press since this one.

Compaine, Benjamin M., and Douglas Gomery. *Who Owns the Media? Competition and Concentration in the Mass Media Industry,* 3d ed. Mahwah, NJ: Lawrence Erlbaum Associates, 2000. 604 pages.

This is the most comprehensive reference on media ownership in the United States. It covers all the content media—newspapers, magazines, radio, the music industry, film, pay television, home video, and online information. The book also deals with legal, economic, technological, and political factors involved in media concentration. Although this is not a book to be read sequentially, it is a book that those with serious interest in concentration of ownership of the media cannot afford to ignore.

Cook, Timothy E. *Governing with the News: The News Media as a Political Institution.* Chicago: University of Chicago Press, 1988. 289 pages.

Cook examines the role of the reporter as a key participant in decision making and the role of the news media as a central political force. He says that the news media are sustained by press officers at every level of government. He says that federal policies have accommodated, regulated, and subsidized news gathering. As a result, news tends to emphasize official actions and largely ignore nonofficial sources. Politicians understand what makes news and how to use the media and use this knowledge to advance their goals.

Crespi, Irving. *The Public Opinion Process: How the People Speak.* Mahwah, NJ: Lawrence Erlbaum Associates, 1997. 190 pages.

The author, former vice president in both the Gallup and Roper organizations, draws on his forty years of experience in public opinion research to define public opinion and how it best can be studied. He points out that public opinion is multidimensional and that the public opinion process involves more than individual opinions. Collective opinion can be a political force, but that depends on the linkages between political and nonpolitical institutions. Trust in government depends on this.

Demers, David Pearce. *The Menace of Corporate Newspapers: Fact or Fiction.* Ames: Iowa State University Press, 1996. 335 pages.

Much has been said and written about the negative impact of corporate owners putting the bottom line ahead of serving the public. Demers argues otherwise, suggesting that "most of the criticism against the corporate newspaper is more myth than fact." He sees what has happened to newspapers as parallel to what has happened to society and is a function of increasing structural pluralism. He examines the research on this topic and finds substantial support for his position.

Denton, Robert E., Jr., ed. *Political Communication Ethics: An Oxymoron?* Westport, CT: Praeger, 2000. 288 pages.

This book does not answer the question posed by the title, although it does deal with campaign ethics. It offers varied perspectives on the state of politics in the United States. Issues covered include rhetoric, media coverage, advertising, and campaign financing.

Denton, Robert E., Jr., ed. *The 1992 Presidential Campaign: A Communication Perspective.* Westport, CT: Praeger, 1994. 263 pages.

This book presents a varied perspective on the 1992 campaign stating with the party conventions and including the debates, political advertisements, television news, electronic town hall meetings, C-SPAN, issues, and images. Of particular interest is the chapter on the party conventions suggesting that the Democratic convention showed unity while the Republican convention showed division between inclusive and exclusive values. Also of interest is Dan Nimmo's analysis of the electronic town hall meetings. He found little resemblance between those events and the traditional New England town hall meetings.

Denton, Robert E., Jr., ed. *The 2000 Presidential Campaign: A Communication Perspective.* Westport, CT: Greenwood, 2002. 284 pages.

This is an analysis of the 2000 campaign with an emphasis on communication. It covers party conflict during the primaries, the conventions, the presidential debates, political advertising, digital democracy, network news coverage, and explanation of the vote. Analyses go beyond the quantitative results and look at the nuts and bolts of this controversial election.

Festinger, Leon. *Conflict, Decision, and Dissonance.* Stanford, CA: Stanford University Press, 1964. 291 pages.

Festinger explains his theory of cognitive dissonance in this book. He suggests that when people make decisions in conflict situations, dissonance arises. This is particularly true if the decision is a difficult one involving choices that are nearly equally desirable. The individual seeks to resolve the dissonance by finding communication that strengthens the position he has taken and by avoiding communication that favors the choice that he did not make. Thus, he found that when a person buys a car, often a difficult choice, he or she responds to the dissonance by seeking advertisements about the make that he or she bought and avoiding advertisements for competing cars. The theory is an important addition to selectivity theory.

Fiss, Owen M. *The Irony of Free Speech.* Cambridge, MA: Harvard University Press, 1996. 98 pages.

The author asks the reader to imagine a society in which the First Amendment is not only a protector of individual liberties, but also a facilitator of the democratic process. He suggests that it is the latter function that is valued most. The author would have the state be the friend, not the foe of free expression. He sees a role for government in helping the media facilitate the democratic process, but laments the recent trend in the opposite direction in recent Supreme Court decisions. He believes the state should assume the responsibility for ensuring that all sides of important public issues have the chance to be heard. He points out, however, that the market orientation of media means that some important issues do not get covered because the media doubt that such coverage will appeal to the public.

Fox, Roy F. *Speak: Three American Voices.* Westport, CT: Praeger, 2001. 225 pages.

The author says three forms of mediated communication—doublespeak, salespeak, and sensationspeak—shape the way we perceive ourselves, culture, and the world. Doublespeak is communication that pretends to tell something but does not. Salespeak combines language, numbers, and persuasion designed to convince a person to buy. Sensationspeak is content designed to shock and is aimed at the gut. Together they form a media effort that may provide a distorted view of reality.

Gelderman, Carol. *All the President's Words: The Bully Pulpit and the Creation of the Virtual Presidency.* New York: Walker Publishing, 1997. 179 pages.

This book traces the role of speechwriters from the presidency of Franklin D. Roosevelt to that of Bill Clinton, a role that has changed considerably. Under Roosevelt, the speechwriters were presidential aides and therefore involved in policy discussion. Harry S. Truman, Dwight Eisenhower, John F. Kennedy, and Lyndon Johnson followed the same pattern. With Richard Nixon, however, speechwriting was a service department with little policy involvement. Ronald Reagan carried this a step further, testing speeches on focus groups. Gerald Ford, Jimmy Carter, and George Bush Sr. all followed Nixon's practice. Bill Clinton reverted to the earlier practice in midterm. The author suggests that having speeches written by people who were not involved in policy discussions leads to confused messages. She points out that the four presidents who kept speechwriters out of policy discussions all were one-term presidents.

Graber, Doris. *Processing Politics: Learning from Television in the Internet Age.* Chicago: University of Chicago Press, 2001. 231 pages.

The title not withstanding, this book is almost entirely about television with little reference to the Internet. The author believes television does more in the way of informing people than most research acknowledges. She suggests that the usual measures of political knowledge are not adequate. She suggests that citizens may be getting from television what they need to be informed of as voters, but that research fails to focus on this type of knowledge. She also suggests that part of the problem lies with the way television handles news. She suggests that television revamp its image and that it focus on audience's special interests.

Graber, Doris, Denis McQuail, and Pipps Norris, eds. *The Politics of News: The News of Politics.* Washington, DC: Congressional Quarterly Press, 1998. 268 pages.

This collection of essays from Harvard University's Joan Shorenstein Center on the Press, Politics, and Public Policy focuses on how news media interact in the political arena. The book deals with how news is produced, but not with how it is received or used by the public.

Halberstam, David. *The Powers That Be.* New York: Alfred A. Knopf, 1979. 769 pages.

This is an inside history of four media giants, the people who made them, and their influence on American politics. The media are *Time,* CBS, the *Washington Post,* and the *Los Angeles Times.* The major figures for each are respectively Henry Luce, William Paley, Phil and Katharine Graham, and Otis Chandler. There are other figures who played important roles with these media, and Halberstam tells of them also. This book is not merely a chronology, but is about the dynamics within these institutions and their effect on the world outside.

Hentoff, Nat. *Free Speech for Me but Not for Thee.* New York: Harper Perennial, 1993. 405 pages.

Like the late Supreme Court justice Hugo Black, Hentoff believes that when the First Amendment says "no law" it means no law. He also believes that the First Amendment is not just about the *New York Times* and CBS News—it also covers school children, librarians, and a host of other people whose activities sometimes are restricted by those who do not understand or at least do not comply with the First Amendment.

Hess, Stephen. *News and Newsmaking: Essays by Stephen Hess.* Washington, DC: Brookings Institution, 1996. 148 pages.

This book is an anthology of columns written by Hess, a senior fellow at the Brookings Institution, between 1980 and 1994. He examines the inner workings of the major news organizations and concludes that the public would get better news if newspeople did a better job of reporting. The book is anecdotal and thus offers a limited perspective, but it is a useful beginning for understanding news processes.

Isaacs, Norman E. *Untended Gates: The Mismanaged Press.* New York: Columbia University Press, 1986. 258 pages.

Norman E. Isaacs, former chairman of the National News Council, writes of the foibles of the media. An indication of his long-standing concern about media performance is that when he was managing editor of the *Louisville Courier-Journal* he appointed the first newspaper ombudsman. In this book he deals with such issues as attitudes of journalists toward their readers and listeners, freebies, the passion for the scoop, the Janet Cooke hoax, the need for internal criticism in newspapers, and other ethical issues faced by the press. He also makes the case for the reestablishment of a press council.

Jamieson, Kathleen Hall. *Dirty Politics: Deception, Distraction, and Democracy.* New York: Oxford University Press, 1992. 335 pages.

The author, who is this country's expert on political advertising, describes the deception of political advertisements and speeches and tells the reader how to use campaign communication without being fooled by it, She describes the use of soft focus, slow motion, patriotic music, and pseudo news spots. She discusses the flaws in news media coverage. She also discusses how consultants create inflammatory advertisements with the hope that the news media will cover them, thus increasing the dissemination of them. Although the book covers campaigns from 1960 on, there is considerable focus on the 1988 campaign and the infamous Willie Horton advertisements. She says it is up to the voters to reject the lies and misleading statements.

Jamieson, Kathleen Hall. *Packaging the Presidency: A History of Criticism of Presidential Campaign Advertising.* New York: Oxford University Press, 1996. 578 pages.

The author deals with the advertising in each presidential campaign from 1952 to 1996. She found that the convention acceptance speeches of candidates were good predictors of what their advertisements would say. She found that public concern about advertisements has been rising, and she believes this is more because of the increasing expense than because of vast differences in content. Although she expresses concerns about certain aspects, she believes that overall advertising in presidential campaigns is a positive force in the American political system.

Johnson, Thomas J., Carol E. Hays, and Scott P. Hays, eds. *Engaging the Public: How Government and the Media Can Reinvigorate American Democracy.* Lanham, MD: Rowman & Littlefield, 1998. 281 pages.

Political scientists and media scholars examine the problem of voter turnout and recommend solutions. The authors challenge such conventional wisdom as that new technologies and talk radio disengage voters and negative campaigns drive voters away. Suggested solutions include expanding civic education, adopting civic journalism's approach to media coverage, encouraging reliance on new media, reducing barriers to registration and voting, reforming campaign finance, and changing press coverage of campaigns.

Johnson-Cartee, Karen S., and Gary A. Copeland. *Manipulation of the American Voter: Political Campaign Commercials:* Westport, CT: Praeger, 1997. 202 pages.

The authors describe the techniques used in political advertisements and the effects they have. They offers examples where appropriate. They deal with positive and negative advertising, political advertisements as narratives, and emotional appeals. They also tell about the power of recorded visual images and the ways in which audio, visual, and narrative images are blended together. The reader thus knows what to expect, but the book does not offer much guidance on how to defend yourself against the efforts of manipulation.

Kendall, Kathleen. *Communication in the Presidential Primaries: Candidates and the Media, 1912–2000.* Westport, CT: Praeger, 2000. 272 pages.

Candidates need to establish momentum early in the primary season, and political communication is one of the best ways, if not the best way. The author looks at communication in five primaries twenty years apart, beginning with 1912. She acknowledges that the primaries have changed, but found that politicians have adapted to those changes. She found that the emphasis on horse race and imagery in political advertisements has been a constant. She also found that media coverage of primaries has been shallow all along, and while she thinks the primary process can be reformed, she doubts that communication will change greatly.

Kerbel, Matthew Robert. *Edited for Television—CNN, ABC and the 1992 Presidential Campaign*. Boulder, CO: Westview, 1994. 246 pages.

The author combines his own monitoring of coverage by these two networks with interviews with some of the journalists involved. What he describes is a process that is almost unmanageable because of newsroom conventions and the rapid pace of coverage. He discusses horse race coverage and the response to it by these two networks that seem to want to reduce it, but can not figure out how to do it. Overall, this book gives an detailed account of television's impact on politics.

Kraus, Sidney. *Televised Presidential Debates and Public Policy*, 2d ed. Mahweh, NJ: Lawrence Erlbaum Associates, 1999. 323 pages.

Kraus is a long-time observer and student of presidential debates. He edited *The Great Debates: Background, Perspectives, Effects*, a book about the 1960 presidential debates and *The Great Debates: Carter vs. Ford*, a book about the 1976 debates. He is an advocate of presidential debates and argues that they may provide more information for the public than either television news or political advertisements on television. He also believes that the debates encourage citizen participation and help voters decide for which candidate to vote.

Lavrakas, Paul J., Michael W. Traugott, and Peter V. Miller, eds. *Presidential Polls and the News Media*. Boulder, CO: Westview, 1995. 266 pages.

This book addresses the oft-spoken claims that polls and media coverage of them trivialize elections. The book argues that polls can produce a more informed electorate, but they concede that media coverage of polls falls short of achieving that. One suggestion offered is that poll stories should be written by the pollsters themselves rather than reporters because then pollsters understand better the limitations of their work. Authors of chapters in the book include some of the major figures in media polling.

Lichter, S. Robert, and Richard E. Noyes. *Good Intentions Make Bad News: Why Americans Hate Campaign Journalism.* Lanham, MD: Rowman & Littlefield, 1996. 303 pages.

This study of broadcast coverage of the 1988 and 1992 presidential elections attempts to show the impact of reforms suggested by Harvard's Barone Center after the 1988 election. They found excessive coverage of the horse race aspect of the 1992 campaign. They also found an imbalance in coverage that favored Bill Clinton—an imbalance they termed "pronounced, sustained, and overt." Lichter, who has long written about "liberal bias," did not blame the 1992 coverage problems on that, but rather on the work routine and how journalists tell stories.

Liebling, A.J. *The Press,* 2d ed. New York: Random House, 1975. 293 pages.

A. J. Liebling wrote press criticism for the *New Yorker* from 1945 to 1963. This book is a collection of his columns, which were mostly about how the press covered or failed to cover politics and government. The failure to cover led him to observe that "by not reporting there are a lot of things you can avoid finding out." He suggests that news in a newspaper was like free lunch in a bar. It was done not out of charity, but because of competition, and feared that the decline of competition in the newspaper business would lead to a decline in news. The topics have changed since Liebling wrote, but the concerns he voiced remain very real.

Lippmann, Walter. *Public Opinion.* New York: Harcourt, Brace, and Company, 1922. 427 pages.

This is widely considered the most important book about political communication ever written. Lippmann talks of the pictures that form the basis for reality as we know it. He discusses how those pictures get there, how stereotypes are formed, what their effect is, and how one can overcome them. He points out that one does not believe what one sees, one sees what one believes. He also discusses the part that government and the media play in defining the world and what the effect of this is on politics and government.

Luntz, Frank I. *Candidates, Consultants, and Campaigns: The Style and Substance of American Electioneering.* New York: Basil Blackwell, 1988. 272 pages.

This book elaborates on the campaign process with an emphasis on the role of consultants, long an interest of the author. He uses a survey of consultants he made to describe the role of consultants. He also discusses the role of political action committees.

McChesney, Robert W. *Rich Media, Poor Democracy: Communication Politics in Dubious Times.* Urbana: University of Illinois Press. 427 pages.

This book is about the effect of concentration of ownership and marketing strategies on media content. He says that they have transferred control of news and information into the hands of a few wealthy investors, corporate executives, and advertisers. He sees these trends continuing with the Internet, and he believes this will lead to further decline in public participation in political processes. He also expresses concern about the disappearance of the notion of broadcast media having a public service obligation.

McCombs, Maxwell, and Amy Reynolds, eds. *The Poll with a Human Face: The National Issues Convention Experiment in Political Communication.* Mahweh, NJ: Lawrence Erlbaum Associates, 1999. 265 pages.

This is an account of the 1996 National Issues Convention, an effort at deliberative polling. The idea was to bring a group of people together, provide information for them, and allow them to deliberate and thus become informed citizens mirroring public opinion as it ought to be. The hope was to influence the presidential campaign of 1996. The effort was not particularly successful, and this book addresses why. There is some indication that too much was expected in the way of opinion change and not enough attention paid to the process of deliberation.

McGinniss, Joe. *The Selling of the President 1968.* New York: Trident Press, 1969. 253 pages.

This account of the campaign for president by Richard Nixon in 1968 suggests that as a candidate, Nixon was sold to the public just like a brand of toothpaste. The author provides such detail about the making of the Nixon image that it was widely assumed he had infiltrated the Nixon staff. In actuality, he simply did a thorough job of getting sources close to Nixon to talk about what was done. What Roger Ailes, Nixon's media advisor, and the rest of the staff did to build the Nixon image was not unique, and similar things are done with all presidential candidates. No other book provides the same kind of insights into campaigns.

Merzer, Martin, et al. *The Miami Herald Report: Democracy Held Hostage.* New York: St. Martin's Press, 2001. 302 pages.

The U.S. Supreme Court, by a 5 to 4 vote, decided that George W. Bush won Florida in the 2000 election and with that was elected president. But who really won Florida? To find out, the *Miami Herald*, Knight Ridder, and *USA Today* sponsored a hand recount of ballots that had been rejected. The recount covered all sixty-seven counties. It did not come to a clear conclusion about whether Bush or Gore won because which ballots should have been counted was a judgment call. There were the infamous chads, dimples, and pinpricks. What constitutes an indication of intent by the voter? What was the fault of the voter and what was the fault of the voting machine? There was also the question of overvotes—a voter picking two candidates. However, some of those were the voter writing in the same name he or she had punched. In all, 3 percent of the ballots were not counted. Both parties picked their spots for recounts, seeking to have recounted what they assumed would help them. The book is an excellent piece of investigative journalism that provides a lot of insight into contemporary politics.

Mutz, Diana C., Paul M. Sniderman, and Richard A. Brody, eds. *Political Persuasion and Attitude Change.* Ann Arbor: University of Michigan Press, 1996. 295 pages.

This is a collection of articles on current research in political persuasion. It is divided into three section—mass media, political elite, and the electorate. Authors of chapters on media effects assume that there are such effects, but find only modest evidence in their own research. The three chapters on elites make the case for the influence of elites on the political process, but do not address the effects of public opinion on the elites. The last section deals with various factors in the public's recognition of issues and why their perception of issues is sometimes flawed.

Newman, Bruce. *The Mass Marketing of Politics: Democracy in an Age of Manufactured Images.* Thousand Oaks, CA: Sage, 1999. 166 pages.

Newman feels that the use of marketing strategies by politicians similar to those of business are the main reason for the decline in political participation, civic engagement, and trust in government. He explains how marketing techniques worked in the presidential campaign of 1980, the Republican revolution in Congress in 1994, and the election of Jesse Ventura as governor of Minnesota in 1998. He goes on to explain how the marketing strategies change after the candidate is elected. He advocates less use of television by candidates and campaign finance reform as means to reverse the trend of less public interest and participation in politics.

Paletz, David. *Media in American Politics: The Contents and Consequences,* 2d ed. New York: Longman, 2002. 416 pages.

A comprehensive examination of media and American politics, which includes discussion of the Internet in thirteen of the fifteen chapters. It deals with the effect of the media on public policy and with the election of 2000. It also includes discussion on police, pornography, terrorism, and violence as political issues.

Pring, George W., and Penelope Canan. *SLAPPs: Getting Sued for Speaking Out.* Philadelphia: Temple University Press, 1996. 279 pages.

SLAPPs are "strategic lawsuits against public participation." They are a threat to freedom of expression because the history of SLAPPs is full of instances of large corporations suing individuals of limited resources. This book is a thorough assessment of this phenomenon, dealing with how SLAPPs have been used, what kinds of problems they pose, and what precautions can be taken to avoid them.

Rozell, Mark J. *The Press and the Bush Presidency.* Westport, CT: Praeger, 1996. 189 pages.

This is an analysis of the coverage of George Bush Sr. during his presidency by six major media—*Time, Newsweek, U.S. News and World Report,* the *New York Times,* the *Washington Post,* and the *Wall Street Journal.* The author found that harsh media treatment of Bush began during his campaign for the presidency. He was criticized for running a mean-spirited campaign, for lacking ideological substance, and for having an undefined agenda. The author also finds the expected in that coverage was very favorable during and immediately after the Persian Gulf War and then deteriorated as economic conditions worsened.

Sabato, Larry J., ed. *Overtime: The Election 2000 Thriller.* New York: Longman, 2001. 288 pages.

This book brings together the accounts of journalists, academics, and campaigners and thus provides a distinctive view of the election that continued long after the polls had closed. It offers insights and analyses that will be new to most readers.

Sanford, Bruce. *Don't Shoot the Messenger: How Our Growing Hatred of the Media Threatens Free Speech for All of Us.* New York: Free Press, 1999. 257 pages.

The author believes that the public distrust of the press and dislike for its practices shown by many surveys may cause some loss of First Amendment protection for the press. He says that the credibility problems of the media are not entirely the result of their practices, but in part are because of what politicians say about media and the willingness of the public to accept those claims. He suggests that the press must focus more on public service and do more to let the public know about their public service

Severin, Werner J., and James K. Tankard Jr. *Communication Theories: Origins, Methods, and Uses in the Mass Media.* 4th ed. New York: Longman, 1997. 424 pages.

The authors cover the wide spectrum of theory in mass communication. They deal with the language issues of perception, encoding, propaganda, and readability; with social-psychological issues such as congruity, cognitive dissonance, persuasion, group norms, voting behavior, and diffusion of information; with media effects issues such as agenda setting, knowledge gap, and uses and gratifications; and they also discuss the role of media in society and media ownership issues.

Shogan, Robert. *Where the Press Goes Wrong in the Making of the President.* Chicago: Ivan R. Dee, 2001. 308 pages.

The author finds that the scoop mentality is a much bigger problem than media bias. The desire to scoop the opposition results in stories that are incomplete and, because of that, misleading. He also feels that while reporters on the campaign trail with the candidates are aware of the efforts of image-making consultants, they do not make the effort they could to go beyond this and provide coverage that enables the reader to ascertain the real differences between the candidates. The author has covered presidential races since 1968 for the *Los Angeles Times.*

Slotnick, Elliot E., and Jennifer A. Segal. *Television News and the Supreme Court.* Cambridge, UK: Cambridge University Press, 1998. 264 pages.

This analysis of coverage of the Supreme Court by television concludes that television news has failed its democratic duty and left the public ill-informed about the Court. The authors find fault with both the Court and the press, but particularly find fault with the tendency for television management to demand simple visual coverage. One result is about reactions to decisions and about the substance of the decisions. The authors also say that the personalities of the justices, the traditions of the Court, and procedures of the judicial system reduce access to information about Court rulings.

Sparrow, Bartholomew. *Uncertain Guardians: The News Media as a Political Institution.* Baltimore: Johns Hopkins University Press, 2000. 277 pages.

The author argues that the press is not a "Fourth Estate" but rather part of an "iron triangle," with the press colluding with government in order to safeguard its own economic interests. Although the press may be an "attack dog" in its coverage of campaigns, it is frequently a "lap dog" in coverage of policy because of the control of relevant information by government. Economic constraints on the media and their dependence on government news releases further limit the media's ability to serve as a watchdog.

Stempel, Guido H., III, and John W. Windhauser. *The Media in the 1984 and 1988 Presidential Campaigns.* Westport, CT: Greenwood, 1991. 222 pages.

This is the largest data set on presidential campaign coverage. It includes the coverage by sixteen major daily newspapers, the three major television networks, and the three major news magazines from Labor Day to Election Day eve in 1984 and 1988. It also includes an analysis of editorials in these two campaigns and a survey conducted in Chicago, Illinois, and Louisville, Kentucky, about editorial endorsements. That survey found that those editorials have relatively little impact. The content analyses found little evidence of bias and little evidence of concern with issues in the coverage. It also found that media pay very little attention to vice-presidential candidates.

Tillinghast, Charles H. *American Broadcast Regulation and the First Amendment.* Ames: Iowa State University Press, 2000. 228 pages.

The author, a lawyer in California for more than thirty years, traces development of broadcast regulation, notes that it has been inconsistent, and suggests that broadcasting has not had First Amendment freedom to the extent that other media have. He also expresses concern about possible further restriction by the government in the future and the impact of concentration of ownership and suggests that restoration of the Fairness Doctrine would serve the public interest.

Wanta, Wayne. *The Public and the National Agenda: How People Learn about Important Issues.* Mahwah, NJ: Lawrence Erlbaum Associates, 1997. 122 pages.

This book approaches agenda setting from the standpoint of the audience, not the communicator. The author focuses on agenda-setting susceptibility. He concludes that how individuals use the media determines the magnitude of agenda-setting effects, and that demographics affect attitudes toward the media, which affects reliance on and use of the media, and thus affects the extent of agenda-setting. He found fewer agenda-setting effects for network television than for newspapers and local television.

Waterman, Richard W., Robert Wright, and Gilbert St. Clair. *The Image Is Everything Presidency: Dilemmas in American Leadership.* Boulder, CO: Westview, 1999. 183 pages.

This book is a journalistic narrative about the increase in the importance of image to the presidency and presidential campaigns. Policy thus becomes a prop to help the image. The authors say that "appearing to be successful may therefore be a more useful strategy than achieving actual policy success." The authors point out that presidents were concerned about their images two centuries ago, but the emphasis has increased recently. The emphasis of the book also is on more recent presidents starting with John F. Kennedy, whom the authors term the "Image v. Reality President, " thus contrasting him with Richard Nixon, whom they term the "Image Is Everything President." The book does not deal with how the presidents achieve these images or with instances in which substance has been more important images.

Weaver, David H., and G. Cleveland Wilhoit. *The American Jour-*

nalist: A Portrait of U.S. News People and Their Work, 2d ed. Bloomington: Indiana University Press, 1991. 276 pages.

Based on a national survey of 2,045 newspaper, television, and radio journalists, this book describes the demographics, background, and attitudes of working newspeople. The book is limited to those who handle news and therefore excludes advertising and public relations people. It enumerates the age, education, race, political leaning, and marital status of journalists as well as their attitudes about their work, their perceptions of the ethical values of their profession, and the impact of technology on their work.

Weaver, David H., and G. Cleveland Wilhoit. *The American Journalist in the 1990s: U.S. News People at the End of an Era.* Mahwah, NJ: Lawrence Erlbaum Associates, 1996. 299 pages.

To the statistical profile of the two editions of *The American Journalist,* the authors add data that show journalists have less autonomy and less job satisfaction, and the percentage of journalists is nearly twice what it was in the first study. They also find that there are twice as many people of color in newsrooms, but otherwise the demographic profile has not changed greatly in the last decade.

Westin, Av. *News Watching: How TV Decides the News.* New York: Simon and Schuster, 1982. 274 pages.

Av Westin, a former network news producer, offers the view of news selection from inside operations. He describes the limitations under which the newsroom operates, starting with limited time. He points out how television news surpasses newspapers in some areas, but not in other areas of coverage. He helps the reader understand what to expect from television news and what one will not get from television news.

White, Theodore H. *The Making of the President, 1960.* New York: Athenaeum Publishers, 1961. 400 pages.

Theodore H. White won the Pulitzer Prize for this detailed description of the 1960 campaign. It provides insights into the workings of a presidential campaign and gives the reader the feel of a presidential campaign that one does not get from day-to-day media coverage. White also lets the reader know what worked and what did not work in that campaign.

Journal Articles

Abrams, Herbert A., and Richard Brody. *"Bob Dole's Age and Health in the 1996 Election: Did the Media Let Us Down?"* *Political Science Quarterly* 113 (Fall 1998): 471–491.

This analysis of coverage of the 1996 presidential campaign by seventeen national and regional newspapers, four television networks, and three news magazines answers the question of the title with a resounding "yes." They found little discussion of Dole's age (seventy-three years old), his prostate cancer, the fact that he had been a smoker for forty years, or the fact that his parents both died of heart problems.

Althaus, Scott, Peter F. Nardull, and Daron R. Shaw. *"Candidate Appearances in Presidential Elections, 1972–2000."* *Political Communication* 19 (January–March, 2000): 49–72.

Despite the impact of television on presidential candidates, this study finds that appearances by candidates have been increasing steadily from 1972 to 2000. Appearances also have increased in geographic scope. Although appearances are concentrated in areas with large populations, most voters live in media markets that received at least one visit by a presidential candidate, and the percentage of voters exposed to intense personal campaigning has been on the rise.

Carter, Sue, Frederick Fico, and Jocelyn A. McCabe. *"Partisan and Structural Balance in Local Television Election Coverage."* *Journalism & Mass Communication Quarterly* 79 (Spring 2002): 41–53.

Much of what voters learn about candidates for state office comes from local television news. This study of four major television stations in Michigan found that coverage of the governor's race averaged less than 4 percent hard news. Horse race coverage dominated, and coverage lacked information from candidates or their supporters about positions on issues.

Culbertson, Hugh M., and Guido H. Stempel III. *"How Media Use and Reliance Affect Knowledge Level."* *Communication Research* 13 (October 1986): 479–602.

For years, surveys by the Roper Organization for the television industry have proclaimed that people get most of their news from television. In other words, people rely on television. This study looks at reliance, media use, and issues knowledge. It found no correlation between reliance and media use. They found a negative relation between reliance on television news and issue knowledge and no relation between reliance on newspapers and issue knowledge. However, use of both media use and issue knowledge were related.

D'Alessio, Dave, and Mike Allen. *Media Bias in Presidential Elections: A Meta Analysis. Journal of Communication* 50 (Autumn 2000): 133–157.

The authors analyzed fifty-nine quantitative studies of presidential-election coverage made since 1948. They looked at gatekeeping bias reflected in story selection and statement bias. They found no significant biases in coverage by newspapers and news magazines, and they found a small amount of bias in television news coverage but concluded that it was not substantial.

Dalton, Russell L., Paul Allen Beck, Robert Huckfeldt, and William Koetzle. *"A Test of Media-Centered Agenda Setting: Newspaper Content and Public Interest in a Presidential Election." Political Communication* 15 (July–September 1998): 463–481.

This analysis of coverage of the 1992 presidential campaign by a representative sample of newspapers found that claims that the media control the public agenda are overstated. Candidates' messages are well represented in newspaper coverage and are independent of the newspaper's editorial endorsement. The authors suggest that agenda setting in a presidential campaign is a transaction process in which elites, the media, and the public converge to a common set of salient issues.

Domke, David, David P. Fan, Michael Fibison, Dhavan V. Shah, Steven Smith, and Mark D. Watts. *"News Media, Candidates and Issues, and Public Opinion in the 1996 Presidential Campaign." Journalism & Mass Communication Quarterly* 74 (Winter 1997): 718–737.

This study has one of the largest databases of political content ever studied. Using a Nexis database, the authors drew a sample of 12,215 newspaper and television stories published by forty newspapers or aired by three television networks between 10 March 1996 and the day after the election. They found that coverage of both Bill Clinton and Bob Dole was positive, with Clinton's slightly more positive. Dole fared better on character and ideology, and Clinton fared far better on horse race. The authors concluded that media coverage is the best explanation for Clinton's victory.

Drew, Dan, and David Weaver. *"Voter Learning in the 1996 Presidential Election: Did the Media Matter?"* Journalism & Mass Communication Quarterly 76 (Summer 1998): 292–301.

This study examines the relation between exposure and attention to news media and information learned about issue positions of Bill Clinton, Bob Dole, and Ross Perot in the 1996 presidential campaign. Results are based on interviews with 534 randomly selected Indiana residents. Attention and exposure to news media had little effect on learning about issues and motivating people to vote. This may reflect the fact that a larger number of respondents indicated they were not very interested in the campaign.

Eveland, William P., Jr., and Dietram A. Scheufele. *"Connecting News Media Use with Gaps in Knowledge and Participation."* Political Communication 17 (April–June 2000): 215–237.

This study found that the knowledge gaps between higher and lower education groups were greater among light users of television news than among heavy users of television news. A similar but weaker pattern was found among light and heavy newspaper readers. Neither television news use nor newspaper news use was related to gaps in voting. However newspaper use but not television news use was related to gaps in political participation.

Gilens, Martin. *"Race and Poverty in America: Public Misperceptions and the American News Media."* Public Opinion Quarterly 60 (Spring 1996): 515–541.

Surveys show that the American public greatly exaggerates the proportion of African Americans among the poor. This study finds that network television news and the news magazines portray the poor as substantially more black than is really the case. Among the poor, the elderly and the working poor are underrepresented, while unemployed working-age adults are overrepresented. These discrepancies are even more true for African Americans, thus creating a distorted image of African Americans.

Goldstein, Ken, and Paul Freedman. *"Lessons Learned: Campaign Advertising in the 2000 Election."* Political Communication 19 (January–March 2000): 5–28.

This analysis of nearly one million television advertisements in the 2000 election found that advertising must be studied at the market level rather than nationally. A large part of the variation in advertisements is because of the variation in the level of competition in various races—increasing competitiveness leads to higher levels of negativity. They also found that the kinds of advertisements broadcast by parties and interest groups differ dramatically from those sponsored by the candidates themselves. Strategic decisions about targeting create unbalanced flows of information in different geographic areas and at different time.

Haller, H. Brandon, and Helmut Norpoth. *"Reality Bites: News Exposure and Economic Opinion."* Public Opinion Quarterly 61 (Winter 1997): 555–575.

This is a study of the effect of news exposure on assessments of economic conditions. Half of the American public admits not getting any economic news, but the authors found that opinions about the economy of those who did not get economic news and those who did are nearly the same.

Halstuk, Martin E., and Bill F. Chamberlin. *"Open Government in the Digital Age: The Legislative History of How Congress Established a Right of Public Access to Electronic Information Held by Federal Agencies."* Journalism & Mass Communication Quarterly 78 (Spring 2001): 45–65.

Freedom of information at the federal government level has been a serious issue for half a century. Computerization of government records presented a new aspect of the issue not adequately covered by existing law. This article traces the history of the legislative effort that led to the passage of the Electronic Freedom of Information Act of 1996. Although a Senate committee report mentioned the problem in 1974, it was not until 1991 that there was an effort to create a statute to deal with the question. The failure of congress to act enabled some federal agencies to hide electronic material for years. The article demonstrates the need for Congress to keep abreast of technology better than it has.

Hughes, William J. *"The 'Not So Genial' Conspiracy: The New York Times and Six Presidential 'Honeymoons,' 1953–1993."* Journalism & Mass Communication Quarterly 72 (Winter 1995): 841–850.

Conventional wisdom is that newly elected presidents enjoy a honeymoon of a couple of months during which media treatment is relatively gentle. This analysis of front-page headlines in the *New York Times* during the first 100 days of six presidents—Eisenhower, Kennedy, Nixon, Carter, Reagan, and Clinton—suggests that all honeymoons are not equal. Eisenhower and Reagan got the most favorable coverage, while Carter and Clinton got significantly less favorable coverage. The author suggests that one reason for this may be that Eisenhower and Reagan came into office with relatively narrow agendas that had popular support, while Clinton and Carter came in with broader agendas including some unpopular items.

Hurd, Robert E., and Michael W. Singletary. *"Newspaper Endorsement Influence on the 1980 Presidential Vote."* *Journalism Quarterly* 61 (Summer 1984): 332–338.

The effect of newspaper endorsements for presidential candidates has been the subject of much discussion, but not so much systematic analysis. This study, however, provided an analysis by looking at endorsements and the vote in major urban centers. Endorsements favored Reagan in this election by a wide margin, but the authors concluded that the impact of this was one vote in a thousand for Reagan. Endorsements thus were not a decisive factor in that election.

Jasperson, Amy E., Dhavan V. Shah, Mark Watts, Ronald J. Faber, and David P. Fan. *"Framing and the Public Agenda: Media Effects on the Importance of the Federal Budget Deficit."* *Political Communication* 15 (April–June 1998): 205–224.

Public opinion polls indicate a dramatic shift in the percentage of people considering the budget issue to be the most important issue facing the country from November 1994 to April 1996. The authors compared results of Roper polls with media content during this period. They concluded that agenda-setting and framing taken together offer the best explanation of media effects on public opinion on this issue.

Johnson, Anne, and Lynda Lee Kaid. *"Image Ads and Issue Ads in U.S. Presidential Advertising: Using Videostyle to Explore Stylistic Differences in Televised Political Ads from 1952 to 2000."* *Journal of Communication* 52 (June 2002): 281–300.

This is a content analysis of 1,213 advertisements from the past thirteen presidential election campaigns. They were coded as either issue advertisements or image advertisements. Key differences in style between the two kinds of advertisements were found. In issue advertisements, the candidate tends to speak for himself, while in image advertisements, an anonymous announcer is usually used. The majority of advertisements were positive, but issue advertisements were more likely to be negative than were image advertisements.

Johnson, Thomas J., Mahmoud A. M. Braima, and Jayanthi Sothirajah. *"Doing the Traditional Media Sidestep: Comparing the Effects of the Internet and Other Nontraditional Media with Traditional Media in the 1996 Presidential Campaign."* Journalism & Mass Communication Quarterly 76 (Spring 1999): 99–179.

This study looks at how heavy users of the Internet and other nontraditional media differ from users of traditional media such as newspapers, television news, radio news, and news magazines in their knowledge of issue positions of the two candidates in 1996. They found nontraditional media had little influence on political knowledge, but more influence on images of the candidates than the traditional media did. They also found that use of nontraditional media was very low, but the authors point out that interest in the campaign also was low.

Kim, Sei-Hill, Dietram A. Scheufele, and James Shanahan. *"Think about It This Way: Attribute Agenda-Setting Function of the Press and the Public's Evaluation of a Local Issue."* Journalism & Mass Communication Quarterly 79 (Spring 2002): 7–25.

The major tenet of agenda-setting research has been that the media do not tell you what to think, they tell you what to think about. This study says otherwise. The media can tell you how to think about the issue as well as what to think about. The study involves a commercial development plan in Ithaca, New York. Newspaper coverage of the issue was analyzed for three months, and then a public opinion survey was made. The content analysis identified six attributes of the issue. The survey showed that the newspaper coverage increased salience of certain aspects, and that this was more true of those who read local news a great deal.

Kim, Sung Tae, David Weaver, and Lars Willnat. *"Media Reporting and Perceived Credibility of Online Polls."* Journalism & Mass Communication Quarterly 77 (Winter 2000): 846–864.

Through a Lexis-Nexis search, the authors show the increase in the use of online polls in the media from five in 1992 to 405 in 1998. They then conducted a telephone survey of 767 adults in northern Virginia and Maryland to see whether or not people trust online polls. They found that 60 percent of their respondents believed that polls in newspapers or on television were more accurate than polls reported on the Internet.

Leshner, Glenn, and Michael L. McKean *"Using TV News for Political Information: Effects on Political Knowledge and Cynicism."* Journalism & Mass Communication Quarterly 74 (Spring 1997): 69–83.

This study of a 1994 U.S. Senate race in Missouri contradicts the claim that television causes a decline in political knowledge and an increase in cynicism. The authors made surveys in the Columbia, Missouri, area in late September and in November just after the election. Although television news use did not correlate with knowledge of candidates in the September survey, in the November survey it had the highest correlation with knowledge of the candidates of any of the mass media. In neither survey does television news use correlate with cynicism.

Lowry, Dennis T., and Jon A. Shidler. *"The Sound Bites, the Biter, and the Bitten: A Two-Campaign Test of the Anti-Incumbent Bias Hypothesis in Network TV News."* Journalism & Mass Communication Quarterly 75 (Winter 1998): 719–729.

This is an analysis of the sound bites in the presidential and vice-presidential coverage of ABC, CBS, CNN, and NBC in the 1992 and 1996 campaigns. The authors concluded that there was only minimal evidence of anti-incumbent bias. They found that Republicans tended to get more negative sound bites than the Democrats, but they also found that nearly half the sound bites were neutral.

McCombs, Maxwell, and Donald L. Shaw. *"The Agenda-Setting Function of the Mass Media."* Public Opinion Quarterly 36 (Summer 1972): 176–187.

This is the study that started agenda-setting research. They did a public opinion survey in Chapel Hill, North Carolina, in which they asked respondents to rank the importance of the various issues in the 1968 presidential campaign. They then did a content analysis of the print media that circulated in Chapel Hill to find out how often those issues were mentioned. The issues then were ranked according to the amount of content, and McCombs and Shaw obtained a high rank correlation between the public preference and the media content. It thus appeared that the media had set the public's agenda about the campaign.

Miller, M. Mark, Julie Andsager, and Bonnie P. Riechert. *"Framing the Candidates in Presidential Primaries: Issues and Images in Press Releases and News Coverage." Journalism & Mass Communication Quarterly* 75 (Summer 1998): 312–324.

Press releases from the 1996 Republican candidates were downloaded from their websites. Coverage of the candidates was analyzed in the *New York Times,* the *Washington Post,* and the *Los Angeles Times.* Although candidate images were distinct in press releases and news stories, candidate positions were represented differently in the releases and the media. Media coverage did include things about the candidates that were not in the news releases, which should be the case because releases do not tell everything.

Mutz, Diana C., and Joe Soss. *"Reading Public Opinion: The Influence of News Coverage on Perceptions of Public Sentiment." Public Opinion Quarterly* 61 (Fall 1997): 431–451.

This study analyzed a newspaper's attempt to move community opinion and bring about policy change on low-income housing. Little change was found in opinion or policy, but the perceived salience of the issue and the perceptions of the dominant opinion climate changed. Thus news organizations by emphasizing an issue may facilitate the changes they seek.

Pinkleton, Bruce E., and Erica Weintraub Austin. *"Individual Motivations, Perceived Media Importance, and Political Disaffection." Political Communication* 18 (No. 3, 2000): 321–334.

Mass media have been blamed for distancing people from the political process and thereby lessening voter turnout. This survey of 592 registered voters in the state of Washington found that political involvement was positively associated with voters' perception of the importance of newspapers and radio talk shows. These in turn were negatively related to cynicism and positively associated with efficacy. This suggests that media can serve as a catalyst for involved citizens making voting decisions.

Rogers, Everett M. *"Reflections on News Event Diffusion Re-*

search." *Journalism & Mass Communication Quarterly* 77 (Autumn 2000): 561–576.

Rogers traces the evolution of diffusion research starting with the study of diffusion of news about Eisenhower's heart attack by Paul Deutschmann and Wayne Danielson. He documents the increase in the number of diffusion studies. He talks about the S curve for time of diffusion and also about the distinction between high salience and low salience events. He sees a continued need for diffusion research and offers suggestions for what he sees as needing to be done.

Salwen, Michael B. *"Effect of Accumulation of Coverage on Issue Salience in Agenda Setting."* *Journalism Quarterly* 65 (Spring 1988): 100–106.

This study looked at the media agenda and the public agenda on environmental issues over a period of thirty-three weeks and found that it took five to seven weeks for the public to adopt the media agenda. The study also found that the correlation between the media agenda and the public agenda increased for a few weeks and then began to decline. This suggests that the public agenda is in constant flux, and putting an issue on the public agenda does not mean that it will stay there until it is resolved.

Schaefer, Todd M. *"The 'Rhetorical Presidency' Meets the Press: The New York Times and the State of the Union Message."* *Journalism & Mass Communication Quarterly* 76 (Autumn 1999): 516–530.

This is an analysis of *New York Times* coverage of State of the Union messages from 1953 to 1996. The author found coverage was not influenced by objective reality and found no evidence of liberal bias. He instead found coverage influenced by what he termed "news biases." This included such things as the president's approval rating and political power. He also found that the *Times* did not seem to show ideological consistency in its coverage.

Shaw, Daron R. *"The Impact of News Media Favorability and Candidate Events in Presidential Campaigns."* *Political Communication* 16 (April–June 1999): 183–202.

This study of the 1992 and 1996 presidential campaigns found that the interaction between events and favorability of news media coverage drives much of the change in voters' preferences.

The favorability of television coverage was particularly important. However, the author suggests that other factors influenced voters, including other types of media effects.

Sheer, Susan A. *"Scenes from the Political Playground: An Analysis of the Symbolic Use of Children in Presidential Campaign Advertising."* Political Communication 16 (January–March 1999): 45–59.

This study examined a sample of political advertisements produced by the two major parties since 1952. The author used the advertisements in campaigns archive of the Annenberg School for Communication at the University of Pennsylvania. She found that the ways children are used symbolically in these advertisements fall into five categories: economic insecurity, poverty, crime, war, and hope for the future. Images of children in poverty were found predominantly in the 1960s, while appeals to economic security were used continuously.

Shoemaker, Pamela J., Martin Eichholz, Eunyi Kim, and Brenda Wrigley. *"Individual and Routine Forces in Gatekeeping."* Journalism & Mass Communication Quarterly 78 (Summer 2001): 233–246.

This is a study of the coverage of fifty major bills passed by the 104th and 105th Congresses. This involved a content analysis of articles form the Lexis-Nexis database, a mail survey of the reporters who wrote those stories, and a mail survey of editors of the forty newspapers that covered the stories. The study found that how editors defined newsworthiness affected the extent of coverage more than any characteristic of reporters. Such variables as gender, ethnicity, years as a journalist, and political ideology did not seem to influence the amount of coverage a reporter gave a story.

Sotirovic, Mira, and Jack M. McLeod. *"Values, Communication Behavior, and Political Participation."* Political Communication 18 (July–September, 2000): 273–300.

Study finds that public affairs reading mediates the positive effects of postmaterialism, while watching entertainment mediates the negative impact of materialism on political participation. The study also found positive effects of reading public affairs in newspapers and negative effects of watching television entertainment on political knowledge and participation. The study also found that values influence political participation because of their effect on communication behaviors.

Stamm, Keith, Michelle Johnson, and Brennon Martin. *"Differences among Newspapers, Television, and Radio in Their Contributions to Knowledge of the Contract with America."* Journalism & Mass Communication Quarterly 74 (Winter 1997): 687–702.

Many studies have documented the contribution of newspapers and television to political knowledge, but seldom have they found such a contribution by radio. This study challenges that assumption. A purposive sample was asked about both exposure to newspapers, television, and radio and attention to news of Congress. Respondents then were asked to answer fifteen questions about the Contract with America. Exposure to newspapers and radio correlated significantly with the score on the Contract with America questions, but exposure to television did not. Attention to Congress in all three media correlated significantly with the score on the questions, and the highest correlation was for radio. The authors conclude that studies testing knowledge gains by media use should include radio.

Stempel, Guido H., III. *"Where People Really Get Most of Their News."* Newspaper Research Journal 11 (Fall 1991): 2–9.

The Roper studies have shown that people say they get most of their news from television. This study looked at national, state, and local news. It found that while people did say that they got most of their news about the president and the congress from television, by a wide margin they said they got most of their news about such things as city council and local schools from newspapers. For state news, people got their news from newspapers and television equally.

Stempel, Guido H., III, Thomas Hargrove, and Joseph P. Bernt. *"Relation of Growth of Use of the Internet to Changes in Media Use from 1955 to 1999."* Journalism & Mass Communication Quarterly 77 (Spring 2000): 71–79.

This national survey shows the huge gain for Internet use between 1995 and 1999. During this period, use of television news and newspapers declined, and it was widely assumed that the Internet was displacing those media. However, this study shows that Internet users were more likely to read newspapers than people who did not use the Internet. The same was true for use of radio news. However, Internet users were less likely to watch local television news than were those who did not use the Internet.

Terkildsen, Nyada, Frauke I. Schnell, and Cristina Ling. *"Interest Groups, the Media, and Policy Debate Formation: An Analysis of Message Structure, Rhetoric, and Sources Cues."* Political Communication 15 (January–March 1998): 45–61.

An analysis of the abortion debate in print media finds media both reporting news and advocating unique policy messages. Group action in structuring issue information is cyclical and often related more to journalistic norms than to pressure group strength. Nearly half of the post–*Roe v. Wade* abortion coverage was framed in the media's terms, not the interest groups. To achieve maximum coverage, groups must understand the media's news criteria and tailor their messages accordingly.

Voakes, Paul. *"Civic Duties: Newspaper Journalists' Views on Public Journalism."* Journalism & Mass Communication Quarterly 76 (Winter 1999): 756–774.

This national survey of newspaper journalists found strong support for four practices associated with civic journalism. Respondents were asked about the practices, but the words "civic journalism" and "public journalism" were not used. The averages for the four practices were 44 percent strongly approved and 36 percent somewhat approved. This is a surprising finding because there has been much criticism of civic journalism or public journalism from newspaper journalists.

Wanta, Wayne, Mary Ann Stephenson, Judy VanSlyke Turk, and Maxwell E. McCombs. *"How Presidents' State of the Union Talks Influenced News Media Agendas."* Journalism Quarterly 66 (Autumn 1989): 537–541.

The president sets the political agenda in his State of the Union message. This study looked at the coverage before and after four State of the Union messages. It found that in two of them—Jimmy Carter's in 1978 and Ronald Reagan's in 1985—the agenda of the speech more nearly matched the pre-speech coverage than the post-speech coverage. In the other two instances, the agenda of the speech was similar to that of the coverage. This suggests that it is possible for either the public or the media to set the agenda for the State of the Union message.

Weaver, David, and Dan Drew. *"Voter Learning in the 1992 Presidential Election: Did the Nontraditional Media and Debates Matter?"* Journalism & Mass Communication Quarterly 72 (Spring 1995): 7–17.

The answer to the question posed by the title of this article is "no." The authors determined this with a study of 504 randomly selected Indiana residents during the last two weeks of the 1992 campaign. They also found that television news exposure had a positive correlation with issue knowledge, but advertisements did not. They also found that attention to television and radio news stories about the campaign and exposure to the three presidential debates were predictors of increased interest in the campaign.

Wyatt, Robert O., Joohan Kim, and Elihu Katz. *"How Feeling Free to Talk Affects Ordinary Political Conversation, Purposeful Argumentation, and Civic Participation."* Journalism & Mass Communication Quarterly 77 (Spring 2000): 99–114.

This article reports a national survey in which respondents were asked how free they felt to talk about nine subjects and how much they did talk about those subjects. It found respondents felt between "very" and "somewhat" free to talk on all nine subjects. Crime was the most frequently talked about subject, with education next. A factor analysis of frequency-of-talk responses produced two factors—political conversation and personal conversation. The study indicates more willingness to talk about political topics that is generally assumed.

Reference Works

American Public Opinion Index. Louisville, KY: Opinion Research Service. Issued annually.

This includes virtually all scientific polls by major polling organizations in the United States. The book is arranged by question topics and. Question wording and sample size are indicated. Answers can be found on a CD-ROM.

Broadcasting & Cable Yearbook. New Providence, NJ: R. R. Bowker. Issued annually.

Broadcasting magazine is the trade publication of the broadcasting industry. This annual is the most complete compilation of information about broadcasting available. It includes listings of AM, FM, and T stations grouped by cities and by states. Listings include affiliation, address, names of major executives, and frequency. The yearbook also includes listings of cable companies, broadcasting groups, and newspaper ownership of broadcasting stations. It also has the Federal Communications Commission regulations.

Decisions of the United States Supreme Court. Charlottesville, VA: Lexis-Nexis. Issued annually. Approximately 320 pages.

This book provides a synopsis of every case heard by the Supreme Court in a given session. The issue, the basis for the decision, and summaries of the majority and minority opinions are included as well as biographies of the justices. This yearbook is indexed both by case names and legal topics.

Editor & Publisher Yearbook. New York: Editor & Publisher. Issued annually.

Editor & Publisher is the trade magazine of the newspaper industry and lists all the daily newspapers by city and state. Listings include circulation, ownership, wire and feature services used, and the names of major executives. It also includes a listing of weekly newspapers, campus newspapers, and Canadian newspapers, as well as a listing of news services, features services, and newspaper groups.

Federal Regulatory Directory. Washington, DC: Congressional Quarterly Press. Issued annually. Approximately 800 pages.

This is a directory of all the key personnel of the federal regulatory agencies. It includes biographies, and in some cases pictures, as well as extensive descriptions of the authority and responsibilities of the various agencies.

Gallup Opinion Index. Wilmington, DE: Scholarly Resources. Compilation of Gallup Polls divided into books covering 1939–1971, 1972–1977, and then each year since.

This is indexed by topics and includes question wording and respondent answers for each question asked by the Gallup Organization in the year.

Hamilton, Neal A. *Presidents: A Biographical Dictionary.* New York: Checkmark Books, 2001. 482 pages.

This book provides extensive biographical material about all of the presidents as well as a general historical perspective on the presidency.

Stempel, Guido H., III, and Jacqueline Nash. *Historical Dictionary of Political Communication in the United States.* Westport, CT: Greenwood, 1999. 171 pages.

This book includes brief biographies of major figures in political communication, and brief descriptions of major events and concepts in political communication.

The Television Industry. Washington, DC: National Association of Broadcasters. Issued annually.

This is a market-by-market review of the television industry. It shows audiences, historical financial data, and revenues for each station in each television market.

Who's Who in American Politics. New Providence, NJ: Marquis Who's Who. Issued annually.

This book provides biographical sketches for political officeholders in state and national government. It also provides state-by-state listings of office holders.

World Almanac and Book of Facts. Mahwah, NJ: World Almanac Books. Issued annually.

Includes statistics on government, business, and education. Also includes election results for current presidential and congressional elections, population figures for cities and counties, Academy Award winners, Pulitzer Prize winners, Nobel Prize winners, and more.

Websites

Americans for Democratic Action
http://www.adaction.org/main.html

Americans for Democratic Action, founded in 1947, is the oldest independent liberal political organization. It is dedicated to individual liberty and economic and social justice. It takes stands on a broad range of domestic, foreign, economic, military, social, and environmental issues. It provides a wide range of material on links to its website.

Archive Election Video
http://wp.netscape.com/election/convention/home.html

This is a collection for videos for Real Player from the 2000 presidential election. Include are CBS news programs as well as a group of videos about the Democrats and another about the Republicans.

Center for Responsible Politics
http://www.opensecrets.org

This website is an encyclopedia of information about campaign contributions broken down by states, candidates, contributors, and issues.

Citizens for Legitimate Government
http://www.legitgov.org

This is a website for an activist liberal group that has protested Bush administration policies in Portland, Oregon, Crawford, Texas, near the Bush ranch, and other places. It contains material claiming the government is not meeting its constitutional obligations.

Conservative News
http://www.conservativenews.org

This website devotes itself to conservative news, but is committed to objectivity. Thus, it is not nonpartisan, but it also is not a polemic. It offers a factual account slanted to the interests of conservatives.

DC's Political Report
http://www.dcpoliticalreport.com

This website includes candidates, results of polls, information on parties, state-by-state information, and links to state party websites.

Democracy Net
http://www.dnet.org

This is a free voter information service conducted by the League of Women Voters. It covers local, state, and national elections and contains issues statements, biographies, and pictures of candidates. The user has the opportunity to ask a question of a candidate.

Democratic National Committee
http://www.democrats.org

This website contains links to various aspects of national politics and to activities and issue positions of the Democratic Party.

Democrats Online
http://www.demsonline.org

This website contains links to all the states and to all the Democratic candidates who have websites. It also provides lists of candidates and election results.

Directory of Political Parties
http://www.politics1.com/parties.htm

This claims to be the most comprehensive guide to American politics. It is one of the broadest because in addition to providing information about the parties, it also provides lists of political consultants, and products and services used by the political parties.

Gallup Poll
http://www.gallup.com

Contains current Gallup Poll questions and results. Indexed by topic, it also contains trend information on various topics and issues going back more than half a century in some cases.

GOP Online
http://www.goponline.net

This website has links to all the states and to Republican candidates who have websites. It also provides lists of candidates and election returns.

League of Women Voters
http://www.lwv.org

The League of Women voters is a nonpartisan group committed to encouraging people to vote and provides information about candidates. The website provides information about local, state, and national elections.

News Directory
http://www.newsdirectory.com

This website lists city and state newspapers that have websites. Links also include listings of television stations, also grouped by cities and states.

Pew Research Center for People and the Press
http://www.people-press.org

This website contains Pew Research Center surveys for the last four years, including question wording and results. It is indexed by topic of specific poll and the focus is on politics and the media.

Political Resources
http://www.politicalresources.net

This website has links to 118 websites on many different political matters. It includes both U.S. and international politics, campaigns, laws, election history, and other topics.

Republican National Committee
http://www.rnc.org

This website contains numerous links to various aspects of national politics, Republican activities, and positions on issues.

Right Now
http://www.rightnow.org

This is a conservative website with a focus on hunger and a related focus on religion.

States
http://www.state.(two letter abbreviation of state).us

Every state in the United States has a website, and they vary somewhat in contents, but most have names of state officials in executive, legislative, and judicial branches. They also contain budget and economic data and education information. Web address for most states is in the form indicated above, but there are these exceptions:

Alabama: http://alaweb.asc.edu
California: http://www.state.ca.us
Hawaii: http://www.hawaii.gov
Kansas: http://www.accesskansas.org/

Missouri: http://www.ecodev.state.mo.us
Washington: http://access.wa.gov

Videos

Civic Journalism: It's (More Than) Just Good Journalism
Type: VHS color
Length: 30 minutes
Date: 1998
Price: Free
Source: Pew Center for Civic Journalism
1101 Connecticut Avenue, NW
Suite 420
Washington, DC 20036–4303

Former syndicated columnist and media critic Hodding Carter III narrates this video, which outlines the philosophy and techniques of civic journalism. Efforts by Charlotte, North Carolina, and Madison, Wisconsin, are featured.

CNN: Election 2000—36 Days That Gripped the Nation
Type: VHS color
Length: 65 minutes
Date: 2001
Price: $15.98
Source: Barnes & Noble
From website http://www.bn.com or from any Barnes & Noble store.

The 2000 presidential election was one for the history books. For thirty-six days, the outcome was mired in debate, technicalities, recounts, and court actions. This video includes not only CNN coverage, but behind-the-scenes footage and interviews with reporters involved, including Julie Wooruff, Bernard Shaw, Jeff Greenfield, Bill Hemmed, and Bill Schneider.

Executive Privilege and Delegation of Powers
Type: VHS color
Length: 60 minutes
Date: 1984
Price: $29.95
Source: Annenberg/CPB
P.O. Box 2345

South Burlington, VT 05407
1-800-LEARNER
Internet: http://www.learner.org

This is part of the Emmy Award–winning, thirteen-program Columbia University series entitled "The Constitution: That Delicate Balance." Political, legal, and media professionals engage in spontaneous debate on the issue of the executive branch's right to have secret meetings and keep documents secret.

From the Airwaves to the Internet
Type: VHS color
Length: 90 Minutes
Date: 1995
Source: The Radio and Television News Directors Foundation
1000 Connecticut Avenue, NW
Washington, DC 20036
(202) 659-6510
Internet: info@rtndf.org

This video examines the effect of changing technology, especially the Internet, on the future of electronic journalism. It features a panel of four television executives with Joe Penman, president of FOX News, as the moderator. The session was part of the opening general session of the Fiftieth Annual International Conference & World Media in New Orleans.

Just the Facts: The Election Process in America
Type: VHS color
Length: 50 minutes
Date: 2002
Price: $16.99
Source: Barnes & Noble
From website http://www.bn.com or at any Barnes & Noble store.

Description of the election process from the primaries through the party conventions and the campaigns, and on to Election Day.

Nomination, Election, and Succession of the President
Type: VHS color
Length: 60 minutes
Date: 1989
Price: $29.95
Source: Annenberg/CPB

P.O. Box 2345
South Burlington, VT 04507
1-800-LEARNER

This video is part of the Emmy Award–winning series "The Constitution: That Delicate Balance." Political, legal, and, media professionals engage in spontaneous and heated debate on the process by which presidents are selected.

PBS Videos
Videos are made and sold for many PBS programs, but the distribution usually is controlled by the station producing the program, not by PBS. There are hundreds of videos. Of particular interest for political communication are "Firing Line," "Frontline," and "NOW" with Bill Moyers.
For "Firing Line," contact NETA
P.O. Box 50008
Columbia, SC 29250
(803) 799-551

For "Frontline," contact WGBH
125 Western Avenue
Boston, MA 02104
(617) 300-3500

For "NOW," contact WNET
450 W. 33d St., 6th Floor
New York, NY 10001
(212) 560-3000

PBS videos also can be found at e-Bay, Barnes & Noble, and other stores. Common list price is $29.95, but store prices may be considerably less.

The People & the Power Game
Type: VHS color
Length: Two tapes totaling 117 minutes
Date: 1996
Source: Bedrock Smith Productions, Inc.
4905 Del Ray Avenue
Beheads, MD 20814
Internet: http://www.pbs.org/powergame/

These tapes are part of the PBS Democracy Project and were aired by South Carolina ETV. The first is "The Lobbies and the Media" and the second is "Presidency & Congress."

Television and the Presidency
Type: VHS color
Length: 90 minutes
Date: 1994
Source: The Freedom Forum First Amendment Center
Vanderbilt University
1207 18th Avenue, South
Nashville, TN 37212

Sander Vancocur narrates this video, which includes virtually all of the living former press secretaries and print and television journalists who covered the White House. It examines the effect of television on the presidency from John F. Kennedy to Bill Clinton, asking who has used it and who has been used by it. The conclusion is that John F. Kennedy and Ronald Reagan used it better than any of the other presidents and Richard Nixon and Jimmy Carter were used by television the most. The tape is in three thirty-minute segments.

Tune in Your Community
Type: VHS color
Length: 17 minutes
Date: 1998
Source: Pew Center for Civic Journalism
1101 Connecticut Avenue, NW
Suite 420
Washington, DC 20036-4303

Some of the country's top television news directors tell how they are creating journalism that builds capacity for grappling with tough community issues. It involves citizens in finding solutions and engages viewers in civic life.

Index

About the Author

Guido H. Stempel III, distinguished professor emeritus in the E. W. Scripps School of Journalism at Ohio University, is currently director of the Scripps Survey Research Center at Ohio University. He is coauthor and coeditor of *Research Methods in Mass Communication*, published in 1981 with a second edition in 1989, he is coauthor and coeditor of the successor to that book, *Mass Communication Research and Theory* (2002) and *Historical Dictionary of Political Communication in the United States* (1999), and he is the author of more than 100 journal articles. He received the Chancellor's Award for Contributions to the Field of Journalism from the University of Wisconsin, the Eleanor Blum Award for contributions to research from the Association for Education in Journalism and Mass Communication, and the Edward J. Trayes Teacher-of-the-Year Award from the Mass Communication and Society Division of the Association for Education in Journalism and Mass Communication.